The Origin and Evolution of Investment Treaty Standards

The Origin and Evolution of Investment Treaty Standards

Stability, Value, and Reasonableness

FEDERICO ORTINO

OXFORD
UNIVERSITY PRESS

OXFORD
UNIVERSITY PRESS

Great Clarendon Street, Oxford, OX2 6DP,
United Kingdom

Oxford University Press is a department of the University of Oxford.
It furthers the University's objective of excellence in research, scholarship,
and education by publishing worldwide. Oxford is a registered trade mark of
Oxford University Press in the UK and in certain other countries

First Edition published in 2019

Impression: 1

Published in the United States of America by Oxford University Press
198 Madison Avenue, New York, NY 10016, United States of America

British Library Cataloguing in Publication Data
Data available

Library of Congress Control Number: 2019947385

ISBN 978–0–19–884263–7

Printed and bound by
CPI Group (UK) Ltd, Croydon, CR0 4YY

Acknowledgements

This book has been a long time coming. It is my attempt at understanding a very chaotic and evolving area of international law. This journey started in the International Investment Agreements Section at UNCTAD in 2003, continued in the Investment Treaty Forum at BIICL between 2005 and 2007 and has persevered at King's College London ever since. Along the way, many people have, in different ways, contributed to the making of the book. In particular, I would like to thank Anna Joubin-Bret, Professor Peter Muchlinski, Professor Christoph Schreuer, Audley Sheppard, and Professor M Sornarajah for having introduced me to the world of investment treaties. For their friendship and insights, I am moreover greatly indebted to the many colleagues at King's College London and beyond, in particular, Lorand Bartels, Megan Bowman, David Caron, Jan Dalhuisen, Piet Eeckhout, Jessica Gladstone, Florian Grisel, Ori Herstein, Holger Hestermeyer, Christoph Kletzer, Petros Mavroidis, Cian Murphy, Nikki Palmer, Mona Pinchis-Paulsen, Lauge Poulsen, Chris Townley, Irit Samet, Karl Sauvant, Michael Schillig, Thomas Schultz, Anthony Sinclair, Johnny Veeder, Guglielmo Verdirame, Gaetan Verhoosel, Philippa Webb, Sam Wordsworth and Lorenzo Zucca. I would like to thank Ceyda Knoebel and two of my former doctoral students, Emily Lydgate and Maria Laura Marceddu, for their invaluable research assistance. I would also like to thank all of my students, who have been a big part of this journey and endured stoically my protracted efforts at ordering chaos.

Finally, I am grateful to my family, in particular, my wife, Maria, and our children, Noah, Elias and Greta, for their unconditional love and support and for helping me keep things in perspective. This book is dedicated to them.

Federico Ortino

London, July 2019

Contents

Table of Cases

List of Abbreviations

BIICL	British Institute of International and Comparative Law
BIT	bilateral investment treaty
CETA	Comprehensive and Economic Trade Agreement
CFIA	Cooperation and Facilitation Investment Agreement
COMESA	Common Market for Eastern and Southern Africa
CPTPP	Comprehensive and Progressive Agreement for Trans-Pacific Partnership
ECHR	European Commission on Human Rights
ECT	Energy Charter Treaty
EIU	Economist Intelligence Unit
FCN	friendship, commerce and navigation
FCTC	Framework Convention for Tobacco Control
FET	fair and equitable treatment
FPS	full protection and security
GATT	General Agreement on Tariffs and Trade
ICJ	International Court of Justice
IFC	International Finance Corporation
ILA	International Law Association
IMF	International Monetary Fund
IPA	Investment Protection Agreement
ISDS	investor–State dispute settlement
JRP	joint review panel
MFN	most favoured nation
MIGA	Multilateral Investment Guarantee Agency
NAFTA	North American Free Trade Agreement
NT	national treatment
OECD	Organisation for Economic Co-operation and Development
PCB	printed circuit board
PCIJ	Permanent Court of International Justice
SPR	single presentation regulation
TTIP	Transatlantic Trade and Investment Partnership
UNCTAD	United Nations Conference on Trade and Development
UNCTC	United Nations Centre on Transnational Corporations
WBG	World Bank Group
WGI	worldwide governance indicator
WHO	World Health Organization

Introduction

This book's principal aim is to provide a conceptual and legal analysis of the distinctive guarantees that emerge from international treaties signed since 1959 for the promotion and protection of foreign investment.

While investment treaties include a variety of different provisions (mainly 'standards'),[1] the focus of this study is principally on those provisions that have caused the greatest controversy, particularly following the exponential increase in claims brought by foreign investors before ad hoc arbitral tribunals alleging the violation of such provisions by the host State.[2] These provisions include the requirements to accord foreign investments 'fair and equitable treatment' (FET) and 'full protection and security' (FPS), the requirement to compensate for 'direct and indirect expropriation', the prohibition of 'arbitrary, unreasonable and discriminatory' measures and the requirement to observe any commitments undertaken by the host State vis-à-vis the foreign investment.[3]

A basic assumption of this study is that, while the international investment law system is a complex system (based on more than 3000 treaties and lacking a formal multilateral institutional structure), investment treaties on the whole (and at least up until the early 2000s) are rather similar in terms of 'objective' and 'content'.

[1] Federico Ortino, 'Refining the Content and Role of Investment "Rules" and "Standards": A New Approach to International Investment Treaty Making' (2013) 28 ICSID Rev 152.

[2] As of the time of writing, the total number of known investor–State arbitrations based on investment treaties has reached 942, two-thirds of which have been concluded and the remaining one are still pending. See United Nations Conference on Trade and Development (UNCTAD) database https://investmentpolicy.unctad.org/investment-dispute-settlement accessed 20 May 2019.

[3] Based on data collected by UNCTAD, it appears that the investment treaty provisions that have been relied the most by investors include: FET (in 83% of the 553 arbitrations), indirect expropriation (71%), FPS (42%), arbitrary, unreasonable or discriminatory measures (33%), observance of obligations (23%), national treatment (23%) and most-favoured-nation (MFN) treatment (18%). See UNCTAD database, 'Breaches of IIAs Provisions Alleged and Fund' https://investmentpolicy.unctad.org/investment-dispute-settlement accessed 20 May 2019. Scholarly publications in the past ten years have focused on several of these treaty provisions: Ioana Tudor, *The Fair and Equitable Treatment Standard in the International Law of Foreign Investment* (OUP 2008); Roland Kläger, *Fair and Equitable Treatment' in International Investment Law* (CUP 2011); Alexandra Diehl, *The Core Standard of International Investment Protection: Fair and Equitable Treatment* (Kluwer Law International 2012); Martins Paparinskis, *The International Minimum Standard and Fair and Equitable Treatment* (OUP 2013); Jonathan Bonnitcha, *Substantive Protection under Investment Treaties: A Legal and Economic Analysis* (CUP 2014); Sebastián López Escarcena, *Indirect Expropriation in International Law* (Edward Elgar 2014); Caroline Henckels, *Proportionality and Deference in Investor–State Arbitration* (CUP 2015); Gebhard Buecheler, *Proportionality in Investor–State Arbitration* (OUP 2015); and Valentina Vadi, *Proportionality, Reasonableness and Standards of Review in International Investment Law and Arbitration* (Edward Elgar 2018).

The Origin and Evolution of Investment Treaty Standards. Federico Ortino, Oxford University Press (2019).
DOI: 10.1093/oso/9780198842637.001.0001

In terms of objective, while the 'object' (or immediate aim) of investment treaties is to afford protection to foreign investments operating in a host State, the 'purpose' (or long-term aim) of such treaties[4] is to encourage capital flows and in turn contribute to the prosperity and development of the contracting parties.

In terms of content, despite the various differences across the more than 3000 investment treaties, there clearly exists a core of investment protection guarantees that are found in the great majority of such treaties, as shown in the mapping exercise carried out by UNCTAD (of more than 2500 investment treaties). In quantitative terms, this core includes provisions on transfer of funds (found in almost 100% of the treaties mapped by UNCTAD), MFN treatment (99%), investor–State dispute settlement (ISDS) (98%), expropriation (98%), subrogation (96%), fair and equitable treatment (FET) (95%), and national treatment (NT) (87%).[5] In qualitative terms, these provisions are, on the whole, rather homogeneous, particularly those on FET and expropriation (certainly at least until the early 2000s). Furthermore, the existence of broadly worded MFN treatment clauses in most investment treaties has contributed to the multilateralization of international investment law.[6]

The present analysis focuses on both the 'origin' and 'evolution' of investment treaty standards. In terms of origin, the work considers the broader context at the time when the first modern investment treaty (the 1959 Treaty between the Federal Republic of Germany and Pakistan for the Promotion and Protection of Investments) was concluded. In terms of evolution, the work examines (a) the many decisions of ad hoc arbitral tribunals that, in the past twenty years, have been called upon to apply these treaties in order to resolve the several hundred investor–State disputes, as well as (b) some of the recent investment treaties that in the past ten to fifteen years have attempted to clarify and/or reform the content and scope of investment protection guarantees.

This study argues that the key investment protection provisions in investment treaties (and thus much of the related controversy) revolve around three distinct concepts: legal stability, investment's value and reasonableness. Accordingly, the main three chapters of the present book attempt to explain the origin and evolution of these key provisions through these three distinct concepts.

Chapter I investigates the extent to which investment treaties include a guarantee of 'legal stability in the strict sense'. A guarantee of legal stability in the strict sense may require (a) the host State to observe its contractual undertakings vis-à-vis the

[4] Isabelle Buffard and Karl Zemanek, 'The "Object and Purpose" of a Treaty: An Enigma?' (1998) 3 ARIEL 311, 326. See Gus Van Harten, Investment Treaty Arbitration and Public Law (OUP 2007) 140.

[5] Other provisions that feature in many investment treaties include provisions on full FPS (84%), non-impairment through unreasonable, arbitrary or discriminatory measures (68%) and observance of obligations (so-called umbrella clauses) (42%). See UNCTAD database 'Mapping of IIA Content' https://investmentpolicy.unctad.org/international-investment-agreements accessed 20 May 2019.

[6] Stephan Schill, *The Multilateralization of International Investment Law* (CUP 2009).

foreign investment (contractual stability); or (b) the host State to avoid subjecting the foreign investment to (adverse) changes in the applicable regulatory framework (regulatory stability). In the presence of any such strict stability guarantee, a breach of the investment treaty would be established if the investor was successful in demonstrating that the host State had either violated its contractual obligations or introduced a change in the underlying regulatory framework negatively affecting the investment. Crucially, justifications advanced by the host State based on the need to act in the public interest are irrelevant for the purposes of establishing host States' responsibility under a strict stability guarantee. This chapter addresses in particular the following three investment treaty provisions: the umbrella clause, the stabilization clause and the FET clause.

Chapter II investigates the extent to which investment treaties require compensation when a host State's measure deprives the investor of the value of its investment. In the presence of a guarantee based on the adverse impact on the (value of the) investment, a breach of the investment treaty is established if the investor is successful in demonstrating that a measure of the host State has caused such deprivation. As in the case of the guarantee of stability in the strict sense, crucially, justifications advanced by the host State based on the need to act in the public interest are also irrelevant for purposes of establishing the host State's responsibility pursuant to a guarantee to protect the value of the investment. This chapter focuses principally on investment treaties' provision on (indirect) expropriation.

Chapter III investigates the extent to which investment treaties include a 'reasonableness' guarantee aimed at requiring fairness and rationality in the conduct of the host State affecting foreign investment. A reasonableness guarantee may include certain fairness requirements that go to the substance of an act or omission of the host State (substantive reasonableness) as well as to the process leading up to the adoption of the relevant conduct under review (procedural reasonableness). While there may be several conditions, a breach of a reasonableness-based provision in an investment treaty will crucially require the investor to demonstrate lack of fairness, justification or rationality in the substantive or procedural aspects of the conduct of the host State under review. Focusing on substantive reasonableness only, this chapter examines the following investment treaty provisions: FPS, FET, non-impairment through arbitrary or unreasonable measures and expropriation.

The book's underlying argument is two-pronged. First, from the very beginning, the protection afforded to foreign investments by modern investment treaties has been exceptionally broad (and, as such, restrictive of the host State's ability to regulate). Such protection included guarantees vis-a-vis the host State's (a) breach of investment contracts and regulatory change; (b) substantial deprivation of the value of the foreign investment; and (c) unreasonable conduct.

Second, while a growing number of investment treaty tribunals as well as new investment treaties have reined in such broad protections, the evolution of key investment treaty provisions has been (and in many ways still is) marred by inconsistency and uncertainty. In particular, the same investment treaty provision has been interpreted by arbitral tribunals as providing different kinds of guarantee. For example, some tribunals have interpreted the provisions on indirect expropriation as a guarantee vis-à-vis the host State's substantial deprivation of the value of the investment and other tribunals as a guarantee vis-à-vis the host State's unreasonable conduct. Similarly, some tribunals have interpreted the FET provision as a guarantee of legal stability in the strict sense and other tribunals as a guarantee vis-à-vis the host State's unreasonable conduct, although it may at times be difficult to decipher what a specific tribunal's position actually is.

Furthermore, while there appears to be a growing preference in arbitral practice (as well as treaty practice) for reasonableness-based guarantees, there is still no clarity with regard to the specific reasonableness test that should be employed in order to review the lawfulness of the host State conduct under an investment treaty. For example, whether for purposes of assessing the existence of an indirect expropriation or for purposes of determining a violation of FET, some investment tribunals have employed a (more deferential) means–ends rationality test, while other tribunals have employed a (more intrusive) proportionality balancing test.

I
Guarantees of Legal Stability in the Strict Sense

Introduction

Stability, whether legal, political, economic, financial or monetary, seems to represent one of the core values of today's society.[1] Unsurprisingly, stability in all the above-mentioned meanings also represents one of the key *desiderata* of economic operators, particularly when they invest in a foreign market. For example, stability with regard to the host State's political environment (political stability) or with regard to the rate of inflation in the foreign market (economic stability) will ensure predictability and reduce the risks that may ultimately undermine the viability of the investor's business venture. With regard to legal stability, foreign investors' focus is on the stability of both the underlying investment contract (contractual

[1] Political stability is one of the six Worldwide Governance Indicators (WGI) according to the World Bank Group (WBG) (https://info.worldbank.org/governance/wgi/#home); ensuring monetary and financial stability is the main goal of the International Monetary Fund (IMF) (https://www.imf.org/external/about/howwedo.htm). For the argument that trade agreements address uncertainty, see Nuno Limão and Giovanni Maggi, 'Uncertainty and Trade Agreements' (2015) 7 AEJ: Microeconomics 1.

The Origin and Evolution of Investment Treaty Standards. Federico Ortino, Oxford University Press (2019).
DOI: 10.1093/oso/9780198842637.001.0002

stability) and the applicable regulatory framework in the host country (regulatory stability). A recent World Bank Group survey confirms that, among the so-called political risks facing foreign investors, 'breach of contract' and 'adverse regulatory change' by the host State represent the most pressing ones.[2]

The concept of stability may, however, be somewhat controversial. Stability as a general value, or even as an aspiration, is more likely to be a 'relative' (or soft) rather than an 'absolute' (strict) concept. According to its dictionary definition, stability in fact highlights the 'state of something that is not easily changed' rather than something that cannot (or should not) be modified. In other words, stability is not understood as a total standstill but more as gradual movement. This definition is also reflected in the notion of stability as one of the formal elements of the rule of law, which is often seen as implying a system of norms that is 'sufficiently resistant to change'[3] or as requiring that the 'demands [that] laws make on citizens should remain relatively constant'.[4] The reference to stability at times expressly included in the preamble of international investment treaties should be understood in this softer sense.[5]

When it comes to investment treaty obligations, there can, however, be two alternative understandings of the concept of legal stability, which highlight two conceptually distinct obligations. According to one view, legal stability may be understood to include an obligation of legal stability in the strict sense (akin to so-called 'freezing clauses' in investment contracts). According to this understanding, the mere failure to preserve the more advantageous regulatory framework applicable to the investment will lead to a violation of the investment treaty (regulatory stability in the strict sense). Similarly, failure to observe a contractual undertaking vis-à-vis the foreign investment will lead to a treaty violation (contractual stability in the strict sense).

According to a second view, the obligation of legal stability may be understood in a softer sense, according to which violation of the investment treaty can only be found if the non-observance of the investment contract or the change in the regulatory framework (detrimental to the foreign investment) cannot be justified by the legitimate exercise of public policy powers.

Early investment tribunals were divided on the question of whether or not investment treaties provided strict legal stability obligations. For example, investment tribunals interpreting the fair and equitable treatment provision in order to address adverse regulatory change contain statements supporting either the 'strict' or 'soft' understanding of a stability obligation. One of the paradigmatic examples of a strict obligation of regulatory stability under the fair and equitable treatment

[2] Multilateral Investment Guarantee Agency (MIGA)–Economist Intelligence Unit (EIU) Political Risk Survey 2013.

[3] Jeremy Waldron, 'The Rule of Law and the Importance of Procedure' (2011) 50 Nomos 3.

[4] Colleen Murphy, 'Lon Fuller and the Moral Value of the Rule of Law' (2005) 24 L Phil 239, 241.

[5] See eg the 1991 United States–Argentina bilateral investment treaty (BIT).

(FET) standard is the 2004 decision in *Occidental v Ecuador I*. Having stated that '[t]he stability of the legal and business framework is [...] an essential element of fair and equitable treatment',[6] the *Occidental v Ecuador I* tribunal found a breach of the FET provision, as the tax framework under which the investment had been made and had been operating 'has been changed in an important manner by the actions adopted by the [Ecuadorian tax authorities]'.[7] The tribunal also noted that a determination of whether there is a breach of the FET standard is premised on whether or not the host State has 'alter[ed] the legal and business environment in which the investment has been made'.[8]

On the other hand, one example adopting a softer, more deferential, interpretation of regulatory stability as part of FET is the 2006 decision in *Saluka v Czech Republic*.[9] In the view of the *Saluka* tribunal, in order to be protected, the investor's expectations 'must rise to the level of legitimacy and reasonableness in light of the circumstances'[10] and a determination of a breach of the FET standard 'requires a weighing of the Claimant's legitimate and reasonable expectations on the one hand and the Respondent's legitimate regulatory interests on the other'.[11]

Similarly, early investment tribunals were divided on the protection provided by the so-called 'umbrella clause'. In particular, tribunals disagreed on whether or not 'a simple breach of contract, or of municipal statute or regulation, by itself, would suffice to constitute a treaty violation on the part of a Contracting Party and engage the international responsibility of the Party'.[12]

It is clear that from the perspective of the foreign investor, a strict stability obligation would afford a very high level of protection vis-à-vis the risk of contractual or regulatory change (as the investor will be compensated for the existence of the contract breach or adverse regulatory change). On the other hand, a soft stability obligation would afford a greater degree of discretion to the host State as, at a minimum, the existence of a treaty violation (and the duty to compensate the investor)

[6] The *Occidental v Ecuador I* tribunal relied on the clear statement found in the preamble of the underlying treaty (the 1993 Ecuador–United States BIT) that FET 'is desirable in order to maintain a stable framework for investment and maximum effective utilization of economic resources'. *Occidental Exploration and Production Company v The Republic of Ecuador* (*Occidental v Ecuador I*), Final Award, 1 July 2004, para 183.

[7] ibid, paras 183–84.

[8] ibid, para 191. See Rudolf Dolzer, 'Fair and Equitable Treatment: Today 's Contours' (2013) 12 Santa Clara J Int'l L 7, 22. See also Rudolf Dolzer and Christoph Schreuer, *Principles of International Investment Law* (2nd edn, OUP 2012) 145.

[9] *Saluka Investments BV v The Czech Republic*, UNCITRAL, Partial Award, 17 March 2006.

[10] ibid, para 304.

[11] ibid, para 306.

[12] *SGS Société Générale de Surveillance SA v Islamic Republic of Pakistan*, ICSID Case No ARB/01/13, Decision on Jurisdiction, 6 August 2003, para 168. But see *SGS Société Générale de Surveillance SA v Republic of the Philippines*, ICSID Case No ARB/02/6, Decision on Jurisdiction, 29 January 2004, para 128: 'To summarize the Tribunal's conclusions on this point, Article X(2) makes it a breach of the BIT for the host State to fail to observe binding commitments, including contractual commitments, which it has assumed with regard to specific investments.'

would depend in relevant part on an assessment of the public policy justification underlying the contractual breach or regulatory change at issue.

The aim of this chapter is to inquire whether—and if so, the extent to which—investment treaties contain guarantees of strict legal stability. More specifically, this chapter asks whether investment treaties contain provisions (a) guaranteeing that contractual undertakings vis-à-vis the foreign investment are respected (contractual stability in the strict sense); and/or (b) ensuring that adverse regulatory changes will not be applied to foreign investments (regulatory stability in the strict sense).

Three main arguments are advanced in this chapter. First, legal stability in the strict sense does represent one of the guarantees in international investment treaties, provided specifically through investment treaties' umbrella clauses (section A) and stabilization clauses (section B). Second, despite an attempt by a few early tribunals to read the FET provision as imposing a strict stability obligation on host States,[13] most investment treaty tribunals faced with the task of interpreting FET, seem to have recognized the need to balance the protection vis-à-vis adverse contractual and regulatory changes and host States' right to regulate in the public interest. However, one can still find recent arbitral decisions where the role of legal stability within the FET standard remains at best ambiguous, and which thus fail to assuage the fears that the FET standard may indeed function as imposing an obligation of stability in the strict sense (section C). Third, investment treaties signed in the past ten years clearly show a retreat of provisions guaranteeing legal stability in the strict sense (section D).

A. Respect of Host State's Undertakings with Regard to Foreign Investments and the Umbrella Clause

While contracts are principally used to define parties' respective rights and obligations, they are drafted in order to bring a level of stability and thus predictability in the parties' contractual relationship. Subject to the usual clauses addressing exceptional events (such as force majeure, or changed circumstances), contracts are legally binding on the parties, they are enforceable before courts and tribunals and remedies are available in case of contractual breaches.

Investment contracts, negotiated by the investor and the host State, are no different: '[i]n principle, it will be the intention of both sides to create a legal framework that will last from the beginning to the end of their common project'.[14]

[13] Some early tribunals have also interpreted the 'full protection and security' as requiring a strict stability obligation. See eg *CME Czech Republic BV v Czech Republic*, UNCITRAL, Partial Award, 13 September 2001, para 613.

[14] Dolzer and Schreuer, *Principles of International Investment Law* (n 8) 82.

However, in the international investment context, contractual mechanisms face particular challenges in providing a high level of stability, as the State party to the contract has the ability to affect unilaterally the terms of the investment contract as well as the likely law applicable to such contract (ie the law of the host State).[15]

International investment treaties have for a long time provided for a clause specifically designed to promote and ensure stability in the strict sense with regard to the contractual relations between foreign investors and host States. The so-called 'umbrella clause' (or 'observance of undertakings clause') requires the host State to observe any obligation it may have entered into with regard to foreign investments.[16] While language varies across the various investment treaties, roughly 40–50% of existing treaties contain an umbrella clause.[17]

The last sentence of Article 7 of the 1959 Germany and Pakistan BIT, the first modern investment treaty, reads as follows: 'Either Party shall observe any other obligation it may have entered into with regard to investments by nationals or companies of the other Party.'[18] While some variations exist, the text of most umbrella clauses in modern investment treaties look similar to the one contained in the very first modern BIT.[19]

As evidenced by Dr Sinclair, the origin of umbrella clauses is to be found in a movement during the 1950s in Western Europe pressing for the sanctity of long-term investment contracts (particularly, concessions)[20] and epitomized in Article II

[15] ibid, 82–6 (pointing to stabilization clauses as a mechanism used in state contracts to preserve the sanctity and stability of the contract; as well as to renegotiation clauses focusing on guaranteeing the economic equilibrium of the contract, rather than its legal stability). See Peter Cameron, *International Energy Investment Law: The Pursuit of Stability* (OUP 2010) 27 noting the in-built vulnerability of the contractual relationship following from the fact that a state has the power under its municipal law to alter the terms of a contract, and indeed to terminate it entirely.

[16] See generally Stephan Schill, 'Enabling Private Ordering—Function, Scope and Effect of Umbrella Clauses in Internationa Investment Treaties' (2009) 18 Mich J Int'l L 1; Thomas Wälde, 'The "Umbrella Clause" in Investment Arbitration: A Comment on Original Intentions and Recent Cases' (2005) 6 JWIT 183.

[17] Katia Yannaca-Small, 'Interpretation of the Umbrella Clause in Investment Agreements' (2006) OECD Working Papers on International Investment, 5–6:

> It is estimated that, of the 2500 or more BITs currently in existence approximately forty per cent contain an umbrella clause. Treaty practice of States does not point to a uniform approach to the treatment of these clauses. While Switzerland, the Netherlands, the United Kingdom and Germany, often include umbrella clauses in their BITs, France, Australia and Japan include umbrella clauses in only a minority of their BITs. Of 35 French BITs examined, only 4 contain an umbrella clause while only 5 out of 20 Australian BITs and 2 of the 9 Japanese BITs examined. Canada is the only OECD member state examined in this study which has never included an umbrella clause in its BITs. [...] 34 of the 41 US BITs examined, based on the former Model, contained an umbrella clause [...] [footnotes omitted].

[18] See Article 7 of the 1959 Germany–Pakistan BIT.

[19] As of 20 May 2019, out of 2571 investment treaties mapped by the United Nations Conference on Trade and Development (UNCTAD), 1107 contain an umbrella clause. See UNCTAD database, 'IIA Mapping Project' http://investmentpolicyhub.unctad.org accessed 20 May 2019.

[20] Anthony Sinclair, 'The Origin of the Umbrella Clause in the International Law of Investment Protection' (2004) 20 Arb Int'l 411, 423–4.

of the 1959 Abs-Shawcross Draft Convention on Investments Abroad[21] and Article 2 of the 1967 Organisation for Economic Co-operation and Development (OECD) Draft Convention on the Protection of Private Property.[22] The purpose was two-fold: (a) to internationalize the investment contract, thus preventing its exclusive subjection to the law of the host State and the risk of unilateral variation by the government; and (b) to provide a remedy in international law for breaches of the contract.[23] In other words, '[f]rom an investor's point of view, the umbrella clause was a natural progression in the law of investment protection beyond negotiated contractual techniques to internationalize and stabilize investment agreements'.[24]

The Notes and Comments to Article 2 of the 1967 OECD Draft Convention explain that the umbrella clause represents an application of the general principle of *pacta sunt servanda*, which also applies to agreements between States and foreign nationals.[25] Accordingly, 'any right originating under such an undertaking [given by the host State in relation to property] gives rise to an international right that the Party of the national concerned or of his successor in title is entitled to protect'.[26]

As noted by FA Mann in 1981, umbrella clauses are of particular importance because they protect 'the investor's contractual rights against any interference which might be caused by either a simple breach of contract or by administrative or legislative acts, and independently of the question whether or no [sic] such interference amounts to expropriation'.[27] According to Mann, the variation of the terms of a contract or license by legislative measures, the termination of the contract or the failure to perform any of its terms are acts that the umbrella clause would render wrongful in international law.[28]

In terms of guaranteeing contractual stability in the strict sense, the umbrella clause has certain peculiar features. First, it only covers the (contractual) undertakings of the host State vis-à-vis the protected investment and thus it does not

[21] Article II reads as follows: 'Each Party shall at all times ensure the observance of any undertakings which it may have given in relation to investments made by nationals of any other Party.'

[22] Article 2, titled 'Observance of Undertakings', reads as follows: 'Each Party shall at all times ensure the observance of undertakings given by it in relation to property of nationals of any other Party.' Incidentally, the OECD Draft Convention, based heavily on the Abs-Shawcross text, greatly influenced the many investment treaties that were signed in the last thirty years of the twentieth century.

[23] Sinclair, 'The Origin of the Umbrella Clause' (n 20) 424. See also Andrew Newcombe and Lluis Paradell, *Law and Practice of Investment Treaties: Standards of Treatment* (Kluwer Law International 2009) 441.

[24] Sinclair, 'The Origin of the Umbrella Clause' (n 20) 425.

[25] Paragraph 1 of the Notes and Comments to Article 2 of the OECD Draft Convention on the Protection of Foreign Property, adopted by the OECD Council on 12 October 1967, reproduced in (1968) 2 Int'l Lawyer 335–6.

[26] ibid, 336. Interestingly, the above explanation refers implicitly to the State-to-State arbitration mechanism only, rather than to the investor-to-State one (Article 7(a)), which is also included in the Draft Convention (Article 7(b)).

[27] FA Mann, 'British Treaties for the Promotion and Protection of Investments' (1981) 52 BYIL 241, 246. See also Rudolf Dolzer and Margrete Stevens, *Bilateral Investment Treaties* (ICSID and Kluwer Law International 1995) 81–2.

[28] Mann, 'British Treaties' (n 27) 246.

include the corresponding undertakings of the foreign investor. Accordingly, the umbrella clause appears to be premised on the assumption that the foreign investor is in need of special protection rather than on the underlying investment contract as a whole.

Second, at least part of the content of the umbrella clause is determined through what appears to be a 'dynamic reference' to any undertakings entered by the host State vis-à-vis the foreign investment (akin to the legislative technique of incorporation by reference often used in domestic or international legal systems).[29] Thus, the content of the undertakings protected by the umbrella clause will need to be determined on the basis of the undertaking's legal system of reference at the time the claim under the umbrella clause is made.[30]

Despite a few initial decisions that were sceptical vis-à-vis the very function of umbrella clauses,[31] investment treaty tribunals have since recognized that umbrella clauses are (at a minimum) more than 'aspirational statements'.[32] While there has been disagreement, particularly with regard to the 'effect' and 'scope' of umbrella clauses, more recently there appears to be a consensus among investment tribunals favouring an interpretation according to which (a) the function of umbrella clauses is 'essentially jurisdictional in that it provides a claimant with access to an arbitral tribunal but does not alter their actual rights';[33] and (b) 'the scope of the umbrella clause extends at least to contractual obligations and potentially beyond, provided that a specific undertaking is entered into with regard to an investment'.[34]

[29] With regard to United States administrative law, see Emily Bremer, 'Incorporation by Reference in an Open-Government Age' (2013) 36 Harv J L & Pub Poly 131 and for WTO law, see Marina Foltea, *International Organizations in WTO Dispute Settlement: How Much Institutional Sensitivity?* (CUP 2012) 60 ss.

[30] In principle, a protected 'undertaking' for purposes of the umbrella clause may stem from both domestic law and international law. Umbrella clauses use different terms, including 'undertaking', 'obligation', or 'commitment'. Dolzer and Stevens have noted that the 'term "obligation" tends not to be defined in the treaties but is generally assumed to include both obligations arising from investment contracts i.e. contracts between a Party and investors from the other Contracting Party, as well as obligations stemming from direct undertakings between the two Contracting Parties': Dolzer and Stevens, *Bilateral Investment Treaties* (n 27) 82. See Newcombe and Paradell, *Law and Practice of Investment Treaties* (n 23) 448–9.

[31] See in particular, *SGS v Pakistan*, Decision on Jurisdiction, 6 August 2003 (n 12).

[32] Jude Antony, 'Umbrella Clauses since *SGS v Pakistan* and *SGS v Philippines*—A Developing Consensus' (2013) 29 Arb Int'l 607, 614.

[33] ibid.

[34] ibid, 638. Interestingly, the Notes and Comments to Article 2 of the OECD Draft Convention seem to include a general undertaking giving rise to legitimate expectations. The Notes specify, first, that the 'undertaking may represent a consensual or a unilateral engagement on the part of the Party concerned' and, second, that 'it must relate to the property concerned; it is not sufficient if the link is incidental'. Moreover, in order to establish the link between the undertaking and the property, the Notes and Comments include the case where, though the undertaking was originally couched in general terms, the national concerned acted in reliance on it. 'In such cases, in accordance with the principles of international law, a situation must be protected in which a Party by its conduct had given rise to a legitimate expectation of the continuance of a particular state of affairs.' See further, Christoph Schreuer, 'Travelling the BIT Route: Of Waiting Periods, Umbrella Clauses and Forks in the Road' (2004) 5 JWIT 231, 250–1; Mann, 'British Treaties' (n 27) 246.

On the basis of this growing consensus, and leaving to one side the still controversial question of privity,[35] the umbrella clause represents a clear example of an investment treaty obligation guaranteeing the stability in the strict sense of the host State's (contractual) undertakings, as it requires the host State to respect, and conform to, any undertakings assumed with regard to the foreign investment. As noted above, whether the undertaking exists *and* whether it has been breached crucially depend on the content of the undertaking itself.[36] In the paradigmatic case of a contract between the host State and the foreign investor, the existence and non-observance of the contractual undertaking for purposes of an umbrella clause claim is determined on the basis of the contract and its applicable law. For example, in *CEF Energia BV v Italy* the tribunal rejected the investor's umbrella claim on the basis of the finding that the contractual breaches alleged by the investor were in fact unilateral modifications permitted by Italian law, as the applicable law to the contracts at issue.[37]

Nevertheless, having determined the existence of an undertaking, failure by the host State to observe such undertaking represents a breach of the investment treaty's umbrella clause.[38] Excluding general exception clauses in the underlying treaties (or circumstances precluding wrongfulness under customary law), the umbrella clause does not require an investment tribunal to take into account the possible reasons that may have justified the host State's conduct. In this sense, an umbrella clause represents a treaty obligation directly guaranteeing the stability in the strict sense of the host State's undertakings.

However, while umbrella clauses guarantee the stability in the strict sense of the host State's undertakings (principally of a contractual nature) entered into with regard to the investment, they do not guarantee regulatory stability in the strict sense. In other words, umbrella clauses may not be able to freeze the regulatory framework governing the foreign investment at the time the investment is made. This is

[35] The issue of privity refers to whether or not the respondent State and the claimant are (either or both) required to be parties to the contract establishing the obligation relied on in the umbrella clause claim. See Antony, 'Umbrella Clauses' (n 32) 639.

[36] The role of an investment treaty tribunal is to determine whether the host State has complied with the relevant undertaking (or obligation). The existence of an exclusive forum selection clause in the underlying source of the obligation may create a potential jurisdictional conflict (say, eg, between the treaty tribunal and the contractual forum). However, such conflict can and should be resolved using the traditional tools, such as *lis alibi pendens*. See Campbell McLachlan, Lis Pendens *in International Litigation* in Collected Courses of the Hague Academy of International Law (Hague Academy of International Law 2009).

[37] *CEF Energia BV v Italy*, SCC Case No 158/2015, Award, 16 January 2019, para 254.

[38] Some tribunals have limited a finding of breach of the umbrella clause to 'governmental' breaches of the underlying obligation (or undertaking), thus excluding 'pure commercial' breaches (see eg *Sempra Energy International v The Argentine Republic*, ICSID Case No ARB/02/16, Award, 28 September 2007, para 310). However, even under this reading, the umbrella clause's fundamental nature and operation does not change; it is still for the host State to respect its undertakings (even if such obligation only applies when the host State exercises 'sovereign' powers, rather than merely acting in its 'commercial' capacity). See Mihir C Naniwadekar, 'The Scope and Effect of Umbrella Clauses: The Need for a Theory of Deference?' (2010) 2 Trade, L Dev 169.

for at least two sets of reasons. First, the host State's wider regulatory framework applicable to the foreign investment does not usually take the form of an 'undertaking' 'entered into by the host State' 'with regard to the investment'. Accordingly, the wider regulatory framework does not come under the protection offered by the umbrella clause. It is true that specific undertakings vis-à-vis foreign investors may be included in domestic law (eg in investment codes of host States) and thus may come under the scope and protection of an umbrella clause (subject to the required link between the undertaking and the specific investment at issue). However, the wider regulatory framework is not protected by an umbrella clause, as it is usually comprised of a complex set of disciplines (rather than undertakings), which may not relate to foreign investments specifically. For example, domestic laws may set a mandatory minimum wage for employees or a corporate tax rate without committing one way or the other whether those laws will be modified in the future.[39]

Second, even in the presence of stabilization commitments (whether in the investment contract or in the host State legislation) made specifically to the foreign investment, these commitments are incorporated in the treaty's umbrella clause only to the extent that they actually exist in, and are valid and enforceable under, the relevant legal system of reference at the time the umbrella clause claim is made. This is again based on the understanding that the content of the umbrella clause is at least in part determined through a dynamic reference to any undertakings entered into by the host State vis-à-vis the foreign investment. Let us assume a stabilization commitment with regard to the mandatory minimum wage is found in the authorization granted to the foreign investment at the time of admission to the host State (ie increases of the minimum wage will not apply to the specific investment). Let us assume further that a later act of Parliament or judgment by the Constitutional Court of the host State declares such commitments void because they are in violation of the constitutional protection of employees or the constitutional principle of parliamentary sovereignty. A claim brought by a foreign investor based on the observance of undertakings clause in an investment treaty (after such act of Parliament or judgment of the Constitutional Court) would likely fail, as the stabilization 'undertaking' itself does not exist any longer at the time the claim is brought. One can imagine a similar effect in the case of a stabilization commitment contained in a domestic investment code at the time the investment was admitted, and which is then abrogated before the treaty claim is brought.[40]

39 See Mann, 'British Treaties' (n 27) 242, 246:

> Thus if the law of the land provides that the State is liable for the torts of its servants this is not an 'obligation arising from a particular commitment' the State may have entered into and may be changed, though in certain circumstances this may become subject to the provisions about expropriation.

40 For a similar real-life scenario, see Rachel Frid de Vries, 'Stability Shaken? Israeli High Court of Justice Strikes Down the Stabilization Clause in the Israeli Government's Gas Plan' (2017) 18 JWIT 332.

B. Regulatory Stability in the Strict Sense and (the Little Known Case of) Investment Treaties' Stabilization Clauses

Under traditional investment treaties, investments are admitted in accordance with the host State's legislation and regulation. As noted in the Introduction, next to breach of contract, one of the most pressing concerns for foreign investors is an adverse change in the host State's regulatory framework applicable to the investment once the investment has been admitted. In order to ensure the stability in the strict sense of such regulatory framework, international investment treaties have, albeit rarely,[41] featured so-called 'stabilization clauses' purporting to freeze the regulatory framework applicable to the covered foreign investments at the time of its admission to the host State. Following the known categorization of contractual stabilization clause,[42] Professor Gazzini has recently referred to such treaty clauses as 'freezing clauses'.[43]

There appears to be very little awareness (let alone examination) of investment treaties' stabilization clauses. In addition to Gazzini's recent note,[44] the only references were found in a 1988 publication by the United Nations Centre on Transnational Corporations (UNCTC) on Bilateral Investment Treaties[45] and in the 1998 sequel prepared by UNCTAD.[46] The latter one states as follows:

> the stabilization clause [...] requires that, if there is a change in the law after the admission of an investor protected under the BIT, and the new law is less favourable to the investor, the pre-existing, more favourable norms remain applicable to

[41] While the present author has not carried out a systematic review of investment treaties, the cursory examination of a few western European treaties (mainly, Italian, Dutch and French treaties) shows that stabilization clauses are relatively rare in such treaties (or are found in older treaties that have since been terminated following the renegotiation between the same contracting parties of a new treaty that does not include such clauses). However, through the operation of the Most Favoured Nation (MFN) clause, their relevance may not be so negligible.

[42] There exist two basic types of contractual stabilization clauses: (a) 'freezing clauses', which freeze the law at the time the contract is executed for the specific investor and any future changes do not apply to the contract at issue; and (b) 'economic equilibrium clauses', which provide that, while future regulatory changes in the host State will apply to the specific investor, the host State agrees to provide compensation to the investor for its compliance with the new law. On contractual stabilization clauses, see further Nagla Nassar, *Sanctity of Contracts Revisited: A Study in the Theory and Practice of Long-Term International Commercial Transactions* (Martinus Nijhoff 1995); Thomas Wälde and George N'Di, 'Stabilising International Investment Commitments' (1996) 31 Tex Int'l L J 215; Piero Bernardini, 'The Renegotiation of the Investment Contract' (1998) 13 ICSID Rev/FILJ 411; Lorenzo Cotula, 'Regulatory Takings, Stabilization Clauses and Sustainable Development' (2008) OECD Investment Policy Perspectives 69; Andrea Shemberg, 'Stabilization Clauses and Human Rights' (2009) International Finance Corporation (IFC) Report.

[43] Tarcisio Gazzini, 'Beware of Freezing Clauses in International Investment Clauses' Columbia FDI Perspectives (N 191, 2017) http://ccsi.columbia.edu/files/2016/10/No-191-Gazzini-FINAL.pdf accessed 20 May 2019.

[44] ibid.

[45] UNCTC, *Bilateral Investment Treaties* (Graham & Trotman in cooperation with the United Nations 1988) 57–8.

[46] UNCTAD, *Bilateral Investment Treaties in the Mid-1990s* (United Nations 1998) 87.

> that investor. Such a clause is intended to protect investors from changes in legislation after their admission.

This lack of awareness is also evident in some of the decisions by investment treaty tribunals that have criticized an interpretation of the FET standard that imposes on States a regulatory stability obligation.[47] For example, the tribunal in *El Paso v Argentina* noted that 'it is inconceivable that any State would accept that, because it has entered into BITs, it can no longer modify pieces of legislation which might have a negative impact on foreign investors, in order to deal with modified economic conditions and must guarantee absolute legal stability'.[48]

Unsurprisingly, and in line with the better-known case of stabilization clauses in investment contracts,[49] there are variations in the drafting of investment treaties' stabilization clauses. An example of a general stabilization clause is Article 11.3 of the 1996 Italy–Jordan BIT, which reads as follows:

> Whenever, after the date when the investment has been made, a modification should take place in laws, regulations, acts or measures of economic policies governing directly or indirectly the investment, the same treatment will apply upon request of the investor that was applicable to it at the moment when the investment had been carried out.[50]

Article 11.3 grants to the foreign investor the right to avoid being subjected to any (prejudicial) change in the applicable regulatory framework after the investment has been made. In the words of Gazzini, such a clause 'provides all investors of the other contracting party a total exemption from unfavourable laws, regulations, acts, or measures of economic policies adopted by host countries [...], it neutralizes the exercise of subsequent regulatory powers to the extent that such exercise is directly or indirectly detrimental to covered investors'.[51]

[47] See section C, 'Strict Stability through the Fair and Equitable Treatment (FET) Standard', below.

[48] *El Paso Energy International Company v The Argentine Republic*, ICSID Case No ARB/03/15, Award, 31 October 2011, para 367. Obviously, one should read this statement as referring to a BIT that does not expressly contain a stabilization clause.

[49] See eg Sotonye Frank, 'Stabilisation Clauses and Foreign Direct Investment: Presumptions versus Realities' (2015) 16 JWIT 88; Katja Gehne and Romulo Brillo, 'Stabilization Clauses in International Investment Law: Beyond Balancing and Fair and Equitable Treatment' (2014) NCCR Trade Working Paper No 2013/46; Shemberg, 'Stabilization Clauses and Human Rights' (n 42).

[50] See also Article 12(3) of the 1998 Italy–Mozambique BIT, which reads as follows:

> Whenever, after the date when the investment has been made, a modification should take place in laws, regulations, acts or measures of economic policies governing directly or indirectly the investment, the same treatment shall apply upon request of the investor that was applicable to it at the moment when the investment was agreed upon to be carried out.

Similar clauses are also contained in Italy's BITs with Angola (1997), Armenia (1998), Azerbaijan (1997, terminated), Bosnia (2000), Cameroon (1999), Kazakhstan (1994), Macedonia (1997), Moldova (1997), Tanzania (2001), Uganda (1997, terminated) and Uzbekistan (1997).

[51] Gazzini, 'Beware of Freezing Clauses' (n 43) 1.

Thus, such a general stabilization clause operates with regard to a wide set of host State's measures as it refers to 'laws, regulations, acts or measures of economic policies governing directly or indirectly the investment'. Interestingly, Article XII.3 of the 2003 Italy model BIT is equally broad as it only refers to 'legislation […] regulating directly or indirectly the investment'.[52]

On the other hand, there exist more limited stabilization clauses in investment treaties that only purport to freeze the host State legislation with regard to certain specific rules. One example of such limited clauses is in connection with the rules on transfer of capital, profits and other payment related to the investment. In these cases, the specific stabilization clause purports to ensure that less favourable laws regulating the repatriation of capital that may be introduced after the investment is made do not apply to the covered investments. For example, Article 2 of the (now terminated) 1965 Belgium–Morocco BIT required each contracting party to authorize the transfer of net profits, interests, dividends and royalties 'in conformity with the regulations promulgated in pursuance of the legislation in force in its territory at the time each investment is made or of any more favourable legislation that may be enacted in the future or of rules agreed upon between the two Parties'.[53]

The stabilization clause may be even narrower, as applying only to the balance of payments exception to the free transfer of capital obligation. For example, Article 6 of the 1982 UK–Paraguay BIT provides as follows:

> Each Contracting Party shall in respect of investments guarantee to nationals or companies of the other Contracting Party the unrestricted transfer to the country where they reside of their investments and returns, subject to the right of each Contracting Party in exceptional balance of payments difficulties and for a limited period to exercise equitable and in good faith powers conferred by its laws existing when this Agreement enters into force.

In these cases, the relevant legislation (being frozen) is the one at the time of the entry into force of the treaty rather than at the time the specific investment is made.[54]

[52] XII.3 of the 2003 Italy model BIT reads as follows: 'After the date when the investment has been made, any substantial modification in the legislation of the Contracting party regulating directly or indirectly the investment shall not be applied retroactively and the investments made under this Agreement shall therefore be protected.' This is the exact language used in the 2004 Italy–Nicaragua BIT (Article XII.3). See further Federico Ortino, 'Italy' in Chester Brown (ed) *Commentaries on Selected Model Investment Treaties* (OUP 2013) 321.

[53] Similarly, Article 6.5 of the 1975 France–Morocco BIT (now terminated) read as follows:

> Le régime juridique régissant ce transfert
> est celui qui est en vigueur au moment de l'agrément pour les transferts effectués pendant une période de dix ans à partir de la date de l'agrément de l'investissement. Toutefois l'investisseur pourra, sur sa demande, bénéficier du régime en vigueur au moment de la réalisation du transfert.

[54] See similarly Article 6 of both the 1982 UK–Cameroon BIT and the 1981 UK–Lesotho BIT.

Investment treaties' stabilization clauses may be bilateral or unilateral in the sense that they may apply reciprocally to both contracting parties, or with regard to the legislation of one contracting party only. For example, Article 4 of the 1974 France–Jugoslavia BIT provides that if new, less favourable legislation should be introduced, investments will continue to be governed by the law in force when they were admitted. However, the reference appears to have been made only to the '*législation yougoslave*'.[55] Similarly, the Protocol to the 1996 Netherlands–Zimbabwe BIT specifies that with respect to the Republic of Zimbabwe, the payments falling under the obligation to guarantee the free transfer under Article 5 of the treaty 'shall be subject to such conditions as to remittability [...] as may have been agreed with the national and fixed in terms of the laws of the Republic of Zimbabwe at the time of admission of the investment'.[56]

A few investment treaties qualify the scope of the stabilization obligation by specifying that the clause is triggered only in the case of 'substantial' modification. This appears to happen in the case of general stabilization clauses. For example, Article XII.3 of the 2004 Italy–Nicaragua BIT prohibits the retroactive application of 'any substantial modification in the legislation of the Contracting party regulating directly or indirectly the investment'. In other words, the requirement that future modification be 'substantial' appears to limit an otherwise broad stabilization obligation (because applicable to a wide set of host States' measures).

Whether the stabilization clause is general or limited, reciprocal or unilateral in scope, it should be noted that the stabilization clause's main objective is to exclude the application of 'prejudicial' changes in the relevant regulatory framework of the host State to any protected investment. Stabilization clauses often provide this expressly,[57] or condition the application of the clause to a request by the foreign investor.[58] In the context of investment contracts, Professor Cameron has referred to this typical feature as the asymmetrical character of stabilization clauses: '[t]he investor is protected against adverse changes but if there are any changes made to the laws or regulations that may have beneficial effects, these are passed on to the investor'.[59] This is in line with so-called 'preservation of rights clauses' often included

[55] Article 4:

> Les ressortissants français, personnes physiques ou morales, bénéficieront pour les investissements visés à l'article 1er de la présente Convention ainsi que pour l'excercice des activités professionnelles et économiques liées à ces investissements, du traitement le plus favorable accordé en la matière à des ressortissants de tout autre pays tiers par la législation yougoslave. Au cas où celle-ci serait modifiée dans un sens moins favorable, lesdits investissements resteront régis par les dispositions en vigueur à la date au ils ont été agrées.

For a similar provision, see 1975 Egypt–Greece BIT.

[56] 'In no case shall treatment of such investments [of nationals of the Netherlands] be less favourable than law no. 1 of 1967, as amended in 1970, permits.' Paragraph 1, Protocol to the 1994 Netherland–Indonesia BIT (terminated).

[57] See eg Article 4 of the 1974 France–Jugoslavia BIT.

[58] See eg Article 11.3 of the 1996 Italy–Jordan BIT or Article 6.5 of the 1975 France–Morocco BIT (now terminated).

[59] Cameron, *International Energy Investment Law: The Pursuit of Stability* (n 15) 82.

in investment treaties, according to which protected investment will benefit from more favourable laws and regulation, that already exist or are introduced in the future.[60]

Based on the various formulations shown above, one can easily imagine a few key interpretative questions that remain open with regard to the content and scope of investment treaties' stabilization clauses. For example, what is the level of change in the regulatory framework necessary in order for the relevant 'modification' to take place? Does a change in the established practice with regard to the interpretation and application of a specific legislation (without any formal amendment) qualify as a 'modification of the legislation regulating the investment'? When does a modification become 'substantial' for purposes of the investment treaty? Given the apparent absence of any decision examining an investment treaty's stabilization clause, it may be difficult to tackle these questions in the abstract (although an examination of the decisions interpreting parallel clauses in investment contracts[61] and in national legislation[62] may constitute a good starting point). For purposes of the present study, it is important to emphasize that such clauses can be categorized as provisions guaranteeing regulatory stability in the strict sense, since their key function is to impose on the host State an obligation to avoid subjecting the protected investment to a prejudicial change in the regulatory framework of the host State. And crucially, as noted with regard to umbrella clauses, excluding general exception clauses in the underlying treaties (or circumstances precluding wrongfulness under customary law), investment treaties' stabilization clauses do not require an investment tribunal to take into account the possible reasons that may have justified the host State's conduct under review.

Brief mention should be made here to those treaty clauses that, while they may at first blush appear as stabilization clauses, upon closer examination are not (at least in a strict sense). The clearest example is Article 10(1) of the Energy Charter Treaty, which provides in relevant part, that 'each contracting Party shall, in accordance with the provisions of this Treaty, encourage and create stable [...] conditions for investors of other Contracting Parties'. As stated by the tribunal in *AES v Hungary*, while the stable conditions in Article 10(1) relate to the framework within which the investment takes place, Article 10(1) 'is not a stability clause'.[63]

[60] See Article 11.2 of the 1996 Italy–Jordan BIT, providing as follows: 'Whenever the treatment accorded by one Contracting Party to the investors of the other Contracting Party according to its laws and regulations or other provisions or specific contract or investment authorizations or agreements, is more favourable than that provided under this Agreement, the most favourable treatment shall apply.'

[61] See Lorenzo Cotula, 'Pushing the Boundaries vs Striking a Balance: Some Reflections on Stabilization Issues in Light of *Duke Energy International Investments v Republic of Peru*' (2010) 7(1) TDM.

[62] See AFM Maniruzzaman, 'National Laws Providing for Stability of International Investment Contracts: A Comparative Perspective' (2007) 8 JWIT 233.

[63] *AES Summit Generation Limited and AES Tisza Erömü Kft v The Republic of Hungary*, ICSID Case No ARB/07/22, Award, 23 September 2010, para 9.3.29 ('A legal framework is by definition subject to change as it adapts to new circumstances day by day and a state has the sovereign right to exercise its powers which include legislative acts'). See section C.

C. Strict Stability through the Fair and Equitable Treatment (FET) Standard

The debate about legal stability in international investment treaties has principally focused on the FET standard.[64] While investment treaties' stabilization clauses are indeed a very rare breed, FET clauses are a common feature of modern international investment treaties. As noted in section A, UNCTAD recent mapping of more than 2500 investment treaties has shown that FET clauses are found in approximately 95% of such treaties.[65] In the paradigmatic case of *Occidental v Ecuador I*, having stated that '[t]he stability of the legal and business framework is […] an essential element of fair and equitable treatment', the tribunal found a breach of the FET as the tax framework under which the investment had been made and had been operating 'has been changed in an important manner by the actions adopted by the [Ecuadorian tax authorities]'.[66]

Legal stability has often been linked to the FET standard through the concept of the protection of the investor's expectations. In one of the leading textbooks on international investment law, the authors identify the 'stability and the protection of the investor's legitimate expectations' as one of the central principles of the FET standard emerging from the practice of investment tribunals.[67] In this context, legal stability has been linked to a broad set of legal sources, including promises, representations, contractual undertakings, administrative decisions and legislative acts. Terms used have included legal framework, legal regime and legal environment.

This section's primary aim is to inquire whether, and the extent to which, investment treaty tribunals have interpreted the FET standard as a guarantee of legal stability in the strict sense. The section puts forward two main arguments. First, despite a limited attempt by a few early investment tribunals to read a strict stability obligation as part of the FET provision (section 1), the majority of investment tribunals appear to have adopted a more nuanced approach by increasingly recognizing the need to safeguard the host State's right to regulate in the public interest

[64] It should be noted that the full protection and security (FPS) provision appears to have also at times been interpreted as imposing a legal stability obligation in the strict sense by those tribunals that have extended the scope of FPS to include 'legal' security and protection. See eg *CME Czech Republic BV v Czech Republic*, Partial Award, 13 September 2001 (n 13) para 613:

> The host State is obligated to ensure that neither by amendment of its laws nor by actions of its administrative bodies is the agreed and approved security and protection of the foreign investor's investment withdrawn or devalued. This is not the case. The Respondent therefore is in breach of this obligation.

See also *National Grid plc v Argentina*, UNCITRAL, Award, 3 November 2008, paras 187–89.

[65] As of 20 May 2019, out of 2571 treaties mapped, the FET clause is not found in at least 131 treaties. See UNCTAD database, 'IIA Mapping Project' http://investmentpolicyhub.unctad.org accessed 20 May 2019.

[66] *Occidental v Ecuador*, Final Award, 1 July 2004 (n 6) paras 183–84.

[67] Dolzer and Schreuer, *Principles of International Investment Law* (n 8) 145.

(section 2). Second, despite investment tribunals' apparently more deferential approach, one can still find (recent) arbitral decisions where the role of regulatory stability within the FET standard remains at best ambiguous, and which thus fail to assuage the fears that the FET standard may indeed function as imposing an obligation of regulatory stability in the strict sense (section 3).[68]

1. Linking FET and legal stability in the strict sense: the early attempt

There exists a line of arbitral decisions that in the early years of the twenty-first century (particularly between 2003 and 2006) appeared to read the FET standard to include a guarantee of legal stability in the strict sense. These tribunals relied principally on (a) statements in treaty preambles linking stability and FET; (ii) the need to protect investors' expectations; and/or (iii) previous arbitral decisions. For example, the tribunal in *Tecmed v Mexico* notoriously stated in a 2003 decision that the FET provision requires the contracting parties to provide to international investments 'treatment that does not affect the basic expectations that were taken into account by the foreign investor to make the investment', including the expectation that the host State acts 'in a consistent manner, free from ambiguity and totally transparently in its relations with the foreign investor'.[69]

In 2004, as noted above, the tribunal in *Occidental v Ecuador I* expressly stated that the stability of the legal and business framework is an essential element of fair and equitable treatment. The tribunal relied on the clear statement found in the preamble of the underlying treaty (the 1993 Ecuador–United States BIT) that FET 'is desirable in order to maintain a stable framework for investment and maximum effective utilization of economic resources'.[70] One of the key questions at issue in *Occidental I* was whether the host State had breached the FET provision by modifying the right of certain exporters to claim a VAT refund. The tribunal explained its finding in the following terms:

> The relevant question for international law in this discussion is not whether there is an obligation to refund VAT, which is the point on which the parties have argued most intensely, but rather whether the legal and business framework meets the

[68] This section draws on and expands upon Federico Ortino, 'The Obligation of Regulatory Stability in the Fair and Equitable Treatment Standard: How Far Have We Come?' (2018) 21 JIEL 845.

[69] *Técnicas Medioambientales Tecmed SA v The United Mexican States*, ICSID Case No ARB (AFA)/00/2, Award, 29 May 2003, para 154. An even earlier tribunal in the context of finding a violation of FET in the context of Article 1105 of the North American Free Trade Agreement (NAFTA), referred to the host State's failure 'to ensure a transparent and predictable framework', as well as to the investor's 'expectation that it would be treated fairly and justly'. *Metalclad Corporation v The United Mexican States*, ICSID Case No ARB(AF)/97/1, Award, 30 August 2000, para 99.

[70] *Occidental v Ecuador I*, Final Award, 1 July 2004 (n 6) para 183.

> requirements of stability and predictability under international law. It was earlier concluded that there is not a VAT refund obligation under international law, except in the specific case of the Andean Community law, which provides for the option of either compensation or refund, but there is certainly *an obligation not to alter the legal and business environment in which the investment has been made.* In this case it is the latter question that triggers a treatment that is not fair and equitable [emphasis added].[71]

In 2005, the tribunal in *CMS v Argentina* similarly affirmed that 'a stable legal and business environment is an essential element of fair and equitable treatment'.[72] The *CMS* tribunal also specifically relied for its interpretation of the FET provision on the preamble of the applicable investment treaty (the 1991 United States–Argentina BIT), where the contracting parties had expressed their agreement 'that fair and equitable treatment of investment is desirable in order to maintain a stable framework for investment and maximum effective use of economic resources'.[73]

A few other decisions in 2006–07, relying on these precedents, followed this line of cases, affirming that the requirement of legal stability is a key element of fair and equitable treatment.[74] In *PSEG v Turkey*, for example, the Tribunal found that the host State conduct had seriously breached the FET obligation in light of 'the "roller-coaster" effect of the continuing legislative changes'.[75] In *Sempra v*

[71] ibid, para 191.

[72] *CMS Gas Transmission Company v The Republic of Argentina*, ICSID Case No ARB/01/8, Award, 12 May 2005, para 274. There is a very similar approach and language in *LG&E Energy Corporation, LG&E Capital Corporation and LG&E International, Inc v Argentine Republic*, ICSID Case No ARB/02/1, Decision on Liability, 3 October 2006, paras 124 and 131 ('Tribunal must conclude that stability of the legal and business framework is an essential element of fair and equitable treatment in this case'); *Enron Corporation and Ponderosa Assets, LP v Argentine Republic*, ICSID Case No ARB/01/3, Award, 22 May 2007, paras 259–60 ('the Tribunal concludes that a key element of fair and equitable treatment is the requirement of a "stable framework for the investment," which has been prescribed by a number of decisions') and *Sempra v The Argentine Republic*, Award, 28 September 2007 (n 38) para 300 ('What counts is that in the end the stability of the law and the observance of legal obligations are assured, thereby safeguarding the very object and purpose of the protection sought by the treaty').

[73] *CMS v Argentina*, Award, 12 May 2005 (n 72) para 274. This is true also for the *LG&E v Argentina* (n 72) and *Enron v Argentina* (n 72) decisions.

[74] *Enron v Argentina*, Award, 22 May 2007 (n 72) paras 259–60 ('the Tribunal concludes that a key element of fair and equitable treatment is the requirement of a "stable framework for the investment," which has been prescribed by a number of decisions'). There is very similar language in *LG&E v Argentina*, Decision on Liability, 3 October 2006 (n 72) paras 124 and 131 ('Tribunal must conclude that stability of the legal and business framework is an essential element of fair and equitable treatment in this case').

[75] *PSEG Global, Inc, The North American Coal Corporation, and Konya Ingin Electrik Üretim ve Ticaret Limited Sirketi v Republic of Turkey*, ICSID Case No ARB/02/5, Award, 19 January 2007, para 250. The *PSEG* tribunal also emphasized the inconsistency of the host State's behaviour (ibid, paras 248–49):

> Inconsistent administrative acts are also evident in this case in respect of some matters. On occasion the administration would ignore rights granted by law as a matter of policy or practice. […] Similar was the situation in respect of the Constitutional Court decision upholding the rights acquired under a contract, which was simply ignored by MENR in its dealings with

Argentina, the tribunal captured the key issue as follows: 'What counts is that in the end the stability of the law and the observance of legal obligations are assured, thereby safeguarding the very object and purpose of the protection sought by the treaty.'[76] The *Sempra* tribunal also discarded the relevance of any justifications for introducing such changes in the legal and business framework. Having found that the emergency legislation implemented by Argentina had, beyond any doubt, substantially changed the legal and business framework under which the investment was decided and implemented, the *Sempra* tribunal concluded that there had been an 'objective breach' of the FET provision, 'even assuming that the Respondent was guided by the best intentions'.[77]

These early decisions' reasoning underlying a requirement of stability in the strict sense stemming from the FET provision appears at best underdeveloped. First of all, while the *Tecmed* decision appears to represent one of the first leading precedents underlying these early decisions establishing a stability obligation, that decision never mentions the concept of 'stability' or 'stable legal framework'; rather, its emphasis is on 'consistency'. In other words, the *Tecmed* tribunal does not appear to prohibit changes in the legal framework in force at the time the investment was made (akin to a stabilization or freezing clause), but rather it seems to impose a laxer requirement of harmonious, predictable or transparent behaviour on the part of the various components of the host State.[78] Furthermore, the *Tecmed* tribunal defines a 'consistent act' as one 'without arbitrarily revoking any pre-existing decisions or permits issued by the State that were relied upon by the investor to assume its commitments as well as to plan and launch its commercial and business activities'.[79] One may still criticize the *Tecmed* consistency standard as being excessive or aspirational,[80] but the point worth making here is that it does not appear to impose a legal stability requirement in the strict sense, as several of the subsequent decisions relying on *Tecmed* actually did.

Second, despite the reference to the relatively well-known legal concept of 'legitimate expectations' in the arguments of the disputing parties,[81] these early tribunals refrained from expressly referring to such concept and instead limited their reference to a broader notion of investors' 'expectations'.[82] Also, these early tribunals adopted differing views with regard to the relationship between the investor's

the Claimants. Such inconsistent acts might be unlawful under Turkish law, but in light of the provisions of the Treaty they are also in breach of the standard of fair and equitable treatment.

[76] *Sempra v Argentina*, Award, 28 September 2007 (n 38) para 300.

[77] ibid, paras 303–04. See also *Enron v Argentina*, Award, 22 May 2007 (n 72) para 268.

[78] *Tecmed v Mexico* (n 69) para 154.

[79] ibid.

[80] Zachary Douglas, 'Nothing if Not Critical for Investment Treaty Arbitration: *Occidental, Eureko* and *Methanex*' (2006) 22 Arb Int'l 27, 28.

[81] See eg *Occidental v Ecuador I* (n 6) para 181.

[82] The tribunal in *LG&E v Argentina* does refer to the investor's 'fair expectations' in one instance. See *LG&E v Argentina*, Decision on Liability, 3 October 2006 (n 72) para 130.

expectations and the stability requirement. Some tribunals appeared to include predictability, consistency or stability as some of the investor's expectations that the treaty provision on FET was aimed to protect. As noted above, the *Tecmed* tribunal stated that FET requires 'to provide to international investments treatment that does not affect the basic expectations that were taken into account by the foreign investor to make the investment', including the expectation that the host State act 'in a consistent manner, free from ambiguity and totally transparently in its relations with the foreign investor'.[83] Other tribunals seemed, instead, to distinguish the 'legal stability' component from the 'protection of the investor's expectations' component of FET. The *LG&E* tribunal, for example, expressly noted that '[i]n addition to the State's obligation to provide a stable legal and business environment, the fair and equitable treatment analysis involves consideration of the investor's expectations when making its investment in reliance on the protections to be granted by the host State'.[84]

Third, some of these early tribunals were not clear whether they conditioned the stability obligation to a certain high level of change and, even more fundamentally, whether they subjected the stability obligation to the existence of a specific commitment by the host State that such change would not occur. The decision in *CMS v Argentina* is the perfect example of this. Having determined that the emergency legislation 'did in fact entirely transform and alter the legal and business environment under which the investment was decided and made',[85] the *CMS* tribunal stated as follows:

> It is not a question of whether the legal framework might need to be frozen as it can always evolve and be adapted to changing circumstances, but neither is it a question of whether the framework can be dispensed with altogether *when specific commitments to the contrary have been made.*[86]

The italicized sentence is particularly important in terms of understanding what kind of obligation the *CMS* tribunal read in to the FET provision. On the one hand,

[83] *Tecmed v Mexico*, Award, 29 May 2003 (n 69) para 154.

[84] *LG&E v Argentina*, Decision on Liability, 3 October 2006 (n 72) para 127. The *LG&E* tribunal seems to contradict itself on this point (ibid, para 131):

> Thus, this Tribunal, having considered, as previously stated, the sources of international law, understands that the fair and equitable standard consists of the host State's consistent and transparent behavior, free of ambiguity that involves the obligation to grant and maintain a stable and predictable legal framework necessary to fulfill the justified expectations of the foreign investor.

[85] *CMS v Argentina* (n 72) para 275.

[86] ibid, para 277. The tribunal in *Sempra v Argentina* (n 38) also appeared to emphasize the magnitude of the change ('The measures in question in this case have beyond any doubt substantially changed the legal and business framework under which the investment was decided and implemented': ibid, para 303). See also the *PSEG v Turkey* tribunal, who did not merely referred to 'legislative changes' but a 'roller-coaster' behaviour on the part of the host State public authorities, specifically noting the 'continuous change in the conditions governing the corporate status of the project' and the 'constant

a reading of FET as imposing a strict stability obligation will entail a treaty violation if the host State introduces any (prejudicial and possibly substantial) changes to the legal framework applicable to the investment. On the other hand, conditioning a violation of the FET provision to a change in the legal framework that goes against a specific stabilization commitment (as hinted by the *CMS* tribunal in the above quoted sentence) would greatly narrow the scope of the strict stability obligation under the FET provision: in this latter sense, a breach of the FET provision would only occur when the host State violates a stabilization commitment given to the investor. In other words, in this narrower sense, the FET provision would have a function similar to that of an umbrella clause. However, aside from the ambiguity, the nature of the norm stemming from either of the two possible interpretations remains the same, as in both cases the FET provision would require the host State either to conform to the (broad) legal framework or only to the (specific) stabilization commitment.

Aside from the lack of clarity and elaboration with regard to its precise origin and scope, it is submitted that there was enough in these early decisions to justify the argument (or fear) that the FET provision can actually embody an obligation of legal stability in the strict sense. Crucially, such an obligation would be principally aimed at protecting foreign investors from (substantial) changes in the legal framework of the host State applicable at the time the investment was made and notwithstanding any possible valid justification that the host State may have had to introduce such changes. In a study published in 2012, UNCTAD concluded that some investment tribunals 'have gone so far as to suggest that any adverse change in the business or legal framework of the host country may give rise to a breach of the FET standard in that the investors' legitimate expectations of predictability and stability are thereby undermined'.[87]

Unsurprisingly, this line of decisions interpreting the FET provision as including a legal stability obligation has not gone without notice. Sornarajah noted that '[t]he breadth of the rule in some awards is staggering and could not have been agreed to by the states concluding the treaties'.[88] Even more broadly, this line of decisions has contributed to some of the criticism vis-à-vis the very concept of the protection of legitimate expectations. Particularly in regard to the first few awards interpreting the FET provision, Potestà noted 'an almost complete lack of analysis as to the reasons for including the protection of legitimate expectations as a sub-element, or indeed the "dominant" sub-element, of fair and equitable treatment'.[89]

alternation between private law status and administrative concession that went back and forth': *PSEG v Turkey* (n 75) para 250.

---

[87] UNCTAD, *Fair and Equitable Treatment: UNCTAD Series on Issues in International Investment Agreements II* (United Nations 2012) 67.

[88] M Sornarajah, *The International Law on Foreign Investment* (3rd edn, CUP 2010) 355.

[89] Michele Potestà, 'Legitimate Expectations in Investment Treaty Law: Understanding the Roots and the Limits of a Controversial Concept' (2013) 28 ICSID Rev/FILJ 88, 121.

Another commentator has more strongly argued that the investment tribunals' interpretation of FET to include the protection of investors' legitimate expectations is 'an invention', as it requires far too high a standard of State conduct 'so far beyond what simple good governance would require'.[90]

2. The majority of investment tribunals have rejected the link between FET and stability in the strict sense

The handful of decisions that, in the infancy of investment treaty arbitration, appeared to read the FET provision to include an obligation of regulatory stability in the strict sense remain limited in number[91] and have been overtaken by a subsequent, large arbitral practice denying the existence of such strict regulatory stability obligation as part of the FET provision.

The initial blow to such an attempt hinged on the rejection of the view that the FET standard protects the investor's general expectation of stability. The tribunal in *Saluka v Czech Republic* was one of the first investment tribunals to politely but firmly reject reading the FET provision as imposing a legal stability obligation.[92] In the view of the *Saluka* tribunal, an interpretation of the FET provision requiring the protection of too large a set of investor's expectations (including the expectation of legal stability) would be 'inappropriate and unrealistic'. In the view of the *Saluka* tribunal, in order to be protected, the investor's expectations 'must rise to the level of legitimacy and reasonableness in light of the circumstances'.[93] Noting that no investor may reasonably expect that the circumstances prevailing at the time the investment is made remain totally unchanged, the *Saluka* tribunal specified that, 'the host State's legitimate right subsequently to regulate domestic matters in the public interest must be taken into consideration as well'.[94]

In 2007, the Annulment committee in *MTD v Chile* referred to the *Tecmed* tribunal's apparent reliance on the foreign investor's unqualified expectations as the source of the host State's obligations as 'questionable'.[95] In other words, investors'

[90] Christopher Campbell, 'House of Cards: The Relevance of Legitimate Expectations under Fair and Equitable Treatment Provisions in Investment Treaty Law' (2013) 30 J Int'l Arb 361, 379.

[91] In one sense, this group of decisions was possibly also limited in authorship, as most of them were rendered by tribunals chaired by Professor Orrego Vicuna (*Occidental v Ecuador I* (n 6), *CMS v Argentina* (n 72), *Enron v Argentina* (n 72) and *Sempra v Argentina* (n 38)).

[92] *Saluka v Czech Republic*, Partial Award, 2006 (n 9) para 302.

[93] ibid, para 304.

[94] ibid, para 305.

[95] *MTD v Chile*, Decision on Annulment, 21 March 2007, at 67:

> The obligations of the host State towards foreign investors derive from the terms of the applicable investment treaty and not from any set of expectations investors may have or claim to have. A tribunal which sought to generate from such expectations a set of rights different from those contained in or enforceable under the BIT might well exceed its powers, and if the difference were material might do so manifestly.

expectations *sic et simpliciter* cannot create legal obligations (including strict stability obligations) unless the protection stems from a treaty provision or general international law.

Furthermore, in 2008, the *Continental* tribunal was the first to oppose reading the FET provision as imposing an obligation of stability in the strict sense in the context of the same US–Argentina treaty that links, in its preamble, FET with the stability of the legal framework. The *Continental* tribunal noted that such reference in the preamble does not constitute a legal obligation in itself, nor can it be properly defined as an object of the treaty. In the view of the tribunal, while stability of the legal framework is undoubtedly conducive to attracting foreign investments, 'it would be unconscionable for a country to promise not to change its legislation as time and needs change, or even more to tie its hands by such a kind of stipulation in case a crisis of any type or origin arose'.[96]

There are plenty of statements in subsequent arbitral decisions rejecting an interpretation of the FET provision that includes a broad legal stability obligation and affirming the host State's prerogative to modify its laws and regulations.[97] For example, in the context of determining a claim based on the FET provision, the tribunal in *Parkerings v Lithuania* stated as follows:

> It is each State's undeniable right and privilege to exercise its sovereign legislative power. A State has the right to enact, modify or cancel a law at its own discretion. Save for the existence of an agreement, in the form of a *stabilisation* clause or otherwise, there is nothing objectionable about the amendment brought to the regulatory framework existing at the time an investor made its

[96] *Continental Casualty Company v The Argentine Republic*, ICSID Case No ARB/03/9, Award, 5 September 2008, para 258 ('Such an implication as to stability in the BIT's Preamble would be contrary to an effective interpretation of the Treaty; reliance on such an implication by a foreign investor would be misplaced and, indeed, unreasonable.') See more recently, *RREEF Infrastructure (GP) Limited and RREEF Pan-European Infrastructure Two Lux Sàrl v Kingdom of Spain*, ICSID Case No ARB/13/30, Decision on Responsibility and Principles of Quantum, 30 November 2018, para 244:

> Moreover, as firmly established in the case-law, an international obligation imposing on the State to waive or decline to exercise its regulatory power cannot be presumed […]. The regulatory power is essential to the achievement of the goals of the State, so to renounce to exercise it is an extraordinary act that must emerge from an unequivocal commitment; more so when it faces a serious crisis.

[97] Several scholars agree: Moshe Hirsch, 'Between Fair and Equitable Treatment and Stabilization Clause: Stable Legal Environment and Regulatory Change in International Investment Law' (2011) 12 JWIT 783, 806 ('In the absence of stabilization clauses, investment tribunals are not inclined to interpret FET clauses as effectively equivalent to stabilization clauses, and regulatory changes alone are insufficient in binding the host states to compensate foreign investors harmed by such changes'); Ursula Kriebaum, 'FET and Expropriation in the (Invisible) EU Model BIT' (2014) 15 JWIT 173:

> In recent years, tribunals have moved towards a more reserved approach concerning the stability limb of fair and equitable treatment and have moved to a more cautious approach concerning the FET standard and the right to regulate. In other words, they have stressed the need for States to maintain a regulatory space.

Also Joshua Paine, 'On Investment Law and Questions of Change' (2018) 19 JWIT 173.

investment. As a matter of fact, any businessman or investor knows that laws will evolve over time.[98]

In a similar vein, the tribunal in *EDF v Romania* stated that the investor 'may not rely on a bilateral investment treaty as a kind of insurance policy against the risk of any changes in the host State's legal and economic framework'.[99] Similarly, the tribunal in *Total v Argentina* stated that the parties to an investment treaty:

> do not thereby relinquish their regulatory powers nor limit their responsibility to amend their legislation in order to adapt it to change and the emerging needs and requests of their people in the normal exercise of their prerogatives and duties. Such limitations upon a government should not lightly be read into a treaty which does not spell them out clearly nor should they be presumed.[100]

Even in the context of Article 10(1) of the Energy Charter Treaty (ECT), which links the FET provision with the obligation to 'encourage and create stable, equitable, favourable and transparent conditions' for foreign investors, the tribunal in *AES v Hungary* excluded the existence of a legal stability obligation.[101]

It is true that many of the tribunals that have expressly excluded a general legal stability obligation stemming out of the FET provision have also expressly recognized the possibility that a legal stability obligation may exist based on a specific stabilization commitment undertaken by the host State. To cite one example, the tribunal in *Total v Argentina* stated as follows:

> In the absence of some 'promise' by the host State or a specific provision in the bilateral investment treaty itself, the legal regime in force in the host country at the time of making the investment is not automatically subject to a "guarantee"

[98] *Parkerings-Compagniet AS v Republic of Lithuania*, ICSID Case No ARB/05/8, Award, 11 September 2007, para 332 [emphasis original]. The tribunal crucially added that the FET provision did, however, prohibit 'for a State to act unfairly, unreasonably or inequitably in the exercise of its legislative power'.

[99] *EDF (Services) Limited v Romania*, ICSID Case No ARB/05/13, Award, 8 October 2009, para 217.

[100] *Total SA v The Argentine Republic*, ICSID Case No ARB/04/01, Decision on Liability, 27 December 2010, para 115. See further Hirsch, 'Between Fair and Equitable Treatment and Stabilization Clause' (n 98) 793–9.

[101] *AES v Hungary*, Award, 23 September 2010 (n 63) para 9.3.29:

> The stable conditions that the ECT mentions relate to the framework within which the investment takes place. Nevertheless, it is not a stability clause. A legal framework is by definition subject to change as it adapts to new circumstances day by day and a state has the sovereign right to exercise its powers which include legislative acts.

> of stability merely because the host country entered into a bilateral investment treaty with the country of the foreign investor.[102]

This statement reminds us of the statement made by the tribunal in *CMS v Argentina*, quoted in section 1, apparently conditioning the legal stability obligation under FET to the existence of a specific stabilization commitment. Could one argue that both decisions similarly stand for an interpretation of the FET provision that merely requires a host State to comply with its specific stabilization commitments? 'Not necessarily' is the answer. There is a crucial difference between the early decisions such as *CMS v Argentina* analysed in section 1 and the decisions such as the one in *Total v Argentina* examined above. Even assuming the narrower reading of the *CMS* decision (according to which a breach of the FET provision will only occur when the host State violates a stabilization commitment given to the investor), such a decision appears to be premised fundamentally on the *CMS* tribunal's express recognition that a stable legal and business environment is an essential requirement of FET. On the other hand, the decision in *Total* (similarly allowing the FET provision to guarantee a specific stabilization commitment undertaken by the host State) rejects the premise based on the stability of the legal regime in force at the time of making the investment. The *Total* decision is instead grounded on the legitimacy or reasonableness of the investor's expectation that such stabilization commitment would be respected. After the sentence quoted above, the *Total* tribunal continues as follows:

> The expectation of the investor is undoubtedly 'legitimate,' and hence subject to protection under the fair and equitable treatment clause, if the host State has explicitly assumed a specific legal obligation for the future, such as by contracts, concessions or stabilisation clauses on which the investor is therefore entitled to rely as a matter of law.[103]

The bulk of the arbitral practice (following from the *Saluka* decision) shows that the starting point of the analysis with regard to the investor's *claim* of (strict) legal stability under the FET provision is the doctrine of legitimate expectations rather than a broad legal stability obligation vaguely linked to investors' expectations.[104] Accordingly, while there is little doubt that, according to arbitral practice,

[102] *Total v Argentina*, Decision on Liability, 27 December 2010 (n 101) para 117. See also *Parkerings v Lithuania* (n 99) para 332 and *Paushok v Mongolia*, Award on Jurisdiction and Liability, 28 April 2011, para 305.

[103] *Total v Argentina*, Decision on Liability, 27 December 2010 (n 101), para 117. See also *Parkerings v Lithuania* (n 99), para 332 ('As a matter of fact, any business or investor knows that laws will evolve over time. What is prohibited however is for a State to act unfairly, unreasonably or inequitably in the exercise of its legislative power.').

[104] See Simon Maynard, 'Legitimate Expectations and the Interpretation of the "Legal Stability Obligation"' (2016) 1 EIL AR 99, 109–11.

the protection of investors' legitimate expectations constitutes a key requirement under FET, this requirement does not in itself entail a guarantee of stability in the strict sense, as investors' expectations are protected only if *legitimate* and *reasonable* under the circumstances.[105] Specifically, one of the factors often referred to by investment tribunals in order to determine the legitimacy of the investor's expectation (of legal stability) is the existence of a specific promise or representation of stability given by the host State and relied upon by the investor. For example, as stated by the tribunal in *EDF v Romania*:

> [e]xcept where specific promises or representations are made by the State to the investor, the latter may not rely on a bilateral investment treaty as a kind of insurance policy against the risk of any changes in the host State's legal and economic framework. Such expectation would be neither legitimate nor reasonable.[106]

Similarly, the tribunal in *Total v Argentina* stated as follows:

> In the absence of some 'promise' by the host State or a specific provision in the bilateral investment treaty itself, the legal regime in force in the host country at the time of making the investment is not automatically subject to a 'guarantee' of stability merely because the host country entered into a bilateral investment treaty with the country of the foreign investor. The expectation of the investor is undoubtedly 'legitimate', and hence subject to protection under the fair and equitable treatment clause, if the host State has explicitly assumed a specific legal obligation for the future, such as by contracts, concessions or stabilisation clauses on which the investor is therefore entitled to rely as a matter of law.[107]

In other words, according to this arbitral practice, the investor's expectation that the general legal framework at the time the investment is made will not be subject to change (detrimental to its investment) does not deserve treaty protection under the FET provision *at least unless* specific promises or representations of stability have been made by the host State.[108]

[105] Caroline Henckels, *Proportionality and Deference in Investor-State Arbitration: Balancing Investment Protection and Regulatory Autonomy* (CUP 2015) 74.

[106] *EDF v Romania*, Award, 8 October 2009 (n 100) para 217.

[107] *Total v Argentina*, Decision on Liability, 27 December 2010 (n 101) para 117.

[108] See also *Parkerings v Lithuania* (n 99) para 332 ('Save for the existence of an agreement, in the form of a stabilization clause or otherwise, there is nothing objectionable about the amendment brought to the regulatory framework existing at the time an investor made its investment'); *Paushok v Mongolia*, Award on Jurisdiction and Liability, 28 April 2011 (n 103) para 305 ('An investor, without an agreement which limits or prohibits the possibility of tax increases, should not be surprised to be hit with tax increases in subsequent years and such an event could not be considered as "unpredictable" ').

A second factor often referred to by investment tribunals in evaluating the legitimacy of investors' expectations worthy of protection under FET is whether the adverse regulatory change under review is in itself 'reasonable' or reasonably related to a legitimate public policy. For example, the tribunal in *Impregilo v Argentina*, whose eminent members disagreed on several key issues, agreed on the following:

> the term 'fair and equitable treatment', as it appears in the present BIT and in other similar BITs, is intended to give adequate protection to the investor's legitimate expectations. […] [T]he legitimate expectations of the investors […] have to be evaluated considering all circumstances. In the Tribunal's understanding, fair and equitable treatment cannot be designed to ensure the immutability of the legal order, the economic world and the social universe and play the role assumed by stabilization clauses specifically granted to foreign investors with whom the State has signed investment agreements. […] The legitimate expectations of foreign investors cannot be that the State will never modify the legal framework, especially in times of crisis, but certainly investors must be protected from unreasonable modifications of that legal framework.[109]

The legal issue identified by the *Impregilo* tribunal was not whether the host State had (substantially) modified the legal framework to the detriment of the foreign investment (as a strict stability obligation would have required); rather, the tribunal focused on whether that modification was indeed reasonable in light of the various circumstances and interests at issue.[110] Similar position was expressed by the tribunal in *Parkerings v Lithuania* as follows:

> It is each State's undeniable right and privilege to exercise its sovereign legislative power. A State has the right to enact, modify or cancel a law at its own discretion. Save for the existence of an agreement, in the form of a stabilisation clause or otherwise, there is nothing objectionable about the amendment brought to the regulatory framework existing at the time an investor made its investment. As a matter of fact, any businessman or investor knows that laws will evolve over time. What is prohibited however is for a State to act unfairly, unreasonably or inequitably in the exercise of its legislative power.[111]

[109] *Impregilo SpA v The Republic of Argentina*, ICSID Case No ARB/07/17, Award, 21 June 2011, paras 285, 290–91.

[110] See Maynard, 'Legitimate Expectations' (n 105) 99, 113–14 for the suggestion to apply a reasonableness test to the legal stability obligation.

[111] *Parkerings v Lithuania* (n 99) para 332. See *Ioan Micula, Viorel Micula, S European Food SA, S Starmill SRL and SC Multipack SRL v Romania*, ICSID Case No ARB/05/20, Final Award, 11 December 2013, para 529:

> The BIT's protection of the stability of the legal and business environment cannot be interpreted as the equivalent of a stabilization clause. In the Tribunal's view, the correct position is that the state may always change its legislation, being aware and thus taking into

Lastly, other tribunals have subjected the protection of the investor's legitimate expectations to a balancing act that takes into account, next to investors' legitimate or reasonable expectations, the host State's right to regulate, too. For example, the tribunal in *Perenco v Ecuador* noted the following:

> Many cases hold that a central aspect of the analysis of an alleged breach of the fair and equitable treatment standard is the investor's reasonable expectations as to the future treatment of its investment by the host State. [...] The search is for a balanced approach between the investor's reasonable expectations and the exercise of the host State's regulatory and other powers.[112]

Based on these various pronouncements, it can be argued that, despite those few early decisions that appeared to easily embrace a strict stability obligation, subsequent arbitral practice has shown more deference vis-à-vis the host State's right to regulate, and supported a softer understanding of a stability obligation under FET. In particular, the focus on (a) the existence of a stabilization commitment or promise; (b) the reasonableness of the host State measure; and/or (c) the need to balance the investor's expectations and the host State's right to regulate represents strong evidence of this softer notion of stability. Under this softer notion, a treaty

> consideration that: (i) an investor's legitimate expectations must be protected; (ii) the state's conduct must be substantively proper (e.g., not arbitrary or discriminatory); and (iii) the state's conduct must be procedurally proper (e.g., in compliance with due process and fair administration).

More recently, see *Charanne and Construction Investments v Spain*, SCC Case No V 062/2012, Award, 21 January 2016, paras 510 and 513:

> [...] under international law [...] in the absence of a specific commitment toward stability, an investor cannot have a legitimate expectation that a regulatory framework such as that at issue in this arbitration is to not be modified at any time to adapt to the needs of the market and to the public interest. [...] an investor has a legitimate expectation that, when modifying the existing regulation based on which the investment was made, the State will not act unreasonably, disproportionately or contrary to the public interest.

---

112 *Perenco Ecuador Limited v The Republic of Ecuador and Empresa Estatal Petróleos del Ecuador (Petroecuador)*, ICSID Case No ARB/08/6, Decision on Remaining Issues of Jurisdiction and Liability, 12 September 2014, para 560. See *Joseph Charles Lemire v Ukraine*, ICSID Case No ARB/06/18, Decision on Jurisdiction and Liability, 10 January 2010, paras 284–85:

> The evaluation of the State's action cannot be performed in the abstract and only with a view of protecting the investor's rights. The Tribunal must also balance other legally relevant interests, and take into consideration a number of countervailing factors, before it can establish that a violation of the FET standard, which merits compensation, has actually occurred: (a) the State's sovereign right to pass legislation and to adopt decisions for the protection of its public interests, especially if they do not provoke a disproportionate impact on foreign investors; (b) the legitimate expectations of the investor, at the time he made his investment [...].

See also *El Paso v Argentina*, Award, 31 October 2011 (n 48) para 358 ('In other words, a balance should be established between the legitimate expectation of the foreign investor to make a fair return on its investment and the right of the host State to regulate its economy in the public interest.'). See further Jonathan Bonnitcha, *Substantive Protection under Investment Treaties* (CUP 2014) 175–90.

violation would be established not because of a (substantial) detrimental change in the host State's legal framework applicable to the foreign investment, but because the legal change was judged 'unreasonable'.[113] While such a reasonableness test may take different forms (including procedural fairness, substantive rationality or proportionality balancing),[114] the distinctive feature of this softer understanding of FET and the obligation of stability is that the analysis will include an examination of the *merit* of the regulatory change.[115]

I will reserve a more detailed examination of the features of this reasonableness-based requirement for chapter III. It suffices here to emphasize that, while the legal environment (including contractual obligations, informal representations or regulatory frameworks) at the time the investment is made will be a relevant factor to be considered by the tribunal in order to establish the host State's liability based on FET,[116] such legal environment will only represent *one* of the relevant factors in the broader balancing exercise to be carried out by the arbitral tribunal. Crucially, among the various other considerations within such balancing, one also finds 'the State's sovereign right to pass legislation and to adopt decisions for the protection of its public interests, especially if they do not provoke a disproportionate impact on foreign investors'.[117]

Finally, it may be useful to highlight the difference between an umbrella clause and a softer understanding of stability under FET. As noted in section 1, a stabilization commitment undertaken by the host State vis-à-vis a specific investment

[113] See *RREEF Infrastructure (GP) Limited and RREEF Pan-European Infrastructure Two Lux Sàrl v Kingdom of Spain*, Decision on Responsibility and Principles of Quantum, 30 November 2018 (n 97) para 263 ('the Tribunal considers that [. . .] the main criterion to be applied for the interpretation of the FET standard is that of reasonableness').

[114] See Valentina Vadi, *Proportionality, Reasonableness and Standards of Review in International Investment Law and Arbitration* (Edward Elgar 2018).

[115] See chapter III showing how investment tribunals have interpreted several treaty provisions, like the FET standard, as reasonableness-based provisions.

[116] See Potestà, 'Legitimate Expectations in Investment Treaty Law' (n 90) 88.

[117] *Lemire v Ukraine*, Decision on Jurisdiction and Liability, 10 January 2010 (n 113) paras 284–85. Similarly, *Perenco Ecuador Limited v The Republic of Ecuador and Empresa Estatal Petróleos del Ecuador (Petroecuador)*, Decision on Remaining Issues of Jurisdiction and Liability, 12 September 2014 (n 113) para 560:

> Many cases hold that a central aspect of the analysis of an alleged breach of the fair and equitable treatment standard is the investor's reasonable expectations as to the future treatment of its investment by the host State. [. . .] The search is for a balanced approach between the investor's reasonable expectations and the exercise of the host State's regulatory and other powers.

See also *Micula v Romania*, Final Award, 11 December 2013 (n 112) para 529:

> The BIT's protection of the stability of the legal and business environment cannot be interpreted as the equivalent of a stabilization clause. In the Tribunal's view, the correct position is that the state may always change its legislation, being aware and thus taking into consideration that: (i) an investor's legitimate expectations must be protected; (ii) the state's conduct must be substantively proper (e.g., not arbitrary or discriminatory); and (iii) the state's conduct must be procedurally proper (e.g., in compliance with due process and fair administration).

See further Bonnitcha, *Substantive Protection* (n 113) 175–90.

in a contract is likely to find protection as such through the guarantee of contractual stability in the strict sense embedded in the umbrella clause. However, that same stabilization commitment will be protected by the FET provision (understood to include a soft stability obligation) only within the strictures of the doctrine of legitimate expectations, which would include the need to take into account the host State's legitimate exercise of regulatory authority.[118] Accordingly, based on the circumstances of the case at issue, the same stabilization commitment may be protected by the umbrella clause but not by the FET provision (if the latter is understood to include a soft stability obligation).

Similarly, the difference between an investment treaty's stabilization clause and a softer understanding of a stability obligation under FET is that, in determining a breach of the FET standard following a (substantial) regulatory change in the host State, only the latter will involve consideration of the host State's right to regulate in the public interest.

3. FET, regulatory change and recent arbitral practice: still in muddy waters

Having reached the conclusion that, despite the few early outliers, most subsequent investment tribunals seem to have embraced a softer, more deferential reading of the FET provision that would exclude a strict stability obligation, this section zooms in on a few recent decisions to determine whether such softer reading has indeed consolidated. Unfortunately, such an examination reveals how several investment tribunals still fail to clearly set out the role of regulatory stability within the FET standard. In particular, they fail (a) to take a clear position on whether or not FET includes a requirement of regulatory stability in the strict sense; (b) to address the precise ambit of, and relationship between, the obligation to provide a stable legal framework and the obligation to protect the investor's legitimate expectations; and (c) to clarify the kind of regulatory change that would qualify for a breach of the FET provision.

(a) Some tribunals' failure to take a clear position on whether or not FET includes a strict stability obligation

In their claims brought against host States, investors still regularly argue for a broad reading of the FET provision that includes an obligation of regulatory stability in the strict sense. More recently, however, investors often put forward two separate grounds in order to claim a breach of the FET provision because of a regulatory change: (a) the host State has violated the obligation to protect investors' legitimate

[118] For an application of the FET (understood as including a soft contractual stability obligation), see *Oxus Gold v Republic of Uzbekistan*, UNCITRAL, 17 December 2015, para 824.

expectations (including the expectation that the regulatory framework would not change during the life of the investment); and (b) the host State has violated the obligation to provide a stable regulatory framework.

For example, in *Philip Morris v Uruguay*, a case involving various legislative measures aimed at restricting the use of brands on cigarette packages, claimants argued, first, that investors' legitimate expectations may rise inter alia from 'general statements, the legal framework, legislation' and that 'specific, explicit promises to an investor [. . .] are not necessary'.[119] Second, while they accepted that 'it is a State's prerogative to exercise its regulatory and legislative powers', claimants argued that those powers 'must not be "outside of the acceptable margin of change" '.[120]

In their pleadings, investors usually refer to any of the early decisions that, as examined in section 1, contained language that appeared to support a broad reading of the FET provision.[121] For example, in *Antaris v The Czech Republic*, a case involving a policy change in the level of government incentive regime in the photovoltaic industry, claimants referred inter alia to *Tecmed, CMS, Occidental I*, and *Enron* to support the proposition that 'the requirements of protection of the investors' basic expectations as to stability are essential elements of the FET standard [and] a host State's policy change may lead to a violation of the FET standard'.[122]

While it is unsurprising that claimants argue for a broad reading of FET and base their arguments on the most supportive precedents, it is nonetheless disappointing that some arbitral tribunals do not take a clearer stance (one way or the other) with regard to the extent to which the FET provision disciplines regulatory change. The tribunals' decisions in *Philip Morris v Uruguay* and *Antaris v The Czech Republic* are good examples of this.

As noted above, the *Philip Morris v Uruguay* tribunal was confronted with the investor's claim that various legislative measures introduced by Uruguay restricting the use of brands on cigarette packages violated the FET provision in the Switzerland–Uruguay BIT principally because (a) the measures were arbitrary; (b) they frustrated the investor's legitimate expectations; and (c) they failed to provide a stable and predictable legal system. Having decided to consider the latter two grounds 'in the same context due to their interrelation',[123] the *Philip Morris v Uruguay* tribunal stated as follows:

> 422. It is common ground in the decisions of more recent investment tribunals that the requirements of legitimate expectations and legal stability as manifestations

[119] *Philip Morris Brands Sàrl, Philip Morris Products SA and Abal Hermanos SA v Oriental Republic of Uruguay*, ICSID Case No ARB/10/7, Award, 8 July 2016, para 342.

[120] ibid, para 346 referring to *El Paso v Argentina*, Award, 31 October 2011 (n 48).

[121] Claimants in *Philip Morris v Uruguay* refer to *Tecmed v The United Mexican States* (n 69) and *Occidental v Ecuador I* (n 6), see Award, 8 July 2016 (n 120) paras 340 and 346.

[122] *Antaris Solar GmbH and Dr Michael Göde v Czech Republic*, PCA Case No 2014-01, Award, 2 May 2018, para 266.

[123] *Philip Morris v Uruguay*, Award, 8 July 2016 (n 120) para 421.

> of the FET standard do not affect the State's rights to exercise its sovereign authority to legislate and to adapt its legal system to changing circumstances.
>
> 423. On this basis, changes to general legislation (at least in the absence of a stabilization clause) are not prevented by the fair and equitable treatment standard if they do not exceed the exercise of the host State's normal regulatory power in the pursuance of a public interest and do not modify the regulatory framework relied upon by the investor at the time of its investment 'outside of the acceptable margin of change.'[124]

While these statements do reflect the greater sensitivity shown by investment tribunals vis-à-vis the host State's right to regulate, one can still find language there that may be perceived as supporting a rather strict obligation of regulatory stability. Particularly, both the tribunal's express reference to a 'requirement of legal stability' (which is in addition to the requirement of legitimate expectations and non-arbitrariness) and its express recognition that a modification of the regulatory framework 'outside of the acceptable margin of change' is indeed prohibited by the FET provision fail to completely clarify whether or not FET includes an obligation of regulatory stability in the strict sense.

The uncertainty in reading the *Philip Morris v Uruguay* award remains, and in fact it is carried over to the tribunal's ultimate findings with regard to the investor's actual claims. In rejecting Philip Morris's FET claim, a majority of the *Philip Morris v Uruguay* tribunal concluded as follows:

> by adopting the Challenged Measures the Respondent has not breached Article 3(2) of the BIT regarding 'legitimate expectations' and the 'stability of the legal framework,' considering that the Claimants had no legitimate expectations that such or similar measures would not be adopted and further considering that their effect had not been such as to modify the stability of the Uruguayan legal framework.[125]

By distinguishing between the legitimate expectation claim and the legal stability claim, and basing its rejection of the latter claim on the finding that the *effect* of the measures under review had not been to modify the stability of the host State's legal framework, one can still advance the argument that the majority of the tribunal appears to accept a reading of the FET provision as a guarantee of regulatory stability in the strict sense.[126]

[124] ibid, paras 422–23.

[125] ibid, para 434; in the tribunal's view, 'the new regulations [have not] modified the legal framework for foreign investments beyond an "acceptable margin of change," as also alleged by the Claimants, considering the limited impact on Abal's business, as found by the analysis of the alleged expropriation of their investment': ibid, para 433.

[126] Another recent example of such (possible) implicit recognition may be found in *Eli Lilly and Company v The Government of Canada*, UNCITRAL, ICSID Case No UNCT/14/2, Final Award, 16

In the second example, the tribunal in *Antaris v The Czech Republic* was confronted with the claim that the host State's modification of its incentive regime in the photovoltaic sector had violated the FET provision in the ECT and the Germany–Czech Republic BIT because the policy change violated the obligation (a) to provide a stable and predictable legal framework; (b) to protect an investor's legitimate expectations; and (c) not to impair the investment through arbitrary and unreasonable behaviour.[127]

The *Antaris* tribunal's analysis begins with the recognition of the existence of a vast arbitral practice (which the disputing parties had referred to) interpreting and applying the FET standard. The tribunal then puts forward thirteen 'general propositions' stemming from such practice, which include the following:

> (1) There will be a breach of the FET standard where legal and business stability or the legal framework has been altered in such a way as to frustrate legitimate and reasonable expectations or guarantees of stability.
>
> [...]
>
> (3) A claimant must establish that (a) clear and explicit (or implicit) representations were made by or attributable to the state in order to induce the investment [...]
>
> (4) An expectation may arise from what are construed as specific guarantees in legislation.
>
> (5) A specific representation may make a difference to the assessment of the investor's knowledge and of the reasonableness and legitimacy of its expectation, but is not indispensable to establish a claim based on legitimate expectation which is advanced under the FET standard.
>
> (6) Provisions of general legislation applicable to a plurality of persons or a category of persons, do not create legitimate expectations that there will be no change in the law; and given the State's regulatory powers, in order to rely on legitimate expectations the investor should inquire in advance regarding the prospects of a change in the regulatory framework in light of the then prevailing or reasonably to be expected changes in the economic and social conditions of the host State.
>
> (7) An expectation may be engendered by changes to general legislation, but, at least in the absence of a stabilization clause, they are not prevented by the fair and equitable treatment standard if they do not exceed the exercise of the

March 2017, paras 386–89. While the tribunal rejected the investor's FET claim as the investor did not demonstrate 'a dramatic change in the law' relating to the utility requirement in Canada's Patent Act, it remains unclear whether such change in the law is all one needs to show to establish a breach of Article 1105 NAFTA or whether the change is a necessary but insufficient requirement for an Article 1105 violation.

[127] *Antaris v Czech Republic*, Award, 2 May 2018 (n 123) paras 262–64.

host State's normal regulatory power in the pursuance of a public interest and do not modify the regulatory framework relied upon by the investor at the time of its investment outside the acceptable margin of change.

(8) The requirements of legitimate expectations and legal stability as manifestations of the FET standard do not affect the State's rights to exercise its sovereign authority to legislate and to adapt its legal system to changing circumstances. [. . .]

While the *Antaris* tribunal does acknowledge that several of these propositions 'overlap with each other' and that its decision to ultimately reject the investors' FET claims 'is not based on all of those propositions', the tribunal fails to recognize the (at least potential) inconsistency of several of those propositions. Apparently more anxious to show a high level of harmony or consistency in the way investment tribunals have so far interpreted the FET provision,[128] the *Antaris* tribunal fails to clarify the extent to which the FET provision disciplines regulatory change. In particular, the tribunal fails to take a clear position on whether, and the extent to which, FET includes an obligation of regulatory stability in the strict sense.

(b) Some tribunals' failure to clearly address the precise ambit of, and relationship between, the obligation to provide a stable legal framework and the obligation to protect the investor's legitimate expectations

It is common (and again unsurprisingly so) that in claiming violation of the FET provision, investors separate between the stability requirement and the obligation to protect investors' legitimate expectations. As noted in section (a), the investors in both the *Philip Morris* and *Antaris* disputes claimed a violation of the FET provision arguing, inter alia, that the regulatory change violated (a) the obligation to provide a stable legal framework; and (b) the obligation to protect the investor's legitimate expectations.[129]

Despite the investors' separate claims, the tribunals in *Philip Morris* and *Antaris* completely failed to elaborate the relationship, if any, between the two allegedly distinct grounds. As noted in section (a), the *Philip Morris* tribunal decided to consider the two arguments in the same context due to their interrelation.[130] Having laid out several propositions with regard to the FET standard, the *Antaris* tribunal believed it unnecessary to decide 'the precise ambit of, and the relationship

[128] The dissenting arbitrator seems to highlight the inconsistency of the tribunal's decision. *Antaris v Czech Republic*, PCA Case No 2014-01, Dissenting Opinion, 2 May 2018.

[129] This happens often independently of whether or not the applicable treaty provides a different textual basis for the two grounds. In *Antaris v Czech Republic*, Dissenting Opinion, 2 May 2018 (ibid), for example, while both the ECT and Germany–Czech Republic BIT were applicable, the existence of distinct language in the former referring to the obligation to 'create stable conditions for investors' does not seem to have justified a different approach with regard to the issue of how FET disciplines regulatory change.

[130] *Philip Morris v Uruguay* (n 120) para 421.

between, [those] propositions'.[131] One can legitimately argue that neither tribunal really believed that there is substantially any difference between the two allegedly distinct grounds.

A similar situation may be found in *Blusun et al v Italy*, another recent dispute involving the photovoltaic sector, where the investor put forward two distinct grounds of violation, one based on legal stability and one on the doctrine of legitimate expectations. Interestingly, the claims in *Blusun et al v Italy* were based exclusively on the ECT. Article 10(1) ECT is quite unique as, in addition to providing the various traditional investment protection standards (including FET and the umbrella clause), it has an introductory reference to 'stable conditions'. Accordingly, Article 10(1) provides that '[e]ach Contracting Party shall, in accordance with the provisions of this Treaty, encourage and create stable, equitable, favourable and transparent conditions for Investors of other Contracting Parties' (first sentence) and '[s]uch conditions shall include a commitment to accord at all times to Investments of Investors of other Contracting Parties fair and equitable treatment' (second sentence). The claimants thus relied separately on Article 10(1), first sentence, with regard to the 'legal stability' claim and on Article 10(1), second sentence, with regard to the 'fair and equitable treatment' claim, with particular emphasis on the doctrine of legitimate expectations.[132]

While the *Blusun* tribunal does appear to have at least attempted to elaborate the relationship between stability and investors' legitimate expectations, the result is nonetheless unsatisfactorily unclear. The *Blusun* tribunal notes, first of all, that (a) all sentences in Article 10(1) embody commitments and neither is merely preambular or hortatory; and (b) the core commitment in Article 10(1) is the FET standard under customary international law and as applied by tribunals.[133] Second, and before examining in turn 'the legal instability claim' and the 'breach of the FET standard under Article 10(1) ECT (legitimate expectations)', the tribunal puts forward the following key conclusion:

> In the absence of a specific commitment, the state has no obligation to grant subsidies such as feed-in tariffs, or to maintain them unchanged once granted. But if they are lawfully granted, and if it becomes necessary to modify them, this should be done in a manner which is not disproportionate to the aim of the legislative amendment, and should have due regard to the reasonable reliance interests of recipients who may have committed substantial resources on the basis of the earlier regime.[134]

[131] *Antaris v Czech Republic* (n 123) para 363.

[132] Interestingly, the claimant in *Philip Morris v Uruguay* (n 120) had equally advanced the two-prong claim (stability and legitimate expectations) but as part of the 'traditional' FET standard found in the Switzerland–Uruguay BIT.

[133] *Blusun SA, Jean-Pierre Lecorcier and Michael Stein v Italian Republic*, ICSID Case No ARB/14/3, Award, 27 December 2016, para 319.

[134] ibid.

Do the two conditions (proportionality of the measure and having due regard to any reasonable reliance interests) refer to the substance of the stability obligation and to the protection the investors' legitimate expectations, respectively? Or does the tribunal consider that those two conditions are in fact part of the same underlying obligation and that there is little point in distinguishing between the two allegedly separate grounds? And in any event, what is the tribunal's view regarding the relation, if any, between 'specific commitment' and investor's 'reasonable reliance'?

These questions remain unanswered as the tribunal's subsequent analysis seems ultimately to rely on the same key conclusion quoted above. In its analysis of the 'legal instability claim', the tribunal examines, for example, the claimants' argument that the Romani Decree (adopted to implement the EU Directive aimed at achieving a share of at least 20% of energy from renewable sources in the EU) was in effect 'a paradigm of the legal instability' addressed by Article 10(1) ECT. The tribunal, however, does not clarify the relationship, if any, between legal stability and legitimate expectations,[135] as the tribunal rejects the investors' legal stability claim by concluding that the Italian measure was 'not disproportionate, did not violate specific commitments [...], and did not breach Article 10(1), first sentence, of the ECT'.[136]

In its analysis of the 'legitimate expectations' claim, the *Blusun* tribunal expressly emphasizes both the 'alternative' nature of the claim at issue and the existence of the issue of the relationship between stability and legitimate expectations.[137] However, first it reiterates (almost verbatim) the key conclusion quoted above ('in the absence of a specific commitment ...').[138] Second, it rejects the (apparently alternative) claim based on the protection of investors' legitimate expectations principally because 'the Respondent made no special commitment to the Claimant with respect to the extension and operation of the FITs, nor did it specifically undertake that relevant Italian laws would remain unchanged'.[139]

Based on the decisions in *Philip Morris, Blusun* and *Antaris*, one remains none the wiser with regard to the precise ambit of, and the relationship between, the obligation to provide a stable legal framework and the obligation to protect the investor's legitimate expectations.

(c) Some tribunals' failure to clarify the kind of regulatory change that qualifies for a breach of the FET provision

A last controversial issue revolves around the kind of regulatory *change* that is required in order to determine a violation of the FET provision. I noted in the

135 ibid, para 338.
136 ibid, para 343.
137 ibid, paras 365–66.
138 ibid, para 372.
139 ibid, para 374.

introduction above the conceptual distinction between a strict and soft notion of legal stability obligation, where the former focuses on the existence of a regulatory change and the latter entails (at least in part) an analysis of the merit (ie fairness or reasonableness) of the measure under review. Crudely put, the two key questions are, respectively, whether a change in regulation has occurred or whether the regulatory change was on its merit unreasonable.

The complication is that, in their FET claims, investors often highlight the magnitude of the regulatory change put in place by the host State by arguing that the host State has 'profoundly altered the stability and predictability of the investment environment',[140] by referring to the legal framework as 'exceptionally unstable'[141] or by describing the regulatory change as 'radical'.[142] Similarly, the claimants in *Blusun v Italy* emphasized the relentlessness of the regulatory changes by describing their claim as follows:

> Our claim is not that Italy's legislation had to remain immutable, unchanged, written in stone. This case is not about regulatory change; it's about regulatory turbulence. It concerns the fact that during the two years between permissible and legally impossible, the legal framework for the project constantly changed, leaving no period of stability in which the requisite capital investment for a project of this size could be realised.[143]

One question here is thus whether these investors are relying on a strict notion of regulatory stability (albeit more limited as only 'substantial' changes will constitute a breach of the FET) or whether they are instead relying on a soft notion of regulatory stability, where those qualifiers ('profound', 'exceptional', 'radical', 'constant') represent (at least implicitly) the evidence of an arbitrary or disproportionate behaviour by the host State.

[140] *CMS v Argentina*, Award, 12 May 2005 (n 72) para 267. See also *El Paso v Argentina*, Award, 31 October 2011 (n 48) para 351, where the tribunal refers to the following quote by the investor:

> Claimant does not call into question Argentina's right to change its laws or regulations. It has never been Claimant's position that the BIT imposes an absolute obligation not to alter the regulatory framework. […] But the complete alteration of the regulatory framework in a manner that does not reasonably protect existing capital investments promoted by the government necessarily frustrates the legitimate expectations of investors.

[141] *Mamidoil Jetoil Greek Petroleum Products Societe SA v Republic of Albania*, ICSID Case No ARB/11/24, Award, 30 March 2015, para 590.

[142] *Eli Lilly and Company v Canada*, Final Award, 16 March 2017 (n 127), para 227 ('Claimant argues that the promise utility doctrine is a radical departure from Canada's traditional utility standard […]'). See also *El Paso v Argentina*, Award, 31 October 2011 (n 48) para 390 ('in [the claimant's] view, the decisions and regulations in issue […] that brought a radical alteration of key rules, effectively eviscerated the existing regulatory frameworks, and therefore exceeded normal regulatory powers'). See also *Eiser Infrastructure Limited and Energía Solar Luxembourg Sàrl v Kingdom of Spain*, ICSID Case No ARB/13/36, Award, 4 May 2017, para 358 ('The drastic changes adopted by Respondent defeated Claimants' legitimate expectations of stability […]').

[143] *Blusun v Italy*, Award, 27 December 2016 (n 134) para 320.

Accordingly, one would expect the competent tribunal to address and clarify this issue. However, an examination of a few recent awards confirms, unfortunately, that the kind of stability obligation being applied by the tribunal remains, at best, far from clear. For example, as noted in section (a) above, while it ultimately rejected the investor's claim, the *Philip Morris v Uruguay* tribunal seems to accept in principle that changes to the regulatory framework are in violation of the FET provision if they are 'outside of the acceptable margin of change'.[144] The tribunal, however, does not clarify what it means by 'acceptable' margin of change: does the regulatory change become 'unacceptable' because it is 'substantial' (or even 'total') or is it unacceptable because the change is 'unreasonable' (or disproportionate)? The tribunal's succinct reasoning for rejecting the investor's FET claim regarding the 'stability of the legal framework', only adds to the uncertainty. The *Philip Morris v Uruguay* tribunal concluded that the regulations under review did not modify the legal framework for foreign investments beyond an acceptable margin of change 'considering the limited impact on [the investor's] business' and 'that their effect had not been such as to modify the stability of the Uruguayan legal framework'.[145] Accordingly, it remains unclear whether the reliance on limited 'impact' and 'effect' indicate that the tribunal was focusing on whether the regulatory change was substantial or unreasonable.

Similarly, the tribunal in *Eli Lilly v Canada* was confronted with a claim that the Canadian court's interpretation of the utility requirement under Canadian patent law, and in particular their adoption of the promise utility doctrine in the mid-2000s, allegedly departing dramatically from prior Canadian patent law, violated, inter alia, the FET standard in Article 1105 NAFTA.[146] While the *Eli Lilly* tribunal ultimately rejected the investor's claim as the investor failed to demonstrate a 'fundamental or dramatic change' in Canadian patent law, it remains unclear what the tribunal meant for a 'dramatic' change. Looking at the various factors examined by the tribunal (including the utility requirement in Canadian jurisprudence, relevant

[144] *Philip Morris v Uruguay*, Award, 8 July 2016 (n 120) para 423:

> changes to general legislation (at least in the absence of a stabilization clause) are not prevented by the FET standard if they do not exceed the exercise of the host State's normal regulatory power in pursuance of a public interest and do not modify the regulatory framework relied upon by the investor at the time of its investment 'outside of the acceptable margin of change'.

It should be noted that the phrase 'outside of the acceptable margin of change' comes from the *El Paso v Argentina* tribunal (n 48), in the context of a long and (perhaps over-) elaborated decision, which contains some apparently conflicting statements: compare 'the legitimate expectations of a foreign investor can only be examined by having due regard to the general proposition that the State should not unreasonably modify the legal framework or modify it in contradiction with a specific commitment not to do so' (para 364) with '[t]here can be no legitimate expectation for anyone that the legal framework will remain unchanged in the face of an extremely severe economic crisis. No reasonable investor can have such an expectation unless very specific commitments have been made towards it or unless the alteration of the legal framework is total' (para 374).

[145] *Philip Morris v Uruguay*, Award, 8 July 2016 (n 120) paras 433–34.

[146] *Eli Lilly and Company v Canada* (n 127).

Canadian regulatory practice and statistical evidence), one can argue that the *Eli Lilly* tribunal was indeed focusing on whether there had been a substantial change in law, rather than whether the change in law was arbitrary or disproportionate.[147] However, some of the tribunal's conclusions (stressing the 'incremental and evolutionary' nature of the change and suggesting some of the reasons that may have led to such change) seem to imply instead a focus on the reasons for (ie reasonableness of) the change.[148]

The tribunal in *Eiser v Spain* was confronted with the claim, brought exclusively under the ECT, where the investors alleged a violation of the FET provision because the drastic changes in the subsidies provided to solar energy producers by the host State defeated the investors' legitimate expectations of stability. The *Eiser* tribunal recognized that 'absent explicit undertakings [...] investment treaties do not eliminate States' right to modify their regulatory regimes to meet evolving circumstances and public needs' and that 'the FET standard does not give a right to regulatory stability per se'.[149] The tribunal, however, added that the FET provision 'does protect from a fundamental change to the regulatory regime in a manner that does not take account of the circumstances of existing investments made in reliance on the prior regime'.[150] While the ECT did not bar Spain from making appropriate changes, the *Eiser* tribunal continued, 'the ECT did protect Claimants against the total and unreasonable change that they experienced here'.[151]

The key question put forward at the beginning of this section presents itself, once again. Is the *Eiser* tribunal relying on a strict notion of regulatory stability (albeit more limited, as only 'fundamental' or 'total' changes will constitute a breach of the FET), or is the tribunal instead relying on a soft notion of regulatory stability where those qualifiers merely represent the evidence of an unreasonable or

[147] See Robert Howse, '*Eli Lilly v Canada*: A Pyrrhic Victory Against Big Pharma' (International Economic Law and Policy Blog, 26 March 2017) https://worldtradelaw.typepad.com/ielpblog/2017/03/eli-lilly-v-canada-a-pyrrhic-victory-against-big-pharma-.html accessed 20 May 2019:

> On those exceptional but usually very important occasions when high courts reconsider well-established judicial doctrines in the face of social, economic, environmental or other forms of rapid change we experience in the world today, they must now beware that any basic or fundamental reorientation of their jurisprudence could force that state's government to pay out millions or even billions to foreign corporations in the guise of an 'expropriation' having occurred [or a breach of the FET provision].

[148] *Eli Lilly v Canada*, Final Award, 16 March 2017 (n 127) para 386:

> Taken as a whole, the evidence before the Tribunal shows that Canada's utility requirement underwent incremental and evolutionary changes [...]. Over those years, there was an increase in the number of utility-based challenges of pharmaceutical patents, which appears to have increased the pace of the development of the law most relevant to that sector.

On the other hand, the fact that the tribunal proceeded next to examine whether the utility requirement under Canadian law is 'arbitrary' may undermine this second reading of what constitutes a 'dramatic' change.

[149] *Eiser v Kingdom of Spain*, Award, 4 May 2017 (n 143) para 362.

[150] ibid, para 363.

[151] ibid.

disproportionate behaviour by the host State? The language used by the tribunal is not helpful in fully understanding the nature of the obligation imposed on the host State through the FET provision.

The ambiguity is somewhat reinforced by the fact that, in its ultimate finding of violation of the FET provision, the *Eiser* tribunal seems to principally stress the regulatory change's dramatic impact on the value of the investment. The tribunal found that a favourable regulatory regime was replaced with 'an unprecedented and wholly different regulatory approach' and that the 'new system was profoundly unfair and inequitable as applied to Claimants' existing investment, stripping Claimants of virtually all of the value of their investment'.[152] It is not clear whether the *Eiser* tribunal's focus on the unprecedented nature of the regulatory change and its impact on the value of the investment shows that the tribunal's finding of violation was based on *the extent of* the regulatory change at issue or *the disproportionate nature of* that change. In other words, it remains unclear whether the tribunal relied on a strict or soft notion of the regulatory stability obligation.[153]

D. Recent Treaty Practice

In recent years, the inclusion of provisions in investment treaties requiring strict legal stability has increasingly dwindle. First, umbrella clauses have very often been omitted in recent investment treaties. An UNCTAD survey of publicly available investment treaties concluded between 2011 and 2015 has found that out of seventy-two treaties only seventeen contain an umbrella clause (and thirteen of those seventeen treaties involved Japan as one of the contracting parties).[154] This roughly adds up to three in every four new treaties not containing an umbrella clause, and contrasts with the pre-2004 treaties statistic of one in every two treaties.[155] Apparently, in 2016 and 2017, out of fifty-four new investment instruments (fifty-two treaties and two model treaties), only two (3.7%) contain an umbrella clause, namely, the Austria–Kyrgyzstan BIT and the Japan–Iran BIT (both signed in 2016).[156]

[152] ibid, para 365.

[153] See *Foresight Luxembourg Solar Sàrl et al v Kingdom of Spain*, SCC Arbitration V (2015/150), Final Award, 14 November 2018, para 398 ('The Majority of the Tribunal concludes that the Respondent's enactment of the New Regulatory Regime constituted a fundamental change to the legal and regulatory framework that crossed the line from a non-compensable regulatory measure to a compensable breach of the FET standard in the ECT').

[154] UNCTAD, 'Taking Stock of IIA Reform' Issues Note (March 2016) 15–19.

[155] See Judith Gill, Matthew Gearing and Gemma Birt, 'Contractual Claims and Bilateral Investment Treaties: A Comparative Review of the *SGS* Cases' (2004) 21 J Int'l Arb 397, n 31. See Raul Pereira de Souza Fleury, 'Umbrella Clauses: A Trend Towards its Elimination' (2015) 31 Art Int'l 679.

[156] See Raul Pereira de Souza Fleury, 'Closing the Umbrella: A Dark Future for Umbrella Clauses?' (Kluwer Arbitration Blog, 13 October 2017) http://arbitrationblog.kluwerarbitration.com/2017/10/13/closing-umbrella-dark-future-umbrella-clauses accessed 20 May 2019. With regard to treaties concluded in 2016, see UNCTAD, *World Investment Report* (United Nations 2017) 121.

Noteworthy is the change in the United States' policy with regard to umbrella clauses, as starting from its 2004 model BIT, United States' treaties omit the umbrella clause. However, it should also be noted that United States' investment treaties adopt a wide jurisdictional clause, including the investor's right to submit to arbitration a claim that the respondent has breached an 'investment authorization' or an 'investment agreement'.[157]

Interestingly, the European Union (EU)'s position on umbrella clauses appears more nuanced. While the agreement with Canada does not contain any umbrella clause (and no broad jurisdictional clause), the 2015 EU draft proposal in the context of the negotiation with the United States for the Transatlantic Trade and Investment Partnership (TTIP)[158] does contain an umbrella clause. The wording is, however, different from the traditional umbrella clauses as it attempts to clarify the various issues that had led to several controversies in arbitral practice. Article 7 of the Chapter on Investment in the EU's draft proposal made public on 12 November 2015 reads as follows:

> Article 7 Observance of written commitments
>
> Where a Party either itself or through any entity mentioned in Article X [Definition of 'measures adopted or maintained by a Party'] has entered into any contractual written commitment with investors of the other Party or with their covered investments, that Party shall not, either itself or through any such entity breach the said commitment through the exercise of governmental authority.[159]

Second, as noted above, investment treaties' stabilization clauses are rare, with the exception perhaps of Italian BITs. The most recent stabilization clause that I could

[157] See eg Article 24.1 of the 2004 US model BIT. Article 1 defines an 'investment agreement' as:

> a written agreement between a national authority of a Party and a covered investment or an investor of the other Party, on which the covered investment or the investor relies in establishing or acquiring a covered investment other than the written agreement itself, that grants rights to the covered investment or investor: (a) with respect to natural resources that a national authority controls, such as for their exploration, extraction, refining, transportation, distribution, or sale; (b) to supply services to the public on behalf of the Party, such as power generation or distribution, water treatment or distribution, or telecommunications; or (c) to undertake infrastructure projects, such as the construction of roads, bridges, canals, dams, or pipelines, that are not for the exclusive or predominant use and benefit of the government.

Article 1 also defines 'investment authorization' as 'an authorization that the foreign investment authority of a Party grants to a covered investment or an investor of the other Party'.

[158] http://trade.ec.europa.eu/doclib/docs/2015/september/tradoc_153807.pdf accessed 20 May 2019.

[159] A footnote clarifies the meaning of 'contractual written commitment' as follows:

> For the purposes if this paragraph, a 'contractual written commitment' means an agreement in writing, entered into by a Party, itself or through any entity mentioned in Article X [Definition of 'measures adopted or maintained by a Party'], with an investor or a covered investment, whether in a single instrument or multiple instruments, that creates an exchange of rights and obligations, binding on both Parties.

find is that contained in the 2004 Italy–Nicaragua BIT. Furthermore, some of the few examples of stabilization clauses in investment treaties are found in early BITs that have since been terminated following renegotiation. Interestingly, the stabilization clause was omitted in the renegotiated treaty.[160]

Third, some recent investment treaties have excluded either expressly or implicitly the possibility to interpret any of the traditional investment protection provisions (including the FET standard) as a guarantee of regulatory stability in the strict sense. A general exclusion of regulatory stability *stricto sensu* may be implied by the investment treaty's recognition, often in the preamble, that the contracting parties retain the right to regulate in the public interest. For example, the preamble of the 2015 Australia–China Free Trade Agreement (FTA) refers to the 'rights of [the] governments to regulate in order to meet national policy objectives, and to preserve their flexibility to safeguard public welfare'. Arguably, reading an FET provision to include a guarantee of regulatory stability in the strict sense would contrast with an interpretation based on the customary rules of treaty interpretation that, in addition to the 'text', rely on the 'context' and 'object and purpose' of the treaty.[161]

Some recent treaties contain express exclusions of regulatory stability in the strict sense. For example, the last sentence of Article 4.1 of the 2014 Columbia–France BIT expressly clarifies the limit of the FET standard as follows: 'Se entiende que la obligacion de otorgar un trato justo y equitativo, no incluye una clausula de estabilizacion juridical ni impide a una Parte Contratante adaptar su legislacion de conformidad con los terminus de este paragrafo.'[162]

Another example of a broad, express exclusion of legal stability *stricto sensu* is Article 8.9 on Investment and Regulatory measures of the 2016 Canada–EU Comprehensive Economic and Trade Agreement (CETA). While paragraph 1 reaffirms the contracting parties' 'right to regulate [...] to achieve legitimate policy objectives', paragraph 2 expressly clarifies that the host State's regulation negatively affecting an investment or interfering with an investor's expectations is not per se prohibited by the investment treaty. Paragraph 2 reads as follows:

> For greater certainty, the mere fact that a Party regulates, including through a modification to its laws, in a manner which negatively affects an investment or interferes with an investor's expectations, including its expectations of profits, does not amount to a breach of an obligation under this Section.[163]

[160] See 1965 Belgium–Morocco BIT, 1975 France–Morocco BIT.

[161] Charalampos Giannakopoulos, 'The Right to Regulate in International Investment Law and the Law of State Responsibility: A Hohfeldian Approach' (*SSRN*, May 2017) 10–11 https://papers.ssrn.com/sol3/papers.cfm?abstract_id=2962686 accessed 20 May 2019.

[162] See similarly Article 4.5 of the 2014 Colombia–Turkey BIT.

[163] Article 9.6, para 5 of the Comprehensive and Progressive Agreement for Trans-Pacific Partnership (CPTPP) provides the same with regard to subsidies or grant ('For greater certainty, the mere fact that a subsidy or grant has not been issued, renewed or maintained, or has been modified or reduced, by a

Furthermore, the inclusion in recent investment treaties of general exception clauses may also be seen as an implicit rejection of strict stability obligations, as these exception clauses would vest on contracting parties at least a margin of regulatory discretion in order to act in the public interest (and notwithstanding any contractual or regulatory stability obligations). For example, one of the two investment treaties concluded in 2016 that include an umbrella clause,[164] features a general exception provision, styled on the general exception of Article XX of the General Agreement on Tariffs and Trade (GATT).[165]

Preliminary Conclusions

This chapter's main findings have been the following. First, legal stability in the strict sense, including both contractual and regulatory stability, represents one of the protections afforded to foreign investment in international investment treaties. It is imposed specifically through umbrella and stabilization clauses, respectively.

Second, despite a limited attempt by a few early investment tribunals to read a strict stability obligation as part of the FET provision, the majority of investment tribunals appear to have adopted a more nuanced approach by increasingly recognizing the need to safeguard the host State's right to regulate in the public interest. However, despite investment tribunals' apparently more deferential approach in their interpretation of FET, one can still find recent arbitral decisions where the role of regulatory stability within the FET standard remains at best ambiguous, and thus fears that the FET standard may function as imposing an obligation of regulatory stability in the strict sense remain.

Third, investment treaties signed in the past ten years clearly show a move away from provisions guaranteeing legal stability in the strict sense, principally by omitting umbrella and stabilization clauses and by narrowing the scope of the substantive protections included in investment treaties.

Three preliminary reflections are advanced. First, the existence of provisions expressly guaranteeing legal stability in the strict sense confirms the conclusion that traditional investment treaties provided, at least in some instances, a remarkably broad level of protection to foreign investments. Furthermore, the existence of such provisions seems to strengthen the argument that other open-ended

Party, does not constitute a breach of this Article, even if there is loss or damage to the covered investment as a result').

[164] See the Agreement between Japan and the Islamic Republic of Iran on Reciprocal Promotion and Protection of Investment, signed on 5 February 2016. The second agreement signed in 2016 featuring an umbrella clause but not a general exception clause is the Austria–Kyrgyzstan BIT.

[165] See Article 13 on General and Security Exceptions of the 2016 Japan–Iran BIT. See further Levent Sabanogullari, *General Exception Clauses in International Investment Law: The Recalibration of Investment Agreements via WTO Flexibilities* (Nomos Verlag 2018).

standards such as FET *should* not be interpreted as imposing a similarly strict legal stability obligation as well. And this argument appears to be valid whether those express strict stability obligations are found in the specific treaty at issue or not.[166]

Second, while the attempt of a few tribunals to read the FET provision as including a legal stability obligation may be used as evidence that investment tribunals have been 'out of control', this is somewhat unfair for two sets of reasons. First of all, legal stability in the strict sense was not exclusively a 'creation' of investment tribunals, as at least some investment treaties did expressly envisage such broad guarantees. In this sense, contracting parties have a much greater responsibility for the existence of legal stability as one of the key obligations found in international investment treaties. While there are several controversial issues when it comes to delineating the scope and effect of investment treaties' umbrella and stabilization clauses, their core function is beyond doubt: to guarantee the stability of the host State's contractual undertakings and regulatory framework, respectively. A second reason why the 'out-of-control' criticism vis-à-vis investment tribunals appears (at least in part) unfair is based on the conclusion that the great majority of investment tribunals have rejected a broad interpretation of the FET provision, recognizing instead the need to safeguard host States' right to regulate in the public interest.

The key criticism that is advanced in this chapter vis-à-vis arbitral practice revolves around investment tribunals' failure to clearly draw a line between strict and soft stability obligation. Based on a review of several arbitral decisions rendered in the past five years, it remains for example, frustratingly unclear whether tribunals perceive the FET provision as imposing a strict stability obligation that focuses on the existence of an adverse regulatory change or a soft stability obligation that focuses instead on the regulatory change's fairness, reasonableness or proportionality. The apparent disregard shown by these investment tribunals of the fundamental difference between a strict stability guarantee and soft stability guarantee is indeed puzzling.

Finally, when it comes to the question of the future of strict legal stability guarantees, one may distinguish between contractual and regulatory stability. While it is hard to imagine that any future investment treaty will include a stabilization clause, the future of umbrella clauses may not appear as bleak, as shown for example by its inclusion in the most recent draft proposal put forward by the EU in the context of the TTIP negotiations. This may be in part because investment tribunals have narrowed the scope of traditional umbrella clauses and in part because

[166] See Louis-Philippe Coulombe, 'Duplicating the Umbrella Clause? Some Thoughts on Contractual Expectations and the Fair and Equitable Treatment Standard' in Ian Laird et al (eds) *Investment Treaty Arbitration and International Law Volume 7* (Juris 2014) 101:

> the fair and equitable standard cannot be construed so as to cover contractual expectations. Such claims should be brought under the umbrella clause. However, where the treaty contains no umbrella clause, or where the latter is inapplicable, the fair and equitable treatment should not be interpreted as a means to fill this void.

some recent investment treaties have included broad general exception provisions capable of preserving a margin of regulatory sovereignty.

However, the appropriateness of including a contractual stability mechanism in an investment treaty will depend on each contracting parties' confidence in the ability (and wisdom) of their public authorities in undertaking commitments with regard to foreign investments. In this regard, one wonders whether future policy makers should consider employing international treaties not simply to strengthen the sanctity of investor–State contracts, but also to introduce some parameters (both procedural and substantive in nature) disciplining the ability of host States to bind themselves through such contracts.

II
Protecting the Value of Investments
The Expropriation Provision

Introduction

Unsurprisingly, a provision requiring host States to compensate for the expropriation of foreign investments is one of the few constants in the more than 3000 international investment treaties concluded in the past sixty years. Professor Vandevelde has pertinently noted:

> An expropriation is the single greatest impairment of the security of an investment. It is an act that eliminates all or substantially all of the value of the investment to the investor. The threat of expropriation was a principal motivating factor in the origin of the BITs.[1]

[1] Kenneth J Vandevelde, *Bilateral Investment Treaties: History, Policy and Interpretation* (OUP 2010) 271.

The Origin and Evolution of Investment Treaty Standards. Federico Ortino, Oxford University Press (2019). © Federico Ortino.
DOI: 10.1093/oso/9780198842637.001.0003

While expropriation provisions in investment treaties recognize the power of host States to expropriate foreign investments, they impose several conditions on the exercise of such power. The most important, and historically the most contested condition for a lawful expropriation, is the standard of compensation.[2] The great majority of investment treaties describe such compensation as 'prompt, adequate and effective', where adequate compensation is generally defined as the 'fair market value' of the expropriated investment.[3]

The most controversial issue when it comes to the expropriation provision in modern investment treaties has been the definition of an expropriation.[4] In other words, what host State measures entitle the investor to compensation?

Most of investment treaties expressly refer to both 'direct' and 'indirect' expropriations. While there is little controversy in relation to 'direct expropriation', which mainly includes the formal transfer of title away from the investor, the concept of 'indirect expropriation' has led to an extensive debate at the level of arbitral practice, scholarship and policy. In oversimplified terms, the debate has mainly focused on the different relevance attributed to the measure's adverse effect on the foreign investment, on the one hand, and the measure's public policy purpose, on the other. Investment treaty tribunals, at least initially, have adopted the former understanding of indirect expropriation, focusing exclusively on an investigation of the extent of the host State measure's adverse effect on the foreign investment (the so-called 'sole-effect' doctrine).[5] This understanding implies that an investment treaty affords foreign investors an extensive (mainly financial) protection vis-à-vis any substantial deprivation of their investments caused by conduct attributable to the host State independently of the public policy objective being pursued by the host State conduct at issue. Professor Sornarajah, one of the first and most authoritative critical voices in the field, referred to this broad understanding of indirect expropriation as 'the centrepiece of foreign investment protection, a theory of absolute protection of foreign investment'.[6]

More recently, an increasing number of investment treaty tribunals (as well as scholars and policy-makers) have recognized the importance of the policy objective of the allegedly expropriatory measure and have rejected an indirect expropriation claim when such measure is a legitimate exercise of the host State right to regulate in the public interest (the so-called 'police powers doctrine'), even if

[2] Andrew Newcombe and Llouis Paradell, *Law and Practice of Investment Treaties: Standards of Treatment* (Kluwer Law International 2009) 369.

[3] Vandevelde, *Bilateral Investment Treaties* (n 1) 273–4.

[4] This is commonly the second branch of the international law on expropriation. The first branch defines the interests that will be protected and the third branch relates to the conditions under which a host State may lawfully expropriate alien property. See Rudolf Dolzer and Christoph Schreuer, *Principles of International Investment Law* (2nd edn, OUP 2012) 99.

[5] Rudolf Dolzer, 'Indirect Expropriation: New Developments?' (2002) 11 NYU Env'l J 64, 65; Krista Nadakavukaren Schefer, *International Investment Law* (2nd edn, Edward Elgar, 2016) 242.

[6] M Sornarajah, *The International Law on Foreign Investment* (3rd edn, CUP 2010) 371.

the measure had a substantial adverse effect on the investment. Under this understanding of indirect expropriation, the focus shifts from the measure's impact on the investment to the legitimacy and soundness of the allegedly expropriatory measure.[7]

While in practical terms, it may be argued that there are nowadays more important treaty provisions protecting foreign investment (particularly the fair and equitable treatment (FET) clause),[8] the controversy over the proper definition of indirect expropriation still highlights the broader debate over the appropriate restraints imposed by international investment treaties on States' regulatory authority for the purposes of promoting the flow of foreign investment and thus the prosperity of the treaty's contracting parties.

The essence of this debate is captured by the discussion within the European Union (EU) on the shape of future EU investment agreements,[9] particularly in the context of the negotiation of the Transatlantic Trade and Investment Partnership (TTIP) between the EU and the United States. The two contracting parties have recognized two key challenges. The first challenge is to find the right balance between granting 'the highest possible level of protection' to foreign investors and safeguarding States' ability 'to adopt and maintain measures necessary to regulate in the public interest to pursue certain public policies'.[10] The second, and equally important, challenge is to improve the clarity and predictability of investment treaties, principally (a) to allow host States and investors to appreciate (and comply with) the rules applicable to their relationship; and (b) to decrease the high level of discretion currently entrusted on to ad hoc investment tribunals to decide the fate of legitimate public regulations.[11]

The aim of this chapter is to trace the origin and evolution of the expropriation provision in modern investment treaties. Three main findings stem from the

[7] Anne Hoffmann, 'Indirect Expropriation' in August Reinisch (ed) *Standards of Investment Protection* (OUP 2008) 164.

[8] Michael Reisman and Rocio Digon, 'Eclipse of Expropriation' in AW Rovine (ed) *Contemporary Issues in International Arbitration and Mediation—The Fordham Papers 2008* (Martinus Nijhoff 2009) 27 et seq.

[9] See August Reinisch, 'The Future Shape of EU Investment Agreements' (2013) 28 ICSID Rev/FILJ 179.

[10] See the 2012 *Statement on Shared Principles for International Investment* by the European Union (EU) and the United States. According to the United Nations Conference on Trade and Development (UNCTAD), if it is to generate sustainable growth and development, promoting and protecting foreign investment has to be accompanied (if not preceded) by the establishment of proper regulatory and institutional frameworks: UNCTAD, *2012 World Investment Report: Towards a New Generation of Investment Policies* (United Nations 2012) 101 ('the key policy challenge is to strike the right balance between regulation and openness').

[11] In its resolution on the future European international investment policy, the European Parliament expressed 'its deep concern regarding the level of discretion of international arbitrators to make a broad interpretation of investor protection clauses, thereby leading to the ruling out of legitimate public regulations'. It thus called on the European Commission 'to produce clear definitions of investor protection standards in order to avoid such problems in the new investment agreements': European Parliament Resolution on the Future of the European International Investment Policy (6 April 2011) 2010/2203(INI), para 24.

present analysis. First, the original aim of the expropriation provision in modern investment treaties was to afford foreign investors a wide level of protection vis-à-vis the host State's conduct that deprived the investor of the value of its investments. There is, indeed, no visible attempt by the treaty drafters to limit the protection afforded with the expropriation provisions in investment treaties to that afforded either under customary law or domestic law. Accordingly, and crucially, the obligation to fully compensate the foreign investor does not disappear when the deprivation of value is the incidental effect of a legislation or regulation aimed at the protection of a legitimate public policy. In other words, based on the expropriation provision in traditional investment treaties, a showing that the host State has deprived the investor of the value of its investment is in principle sufficient to justify a finding of compensable expropriation.[12]

Second, while many investment treaty tribunals have initially and enthusiastically adhered to this broad understanding of (indirect) expropriation in line with the so-called 'sole-effect' doctrine, an increasing number of investment treaty tribunals have more recently adopted a more cautious approach. First, tribunals have limited the scope of the protection offered by the expropriation provision in investment treaties by restricting the notion of expropriatory effect. Key refinements in this context have been, for example, (a) increasing the extent of the required deprivation; (b) relying on the overall investment as the denominator in the deprivation equation; and (c) restricting the relevant object of the deprivation, thus reducing the relevance of the value of the foreign investment. Second, tribunals have also (dramatically) limited the scope of protection of the expropriation provision by fundamentally modifying its original nature. With the increasing relevance of the public policy of the allegedly expropriatory measure (pursuant to the 'police powers' doctrine), a determination of indirect expropriation is increasingly premised on an inquiry over the soundness and legitimacy of the measure under review, rather than merely on its adverse impact on the (value of the) investment. In other words, from a guarantee of the value of the protected foreign investment, provisions on (indirect) expropriation have been interpreted as a guarantee vis-à-vis the host State's unreasonable conduct.

[12] Two other common provisions in international investment treaties should be mentioned in this context. First, in the very first investment treaty arbitration, the claimant argued unsuccessfully that the 'full protection and security' clause in the *United Kingdom v Sri Lanka* established the host State's strict liability for any losses suffered by the investor: *Asian Agricultural Products Limited v Republic of Sri Lanka*, ICSID Case No. ARB/87/3, Award, 27 June 1990. See Giuditta Cordero Moss, 'Full Protection and Security' in August Reinisch (ed) *Standards of Investment Protection* (OUP 2008) 131–50; Stanimir A Alexandrov, 'The Evolution of the Full Protection and Security Standard' in Meg Kinnear (ed) *Building International Investment Law: The First 50 Years of ICSID* (Kluwer Law International 2015) 319–30. Second, some of the so-called 'compensation-for-losses' clauses include an obligation to compensate for losses suffered by foreign investors due to war or a state of national emergency, revolt, insurrection or riot in case the losses stem from requisitioning by host State forces or authorities. See further Facundo Perez-Aznar, 'Investment Protection in Exceptional Situations: Compensation-for-Losses Clauses in IIAs' (2017) 28 ICSID Rev/FILJ 696.

Third, the (r)evolution in the practice of investment treaty tribunals towards a focus on the soundness and legitimacy of the allegedly expropriatory measure has proceeded alongside a similar evolution with regard to the practice of investment treaty-making, which started with the adoption of the United States and Canada model BITs in 2004.

A. The Origin of the Concept of Expropriation in Modern Investment Treaties

This section examines the text of expropriation provisions found in modern investment treaties. It focuses also on the broader context at the time when the first bilateral investment treaty (the 1959 Germany–Pakistan BIT) was concluded. As expropriation provisions in most existing investment treaties have remained relatively unchanged over the years (at least throughout the second half of the twentieth century), any insight that can be obtained from the early years of modern investment treaties can play an important role in understanding one of the core provisions of the international investment law regime.

This section will try to show that the original aim of the expropriation provision in modern investment treaties was to afford the foreign investor a broad level of protection vis-à-vis the host State's conduct that deprived the investor of the value of its investments. In other words, a showing that the host State has entirely (or substantially) deprived the investor of the value of its investment is in principle sufficient to justify a finding of compensable expropriation.

1. Textual emphasis on adverse 'effect' on the foreign 'investment'

From the very early days, expropriation provisions in modern investment treaties appear to have adopted a potentially broad notion of 'expropriation'. This is for at least two reasons, which are directly linked with the first two branches of the international law of expropriation: the definition of the object of protection and the definition of expropriation.

While investment treaties (at least until very recently) do not normally provide a definition of 'expropriation', from the very beginning investment treaties more or less expressly extended the treaty protection beyond transfers of title (so-called formal or direct expropriations) to include host States' measures that have expropriatory effect. The very early investment treaties included references to 'indirect' expropriation, deprivation or dispossession, as well as 'act tantamount to expropriation' or 'measure having equivalent effect'. For example, while the text of Article 3 of the 1959 Germany–Pakistan BIT required that 'Nationals or companies of either Party shall not be subjected to expropriation of their investments in the territory of the other Party' unless the usual conditions (including compensation) are met, the relevant Protocol clarified the notion of 'expropriation' in the following terms: 'the term "expropriation" [...] shall also pertain to acts of sovereign power, which are tantamount to expropriation, as well as measures of nationalization'. Article IV of the 1964 Italy–Guinea BIT referred to 'expropriation', 'other restrictions' and 'measures having equivalent effect'. It reads as follows:

> Les investissements des ressortissants et des Sociétés de chacun des deux Etats contractants effectués dans le territoire de l'autre Etat contractant, de même que les bénéfices y relatifs, ne pourront être expropriés ni soumis à d'autres restrictions, que dans le cas d'un intérêt public évident et démontré et contre versement d'une indemnité égale à la valeur des biens expropriés. [...] Le terme 'expropriation' comprend également tout acte on toute mesure ayant un effet analogue à celui de l'expropriation et de la nationalisation.

Article 3 of the 1964 Benelux–Tunisia BIT (now terminated) required the payment of effective and adequate compensation '[w]here one Party expropriates or nationalizes investments, property, rights or interests belonging to nationals or corporations of the other Contracting Party or takes any other measure which results directly or indirectly in the dispossession of such nationals or corporations'.

The two documents that best reflected the original position of capital-exporting countries and influenced the evolution of modern investment treaties confirm this potentially broad definition of expropriation. Article III of the 1959 Abs-Shawcross Draft Convention on Investment Abroad provided that 'No Party shall take any measures against nationals of another Party to deprive them directly or indirectly of their property' provided that such measures are inter alia accompanied by the payment of compensation. Article 3 on the Taking of Property of the 1962 Organisation for Economic Co-operation (OECD) Draft Convention on the protection of foreign property stated that 'No Party shall take any measures depriving, directly or indirectly, of his property a national of another Party' unless the usual conditions are complied with. Interestingly, the accompanying Notes to the OECD Draft Convention made express reference to the concept of 'creeping expropriation' as recently practiced by certain States and defined it as follows: 'Under it, measures otherwise lawful are applied in such a way as to deprive ultimately the alien of the enjoyment or value of his property, without any specific act being identifiable as outright deprivation.' The references to 'measures otherwise lawful' and to the deprivation of the 'enjoyment or value' of the investor's property are here noteworthy, as they confirm a focus on the ultimate impact of the host State measure on the *value* of the investor's property.

Second, the scope of 'expropriation' in modern investment treaties was, from the very beginning, a broad one because expropriation provisions, specifically, and investment treaties, more generally, focused expressly on 'property' or 'investment' rather than on 'property rights'.[13] The expropriation provisions in the 1959 Abs-Shawcross Draft Convention and the 1962 OECD Draft Convention refer to 'property', which is defined in both conventions as 'all property, rights and interests'.[14] Moreover, the Notes and Comments to Article 9 of the OECD Draft Convention explains that such definition 'is meant to be used in its widest sense which includes, but is not limited to, investments'.

Investment treaties have traditionally used very broad 'asset-based' definitions of investment, covering:

> not only capital (or the resources) that has crossed borders with a view towards the creation of an enterprise or the acquisition of control over an existing one, but also most other kinds of assets of the enterprise or of the investor, such as property and property rights of various kinds, non-equity investment, including several types of loans and portfolio transactions, as well as other contractual rights, including sometimes rights created by administrative action of a host State (licenses, permits, etc.).[15]

The expropriation provision of the 1959 Germany–Pakistan BIT, cited above, referred to 'investment' and Article 8.1(a) thereof defined the term 'investment' to comprise 'capital brought into the territory of the other Party for investment in various forms in the shape of assets such as foreign exchange, goods, property rights, patents and technical knowledge', and it would 'also include the returns derived from and ploughed back into such "investment" '.

From the 1980s, express references in the expropriation provision to measures having equivalent 'effect' on 'investments' become commonplace, confirming the potentially broad scope of (indirect) expropriation. In its mapping of almost 2000 investment treaties, UNCTAD has found that an express reference to 'indirect' expropriation is contained in more than 95% of the treaties examined. For example, Article 4(2) of the 1984 Germany–Burundi BIT states: 'Investment by nationals or companies of either Contracting Party shall not be expropriated, nationalized or subjected to any other measure the effects of which would be tantamount to expropriation or nationalization in the territory of the other Contracting Party.' Similarly, Article 6 of the 1990 Switzerland–Czechoslovakia BIT on 'Dispossession, Compensation' reads as follows: 'Neither of the Contracting parties shall take, either directly or indirectly, measures of expropriation, nationalization or any other measure having the same nature or the same effect against investments of investors

[13] August Reinisch, 'Expropriation' in Peter Muchlinski, Federico Ortino and Christoph Schreuer (eds) *The Oxford Handbook on International Investment Law* (OUP 2008) 410.

[14] See Articles IX(b) and 9(c), respectively.

[15] UNCTAD, *Scope and Definition* (United Nations 2011) 21–2.

of the other Contracting Party' unless the usual conditions applied. Article 13.1 of the 1994 Energy Charter Treaty (ECT) states that 'Investments of Investors of a Contracting Party in the Area of any other Contracting Party shall not be nationalized, expropriated or subjected to a measure or measures having effect equivalent to nationalization or expropriation.'[16]

Throughout the last part of the twentieth century, there are only very few investment treaties that provide more details on the concept of (indirect) expropriation (beyond the reference to 'measures having equivalent effect'). Even these treaties adopt a very broad approach by focusing particularly on whether the host State measure at issue have the effect of depriving the investor of the 'ownership', 'control', 'management', 'benefit' or 'economic value' of its investment. For example, Article III, paragraph 1, of the 1986 US–Egypt BIT included in the definition of expropriation:

> any other measure, direct or indirect (including, for example, the levying of taxation, the compulsory sale of all or part of such an investment, or impairment or deprivation of management, control or economic value of such an investment by the national or company concerned), if the effect of such other measure, or a series of such other measures, would be tantamount to expropriation or nationalization.[17]

Similarly, Article 159, paragraph 4, of the 1993 Treaty Establishing the Common Market for Eastern and Southern Africa (COMESA) elaborates on the concept of 'expropriation' by focusing on whether the State measure has 'the effect of depriving an investor of his ownership or control of, or a substantial benefit from his investment'. Article 159.4 goes even further by stating that expropriation shall include:

> all forms of expropriation such as nationalisation and attachment as well as creeping expropriation in the form of imposition of excessive and discriminatory taxes, restrictions in the procurement of raw materials, administrative action or omission where there is a legal obligation to act or measures that frustrate the exercise of the investor's rights to dividends, profits and proceeds or the right to dispose of the investment.[18]

Even in the few treaties where there is no express reference to 'indirect' expropriation, the language employed is often potentially equally broad. For example, according to Article 9 of the 1970 Netherlands–Kenya BIT adequate compensation is due for 'Any measures of nationalisation or expropriation, taken by either

[16] See also 1994 ECT.
[17] This provision is almost identical to Article 3 of the 1982 United States Model BIT.
[18] See UNCTAD, *Bilateral Investment Treaties in the Mid-1990s* (United Nations 1998) 65–6.

of the Contracting Parties affecting the investments, goods, rights or interests of their respective nationals in the territory of each other'. Similarly, Article 6.1 of the 1982 Sweden–Sri Lanka BIT states that 'Neither Contracting Party shall take any measures depriving nationals or companies of the other Contracting Party of an investment.'

2. What relevance for the host State measure's public purpose?

One noticeable feature of modern investment treaties (at least when it comes to those concluded in the second half of the twentieth century) is the absence of any express reference to the legitimate purpose of the allegedly expropriatory measure as one of the factors to be considered in determining the very existence of expropriation (particularly in those cases where there was no formal interference in the legal title to the investor's property).[19] Reference to whether the measure had been taken for a 'public purpose'[20] only features as one of the conditions making the expropriation lawful (that is part of the so-called third branch of the law on expropriation).

This is surprising (and thus noteworthy), as the relevance of the public purpose of the allegedly expropriatory measure in determining the very existence of an expropriation under international law was well known at the time modern investment treaties started appearing. In his commentary to the Abs-Showcross Draft Convention, Professor Schwarzenberger argued about the importance of the purpose of the measure in determining an 'indirect deprivation of property'. Professor Schwarzenberger first recognized the difficulty in determining 'where indirect deprivation of property ends and, for instance, planning legislation, or property law reform begins', and praised the Draft Convention's attempt to cover 'surreptitious forms of confiscation'.[21] He then stated that 'whether an act of state […] constitutes an illegal interference with property rather than an unchallegeable exercise of state power, largely depends on the purpose of the measure'.[22]

[19] In one of the earlier decisions, the tribunal in *Saluka v Czech Republic* expressly acknowledged that Article 5 of the Netherlands–Czech Republic BIT 'is drafted very broadly and does not contain any exception for the exercise of regulatory power'. *Saluka Investments BV v The Czech Republic*, UNCITRAL, Partial Award, 17 March 2006, para 254. As noted below, the *Saluka* tribunal went on to import into the investment treaty provision on expropriation the customary doctrine of police powers.

[20] While there was no mention in the 1959 Abs-Shawcross Draft Convention, the 1963 OECD Draft Convention referred to 'public interest'. The 1959 Germany–Pakistan BIT referred to 'public benefit'.

[21] Georg Schwarzenberger, 'The Abs-Shawcross Draft Convention on Investment Abroad: A Critical Commentary' (1960) 9 J Pub L 147, 157 ('Whenever [confiscation] is the real object, the label of the ostensible action taken is of little consequence').

[22] ibid, 157. Noting moreover, that 'any judgment on matters of this kind is itself greatly influenced by nonlegal considerations', Professor Schwarzenberger ended his brief comments on 'indirect deprivation' with the following (ominous) statement: 'Under the Draft Convention, the last word would be with "the Umpire" of the Arbitral Tribunal.'

Next to a recognition that a 'taking of property' included both an 'outright taking of property' and 'any unreasonable interference with the use, enjoyment, or disposal of property', the 1961 Harvard Draft Convention on the International Responsibility of States for Injuries to Aliens also provided for an exception based on the ability of States to pursue certain legitimate public policies without the need to afford compensation to affected aliens (the so-called 'police powers' doctrine). Article 10.5 of the Harvard Draft Convention stated in relevant part as follows:

> […] a deprivation of the use or enjoyment of property of an alien which results from the execution of the tax laws; from a general change in the value of currency; from the action of the competent authorities of the State in the maintenance of public order, health, or morality; or from the valid exercise of belligerent rights; or is otherwise incidental to the normal operation of the laws of the State shall not be considered wrongful […].[23]

While acknowledging 'the extreme difficulty' of deciding what constitutes an expropriation, in his seminal 1962 article, Professor Christie noted that a finding of expropriation may be avoided 'if the State whose actions are the subject of complaint had a purpose in mind which is recognised in international law as justifying even severe […] restrictions on the use of property'.[24] While he subjected it to the conditions that the reasons given are valid and bear some plausible relationship to the action taken, Christie recognized that a particular interference with an alien's enjoyment of his property may be justified by the 'police powers' doctrine.[25]

The police powers doctrine found endorsement in the 1987 Third Restatement of the Foreign Relations Law of the United States, which state as follows: 'A State is not responsible for loss of property or for other economic disadvantage resulting from bona fide general taxation, regulation, forfeiture for crime, or other action of the kind that is commonly accepted as within the police powers of states, if it is not discriminatory.'[26]

[23] Article 10.5 subjected the operation of the exception on four conditions:

> (a) it is not a clear and discriminatory violation of the law of the State concerned; (b) it is not the result of a violation of any provision of Articles 6 to 8 of this Convention; (c) it is not an unreasonable departure from the principles of justice recognized by the principal legal systems of the world; and (d) it is not an abuse of the powers specified in this paragraph for the purpose of depriving an alien of his property.

[24] George C Christie, 'What Constitutes a Taking of Property under International Law' (1962) 38 BYIL 307, 330–1.

[25] ibid, 338. See also Rosalyn Higgins, *The Taking of Property by the State: Recent Developments in International Law* in Collected Courses of the Hague Academy of International Law (Brill-Nijhoff 1982) vol 176, chapter iv (where Professor Higgins appears to take the view that, while the measure's legitimate aim is relevant in determining the existence of an indirect taking, it should not be determinative).

[26] American Law Institute, Restatement (Third) Foreign Relations of the United States (1987), vol 1 (RLA-257), para 712, comment (g). See also Charles N Brower, 'Current Developments in the Law of Expropriation and Compensation: A Preliminary Survey of Awards of the Iran-United States Claims Tribunal' (1987) 21 Int'l L 639, 643–4:

The relevance of the public purpose in defining expropriation is also a clear feature of the parallel rules in domestic legal orders. In another seminal article investigating the notion of indirect expropriation under international law, featuring in the very first issue of the *ICSID Review*, Professor Dolzer relied on a comparative survey of the laws of the United States of America, the United Kingdom, France and the Federal Republic of Germany in order to detect any general principles of law as a subsidiary source of international law.[27] Despite acknowledging the difficulty of the task at hand, Dolzer concluded that, at least in certain situations, 'the police power in its various forms generally overrides property rights'.[28] He noted that when the measure at issue prohibits for the future an economic use, which has been made in the past, 'the various domestic orders uniformly indicate, in principle, that no compensation is due when the measure is necessary in order to protect the public from a danger arising from the property'.[29]

This conclusion is confirmed by Professor van der Walt's 1999 comprehensive comparative analysis of constitutional property clauses.[30] Van der Walt's analysis covers more than twenty domestic and supranational systems, including Germany, the Council of Europe, India, Japan, South Africa, Switzerland and the United States of America. The study emphasizes that the distinction between 'police-power regulation of the use of property' and 'eminent-domain expropriation of property' is fundamental to all property clauses, because only the latter is compensated as a rule.[31] In van der Walt's view, while it is normally said that the state can legitimately impose restrictions or limitations on the use and exploitation of private property, in terms of the police power, to protect the rights and interests of others and the public interest, 'the distinction between compensated, eminent-domain expropriations and police-power regulatory limitations of property is perhaps the most controversial and difficult issue in the whole of constitutional property'.[32]

Moreover, the domestic comparative analysis shows that the constitutional dilemma (ie drawing the line between compensated expropriations and police-power regulatory limitations of property) often finds recognition in the constitutional text. This is for at least two reasons. First, the 'expropriation clause' usually only constitutes one part of the constitutional property provision, the other two parts being, in the categorization put forward by van der Walt, the so-called

> Most Cases brought before the Tribunal, however, involve the gray area of expropriation in which no formal taking is announced by the host government [. . .]. The Tribunal's decisions vary slightly in their discussion of the degree of interference necessary to a finding of expropriation, but the most common benchmark appears to be reasonableness.

[27] Rudolf Dolzer, 'Indirect Expropriation of Alien Property' (1986) 1 ICSID Rev/FILJ 41.
[28] ibid, 62.
[29] ibid, 63.
[30] AJ van der Walt *Constitutional Property Clauses: A Comparative Analysis* (Kluwer Law International 1999).
[31] ibid, 17.
[32] ibid, 17–19.

'guarantee clause' and the 'regulation clause'.[33] For example, the constitutional property provision of the 1949 German Basic Law (Article 14) contains all three clauses as follows: the guarantee clause is found in paragraph 1, first sentence ('Property […] shall be guaranteed'); the regulation clause is found in paragraph 1, second sentence ('Their content and limits are determined by law') and in paragraph 2 ('Property entails obligations. Its use should also serve the public interest'); and the expropriation clause is found in paragraph 3 ('Expropriation shall only be permissible for a public necessity. It may only be ordered by or pursuant to a law, which determines the nature and extent of compensation. Compensation shall reflect a fair balance between the public interest and the interests of those affected. In case of dispute regarding the amount of compensation recourse may be had to the ordinary courts').[34]

The second reason is that, again usually, the constitutional property provision does not contain any definition of expropriation (beyond references to 'expropriation', 'taking', 'deprivation', 'compulsory acquisitions' or 'compulsory dispossessions')[35] or any definition of regulation (beyond references to 'limitation' or 'restriction'). For example, Article 42, paragraphs 2 and 3, of the 1947 Italian Constitution only refers to 'expropration' and 'limitations' as follows:

> Private property is recognized and guaranteed by laws which prescribe the manner in which it may be acquired and enjoyed and its limitations, with the object of ensuring its social function and of rendering it accessible to all. Private property, in such cases as are prescribed by law and with provisions for compensation, may be expropriated in the general interest.[36]

Similarly, Article 22*ter*, paragraph 2, of the 1874 Swiss Federal Constitution attributes the Confederation and the Cantons by legislation and for reasons of public interest, the power to 'make provision for expropriation and restrictions on property'.[37]

In other words, contrary to the vast majority of international investment treaties, the constitutional property provisions do not appear to employ expressly concepts

[33] ibid, 11–20.

[34] ibid, 123.

[35] Article 5 of the 1867 Austria's Basic Law, 'Property law is inviolable. Expropriation against the will of the owner can only occur in cases and in the manner determined by law': Van der Walt, *Constitutional Property Clauses* (n 30) 74 et seq.

[36] See van der Walt, *Constitutional Property Clauses* (n 30), 532. See also Article 33, paras 2 and 3, of the 1978 Spanish Constitution, 'The social function of [the right to private property] shall determine the limits of their content in accordance with the law. No one may be deprived of this property and rights except for justified cause of public utility or social interest after proper indemnification in accordance with the provisions of law': Van der Walt, *Constitutional Property Clauses* (n 30) 571.

[37] See van der Walt, *Constitutional Property Clauses* (n 30) 359 et seq. It is interesting to note that Article 22*ter*, para 3, requires the payment of 'fair compensation' for 'cases of expropriation and restriction of property equivalent to expropriation'.

such as 'indirect expropriation', or more fundamentally, 'measures having equivalent effect to' expropriation.

In conclusion, the lack of any visible attempt by the treaty drafters to limit the protection afforded by the expropriation provision on the basis of the host State's right to regulate in the public interest (as it was, at the time, under both customary international law and the constitutional laws of many countries), in conjunction with the express reference in the text of investment treaties to 'indirect expropriation' and 'measures having equivalent effect', makes a broad reading of the concept of expropriation in investment treaties very much plausible.[38]

B. Indirect Expropriation in Investment Arbitral Practice: 'Sole-Effect' versus 'Police Powers'

This section focuses on the interpretation and application by investment treaty tribunals of the expropriation provision in investment treaties in the past twenty years. It argues that arbitral practice registered early on a split in how to define the concept of indirect expropriation, with a majority of tribunals relying upon the adverse effect of the host measure under review (according to the so-called 'sole-effect' doctrine) and a minority considering, in addition to the adverse effect on the protected investment, the measure's public policy purpose (according to the so-called 'police powers' doctrine). While the split continues today, the tables have turned, as today's prevalent approach in the arbitral practice with regard to the definition of an indirect expropriation appears to be one that gives relevance to the public policy purpose of the allegedly expropriatory measure.

1. Initial interpretations and the exclusive relevance of the measure's (adverse) economic effect

There is little doubt that the very first decisions addressing claims of indirect expropriation based on international investment treaties focused exclusively on an assessment of the economic effect or impact of the allegedly expropriatory measure on the foreign investment. The decisions in *Saar Papier, Goetz, Pope and Talbot* and *Metalclad*, rendered between October 1995 and August 2000 and analysed below, confirm this point.

In *Saar Papier v Poland*, one of (if not) the first investment treaty decisions involving a claim of indirect expropriation, the issue before the arbitral tribunal was

[38] Dolzer, 'Indirect Expropriation' (n 5) 92 ('The wording of the existing treaties, however, does not lend itself to the argument that the standards of treaty law should be different from those of general international law').

whether the prohibition on importation of recycled paper, pursuant to a statutory amendment that prohibited the importation of 'waste' from abroad, constituted a 'measure the effects of which would be tantamount to expropriation' pursuant to Article 4(2) of the 1989 Germany–Poland BIT.[39] Based on its own understanding of general (particularly German) administrative law, the *Saar Papier* tribunal believed that a reasonable interpretation of the expropriation provision of the applicable treaty is one that looks at the 'economic effect' of the measures. The tribunal stated as follows:

> The effect of an expropriation is to take away the entirety of an investment made by an investor. Measures similar to expropriation must be deemed to be measures that have an economic impact that is comparable to the economic impact of an expropriation.[40]

The tribunal found that the economic reality was that, while it was technically feasible to convert the factory to producing tissue paper from either new pulp or from (inferior-quality) waste paper collected locally, neither of these courses was economically feasible. Since 'the lifeblood of the factory was cut off by Poland', the tribunal concluded that the conduct under review 'had an effect equivalent to that of an expropriation'.[41]

Confronted with the host State's revocation of the investor's free zone status without any formal taking of property, the tribunal in *Goetz v Burundi* held that the government's action fell under the (rather broad) concept of 'measures having an effect similar to a measure depriving of or restricting property' pursuant to Article 4 of the 1989 Belgium–Luxembourg–Burundi BIT, as it deprived the investment of all utility. The tribunal noted as follows:

> Dès lors que [. . .] la révocation du certificat d'entreprise franche les a contraints à arrêter toute activité [. . .], ce qui a privé de toute utilité les investissements réalisés et dépouillé les investisseurs requérants du bénéfice qu'ils pouvaient attendre de leurs investissements, la mesure litigieuse peut être regardée comme une 'mesure

[39] Polish customs authorities had prohibited the importation of 'makulatura' (recycled or waste paper), claiming that it was 'waste'. *Saar Papier Vertriebs GmbH v Poland*, UNCITRAL, Award, 16 October 1995, para 51. The Ad Article 4 of the Protocol of the 1989 Germany–Poland BIT stated as follows: 'The investor shall also have a claim to compensation in the event of expropriation or a comparable measure within the meaning of paragraph 2 of Article 4 which impairs the economic activity of the enterprise in which he is participating, if his investment is simultaneously also affected thereby.'

[40] *Saar Papier v Poland*, Award, 16 October 1995 (n 39), para 84. The tribunal noted that Poland had 'agreed that an expropriation of the main asset of a company would be equivalent to the expropriation of the shares of that company'. Poland had 'also agreed that a prohibition of access to the main asset of a company would be equivalent to the expropriation of that asset and therefore equivalent to an expropriation of the shares of the company': ibid, para 85.

[41] ibid, para 89. The tribunal reached the same conclusion, applying a second approach based on the principle of protection of 'good faith reliance' or legitimate expectations. See ibid, paras 92–94.

> ayant un effet similaire' à une mesure privative ou restrictive de propriété au sens de l'article 4 de la Convention d'investissement.[42]

While it eventually rejected the investor's indirect expropriation claim for lack of a sufficiently restrictive interference,[43] the tribunal in *Pope and Talbot v Canada* clearly affirmed that non-discriminatory regulation in the pursuit of public policy may constitute expropriation under Article 1110 of the North American Free Trade Agreement (NAFTA) (and thus require compensation) depending on the magnitude or severity of the regulation's effect (ie substantial interference) on the investor's property interests. The tribunal noted:

> [...] the scope of [article 1110] does cover non-discriminatory regulation that might be said to fall within an exercise of a state's so-called police powers. However, the Tribunal does not believe that those regulatory measures constitute an interference with the Investment's business activities substantial enough to be characterized as an expropriation under international law. Finally, the Tribunal does not believe that the phrase 'measure tantamount to nationalization or expropriation' in Article 1110 broadens the ordinary concept of expropriation under international law to require compensation for measures affecting property interests without regard to the magnitude or severity of that effect.[44]

Similarly, the tribunal in *Metalclad v Mexico*, reviewing both the refusal of a Mexican municipality to grant a waste-landfill construction permit and a so-called Ecological Decree issued by the governor of the Mexican State, put forward

[42] *Goetz and Consorts v Burundi*, ICSID Case No. ARB/95/3, Decision on Liability, 2 September 1998, para 124 (note that the 1998 decision is contained in the 29 January 1999 Award embodying the Parties' Settlement Agreement).

[43] *Pope and Talbot v Canada*, Interim Award, 28 June 2000, para 102:

> Even accepting (for the purpose of this analysis) the allegations of the Investor concerning diminished profits, the Tribunal concludes that the degree of interference with the Investment's operations due to the Export Control Regime does not rise to an expropriation (creeping or otherwise) within the meaning of Article 1110. While it may sometimes be uncertain whether a particular interference with business activities amounts to an expropriation, the test is whether that interference is sufficiently restrictive to support a conclusion that the property has been 'taken' from the owner [...].

[44] ibid, para 96. It is not fully clear whether the *Pope & Talbot* tribunal does, however, leave the door open, even if slightly, for the application of a *limited* police powers exception (ibid, para 99):

> Canada appears to claim that, because the measures under consideration are cast in the form of regulations, they constitute an exercise of 'police powers,' which, if non-discriminatory, are supposedly beyond the reach of the NAFTA rules regarding expropriations. While the exercise of police powers must be analyzed with special care, the Tribunal believes that Canada's formulation goes too far. Regulations can indeed be exercised in a way that would constitute creeping expropriation [...]. Indeed, much creeping expropriation could be conducted by regulation, and a blanket exception for regulatory measures would create a gaping loophole in international protections against expropriation.

an interpretation of indirect expropriation for purposes of Article 1110 NAFTA focusing on the allegedly expropriatory measures' (adverse) effect. According to the *Metalclad* tribunal, expropriation under NAFTA also includes 'covert or incidental interference with the use of property which has the effect of depriving the owner, in whole or in significant part, of the use or reasonably-to-be-expected economic benefit of property even if not necessarily to the obvious benefit of the host State'.[45]

The *Metalclad* tribunal first found that the Municipality's denial of the construction permit amounted to an indirect expropriation as it 'effectively [. . .] prevented the Claimant's operation of the landfill'.[46] However, the tribunal repeatedly stressed in this context what it had already established in its analysis under fair and equitable treatment: the Municipality lacked the authority for siting and permitting a hazardous waste landfill. In other words, in the view of the *Metalclad* tribunal, the conduct of the municipality was 'unlawful' under Mexican law.[47] In addition to the measure's substantial adverse effect on the investment, was thus the measure's lack of legality an essential element for a finding of indirect expropriation? Was this really an application of the so-called 'sole-effect' doctrine as put forward by the tribunal in its often-quoted passage? This remains to some extent unclear.[48]

However, the *Metalclad* tribunal's reliance on the 'sole-effect' doctrine seems to be reinforced by the same tribunal's obiter dictum with regard to Mexico's second measure under review, the State Governor's Ecological Decree. The *Metalclad* tribunal concluded that the Ecological decree constitutes an act tantamount to expropriation expressly excluding the relevance of the motivation or intent behind the allegedly expropriatory measure and without enquiring whether such measure was lawful under Mexican law. The tribunal noted as follows:

> The Tribunal need not decide or consider the motivation or intent of the adoption of the Ecological Decree. Indeed, a finding of expropriation on the basis of the Ecological Decree is not essential to the Tribunal's finding of a violation of NAFTA Article 1110. However, the Tribunal considers that the implementation

[45] *Metalclad Corporation v The United Mexican States*, ICSID Case No ARB(AF)/97/1, Award, 30 August 2000, para 103.

[46] ibid, para 106.

[47] '[. . .] the Municipality's denial of the construction permit without any basis in the proposed physical construction or any defect in the site, and extended by its subsequent administrative and judicial actions regarding the *Convenio*, effectively and unlawfully prevented the Claimant's operation of the landfill': ibid, para 106.

[48] Dolzer, 'Indirect Expropriation' (n 5) 91 ('One provisional conclusion which may also be drawn from our review of those cases which focus on the "sole effect doctrine" concerns a certain sparsity in argument, or absence of an attempt to lay the methodological foundations for the doctrine in these cases.')

> of the Ecological Decree would, in and of itself, constitute an act tantamount to expropriation.[49]

While in none of the four above-mentioned decisions did the tribunal expressly endorse the so-called 'sole-effect doctrine', it is difficult to dispute that such doctrine accurately describes the approach undertaken by those four tribunals. This is particularly so, not just because 'effect' was the key (if not the only) factor mentioned in the various determinations of indirect expropriation, but also because in three of those four cases, the tribunal concluded that the measures under review constituted expropriation pursuant to the respective applicable treaties, once it had found that they had an (at least substantial) adverse effect on the foreign investment.[50]

2. The relevance of the measure's purpose in assessing the existence of an indirect expropriation

The very initial exclusive focus on the adverse effect on the investment was quickly supplemented (but not substituted) by investment treaty decisions that expressly recognized, next to such adverse effect, the relevance (and sometimes precedence) of the public policy purpose of the allegedly expropriatory measure.[51] The decisions in *SD Myers, Feldman* and *Tecmed*, rendered between November 2000 and May 2003 and analysed below, confirm this point.

[49] *Metalclad v Mexico*, Award, 30 August 2000 (n 45) para 111. See Yves Fortier and Stephen Drymer, 'Indirect Expropriation in the Law of International Investment: I Know It When I See It, or Caveat Investor' (2004) ICSID Rev 293, 313 who, based on such statement, affirmed that the *Metalclad* tribunal 'clearly applied the sole effect test and held that the intent behind the adoption of the decree was extraneous to a determination under NAFTA Article 1110'. Another contemporaneous decision that is often used in support of the sole-effect doctrine is *Compañía del Desarrollo de Santa Elena, SA v Costa Rica*, Case No ARB/96/1, Award, 17 February 2000, based on the tribunal's following statement (ibid, para 73):

> Expropriatory environmental measures—no matter how laudable and beneficial to society as a whole—are, in this respect, similar to any other expropriatory measures that a state may take in order to implement its policies: where property is expropriated, even for environmental purposes, whether domestic or international, the state's obligation to pay compensation remains.

However, those statements should be seen in light of the *Santa Elena* tribunal's exclusive task of determining the amount of compensation owed by Costa Rica for the 'direct' expropriation of the investor's property rather than for purposes of determining the existence of an expropriation. Note, nonetheless, the tribunal's acknowledgement of the existence of 'ample authority for the proposition that a property has been expropriated when the effect of the measures taken by the state has been to deprive the owner of title, possession or access to the benefit and economic use of his property': ibid, para 77.

[50] See Ben Mostafa, 'The Sole Effects Doctrine, Police Powers and Indirect Expropriation under International Law' (2008) 15 Aust J Int'l L 267.

[51] Dolzer, 'Indirect Expropriation' (n 5) 90–1.

In *SD Myers v Canada*, one of the claims was that the export ban introduced by Canada on the export of printed circuit board (PCB) waste to the United States for remediation amounted to a measure tantamount to expropriation pursuant to Article 1110 of NAFTA. Interpreting Article 1110 'in light of the whole body of state practice, treaties and judicial interpretation',[52] the *SD Myers* tribunal emphasized the appropriateness for tribunals to examine 'the purpose and effect of governmental measures'.[53] The tribunal also noted that the 'general body of precedent usually does not treat regulatory action as amounting to expropriation', but while regulatory conduct by public authorities is unlikely to be the subject of legitimate complaint under Article 1110 NAFTA, the tribunal did not rule out that possibility.[54] While the tribunal believed that Canada's export ban was indeed a protectionist measure (thus environmental protection was not its principal aim),[55] it nonetheless rejected the investor's expropriation claim for lack of the necessary deprivation, as the ban had only been a temporary one.[56] This decision thus shows that lack of the required (high) level of adverse effect will make the assessment of the purpose of the allegedly expropriatory measure irrelevant or unnecessary.

The tribunal in *Feldman v Mexico*[57] acknowledged that measures 'tantamount to expropriation' in Article 1110 NAFTA 'potentially encompass a variety of government regulatory activity that may significantly interfere with an investor's property rights'.[58] However, the *Feldman* tribunal also recognized the difficulty in drawing the boundaries of the concept of indirect expropriation. The tribunal noted as follows:

> However, it is much less clear when governmental action that interferes with broadly-defined property rights […] crosses the line from valid regulation to

[52] The tribunal referred in agreement to the statement in *Pope & Talbot* (n 43), according to which 'the drafters of the NAFTA intended the word "tantamount" to embrace the concept of so-called "creeping expropriation," rather than to expand the internationally accepted scope of the term expropriation': *SD Myers v Canada*, Partial Award, 13 November 2000, para 286.

[53] *SD Myers v Canada*, Partial Award, 13 November 2000 (n 52), paras 280–1. At para 285:

> The primary meaning of the word 'tantamount' given by the Oxford English Dictionary is 'equivalent.' Both words require a tribunal to look at the substance of what has occurred and not only at form. A tribunal should not be deterred by technical or facial considerations from reaching a conclusion that an expropriation or conduct tantamount to an expropriation has occurred. It must look at the real interests involved and the purpose and effect of the government measure.

[54] ibid, para 281.

[55] ibid, para 162 and Separate Opinion by Dr Bryan Schwartz, 12 November 2000, paras 218–19.

[56] *SD Myers v Canada*, Partial Award, 13 November 2000 (n 52), paras 284 and 287.

[57] *Marvin Roy Feldman Karpa v United Mexican States*, ICSID Case No ARB(AF)/99/1, Award, 16 December 2002.

[58] ibid, para 100.

> a compensable taking, and it is fair to say that no one has come up with a fully satisfactory means of drawing this line.[59]

While the *Feldman* tribunal noted that there are many ways in which governmental authorities may force a company out of business or significantly reduce the economic benefits of its business, it admitted that 'governments must be free to act in the broader public interest through protection of the environment, new or modified tax regimes [. . .], imposition of zoning restrictions and the like'.[60] It continued: 'Reasonable governmental regulation of this type cannot be achieved if any business that is adversely affected may seek compensation, and it is safe to say that customary international law recognizes this.'[61] The tribunal eventually rejected the expropriation claim, based on several factors that 'tip the expropriation/regulation balance away from a finding of expropriation'.[62]

The tribunal in *Tecmed v Mexico* is another early decision that relies on both the effect and purpose of the measure under review in order to determine the existence of an indirect expropriation for the purposes of the Spain–Mexico BIT. According to the *Tecmed* tribunal, the first step in an expropriation analysis is to determine whether the measure under review (in the specific case, the non-renewal of a permit to operate a waste landfill) 'radically deprived [the investor] of the economical use and enjoyment of its investments, as if the rights related thereto—such as the income or benefits related to the landfill or to its exploitation—had ceased to exist'.[63] Having established that the measure under review had such expropriatory effects, the tribunal then moved to the second step of the expropriation analysis, aimed at establishing whether the same measure, 'due to its characteristics and

[59] ibid.

[60] ibid, para 103.

[61] ibid. The tribunal noted that while the language of the Restatement differs considerably from Article 1110 NAFTA, many of the essential substantive elements are the same, particularly the concept of a taking and the conditions: ibid, para 104.

[62] ibid, para 111:

> This Tribunal's rationale for declining to find a violation of Article 1110 can be summarized as follows: (1) As *Azinian* suggests, not every business problem experienced by a foreign investor is an expropriation under Article 1110; (2) NAFTA and principles of customary international law do not require a state to permit 'gray market' exports of cigarettes; (3) at no relevant time has the IEPS law, as written, afforded Mexican cigarette resellers such as CEMSA a 'right' to export cigarettes (due primarily to technical/legal requirements for invoices stating tax amounts separately and to their status as non-taxpayers); and (4) the Claimant's 'investment,' the exporting business known as CEMSA, as far as this Tribunal can determine, remains under the complete control of the Claimant, in business with the apparent right to engage in the exportation of alcoholic beverages, photographic supplies, contact lenses, powdered milk and other Mexican products—any product that it can purchase upon receipt of invoices stating the tax amounts—and to receive rebates of any applicable taxes under the IEPS law.

[63] *Técnicas Medioambientales Tecmed, SA v The United Mexican States*, ICSID Case No ARB (AF)/00/2, Award, 29 May 2003, para 115 ('In other words, if due to the actions of the Respondent, the assets involved have lost their value or economic use for their holder and the extent of the loss [. . .]').

considering not only its effects, is an expropriatory decision'.[64] It acknowledged the relevance of whether the alleged expropriatory measure was in the exercise of the host State's police powers. The *Tecmed* tribunal noted, in very clear terms, as follows:

> The principle that the State's exercise of its sovereign powers within the framework of its police power may cause economic damage to those subject to its powers as administrator without entitling them to any compensation whatsoever is undisputable.[65]

The tribunal further clarified that a finding of expropriation is dependent on 'whether such measures are reasonable with respect to their goals, the deprivation of economic rights and the legitimate expectations of those who suffered such deprivation' and, referring to the jurisprudence of the European Convention on Human Rights (ECHR), that 'there must be a reasonable relationship of proportionality between the charge or weight imposed to the foreign investor and the aim sought to be realized by any expropriatory measure'.[66]

Following an extensive analysis of the reasons alleged by the Mexican government for the disputed measure (particularly, the company's numerous infractions of the terms of its permit, the protection of the environment and public health, and community pressure and demonstrations against the location of the landfill near an urban centre), the tribunal eventually found in favour of the investor, as it concluded that the various reasons alleged by the respondent were not sufficient justification to deprive the foreign investor of its investment without compensation.[67]

3. 'Sole effect' versus 'police powers': an enduring but evolving inconsistent arbitral tribunal practice

While *SD Myers, Feldman* and *Tecmed* acknowledged the relevance of the purpose of the measure under review (referred to as the 'police powers' doctrine), other contemporaneous tribunals continued to apply the sole-effect doctrine for the purposes of determining the concept of indirect expropriation. For example, the tribunal in *Lauder v Czech Republic* noted that indirect expropriation 'is a measure that does not involve an overt taking, but that effectively neutralizes the enjoyment

[64] ibid, para 118.
[65] ibid, para 119.
[66] ibid, para 122.
[67] ibid, paras 123–51. See further the analysis in chapter III. Another early and often-cited decision expressly adopting the police powers doctrine is *Saluka Investments BV v The Czech Republic*, Partial Award, 17 March 2006 (n 19), para 255 ('It is now established in international law that States are not liable to pay compensation to a foreign investor when, in the normal exercise of their regulatory powers, they adopt in a non-discriminatory manner bona fide regulations that are aimed at the general welfare').

of the property'.[68] The tribunal eventually rejected the investor's claim, as the investor had not brought 'sufficient evidence that any measure or action taken by the Czech Republic would have had the effect of transferring his property or of depriving him of his rights to use his property or even of interfering with his property rights'.[69]

Similarly, the tribunal in *Middle East Cement Shipping and Handling v Egypt* found in favour of the investor, as the investor was deprived by respondent's measures 'of parts of the value his investment'.[70] The tribunal's view on indirect expropriation is as follows:

> When measures are taken by a State the effect of which is to deprive the investor of the use and benefit of his investment even though he may retain nominal ownership of the respective rights being the investment, the measures are often referred to as a 'creeping' or 'indirect' expropriation or, as in the BIT, as measures 'the effect of which is tantamount to expropriation'.[71]

The *Waste Management v Mexico II* tribunal appears to rely on the measure's effect only. According to the *Waste Management II* tribunal, the phrase 'tantamount to nationalization or expropriation' in Article 1110 NAFTA 'was intended to add to the meaning of the prohibition, over and above the reference to indirect expropriation'.[72] The broad reading of expropriation by the *Waste Management II* tribunal was also based on a contextual reading of Article 1110(8) NAFTA, which reads as follows:

> For purposes of this Article and for greater certainty, a non-discriminatory measure of general application shall not be considered a measure tantamount to an expropriation of a debt security or loan covered by this Chapter solely on the ground that the measure imposes costs on the debtor that cause it to default on the debt.

The *Waste Management II* tribunal noted that the existence of such a clarification confirmed the broad meaning of expropriation in Article 1110, as otherwise it is difficult to see why Article 1110(8) was necessary. The tribunal noted as follows:

> As a matter of international law a 'non-discriminatory measure of general application' in relation to a debt security or loan which imposed costs on the

[68] *Ronald S Lauder v Czech Republic*, UNCITRAL, Award, 3 September 2001, para 200.
[69] ibid, para 202.
[70] *Middle East Cement Shipping and Handling v Egypt*, ICSID Case No ARB/99/6, Award, 12 April 2002, para 107.
[71] ibid.
[72] *Waste Management, Inc v Mexico II*, ICSID Case No ARB(AF)/00/3, Award, 25 June 2003, para 144.

> debtor causing it to default would not be considered expropriatory or even potentially so. It is true that paragraph (8) is stated to be 'for greater certainty', but if it was necessary even for certainty's sake to deal with such a case this suggests that the drafters entertained a broad view of what might be 'tantamount to an expropriation.'[73]

While not stated expressly, the *Waste Management II* tribunal appears to suggest that Article 1110 NAFTA may have adopted a notion of expropriation that is broader than the one applicable under customary international law, which, under the police powers doctrine, would exclude non-discriminatory measures of general application.

Accordingly, by 2003, the dozen decisions by investment treaty tribunals already registered a split in the relevant definition of indirect expropriation: whereas a majority had referred and relied upon the *effect* of the host State's measure under review, some tribunals had been willing to consider the measure's *purpose*, in addition to its adverse impact on the protected investment.[74] Famously, the Annulment committee in *Patrick Mitchell v Congo* highlighted that the choice between the sole-effect doctrine and the police powers doctrine rests in the tribunal's 'freedom of judgement'.[75]

While the success rate of an investment treaty claim based on indirect expropriation has been overall rather low (around fifty decisions out of slightly more than 300 arbitrations, or approximately 17%),[76] it should not come as a surprise that in most of the successful cases the tribunal has adopted an interpretation of indirect expropriation based on (a version of) the sole-effect doctrine. Aside from the *Tecmed* decision, noted in section 2, one can find only a handful of arbitral decisions where the tribunal, having clearly endorsed the relevance of the public

[73] ibid. Similarly, some tribunals have excluded the relevance of the measure's public purpose by relying on a contextual interpretation of indirect expropriation. These tribunals have focused on the reference to 'public purpose' as one of the conditions for a lawful expropriation. In the words of the *Vivendi* tribunal, 'If public purpose automatically immunises the measure from being found to be expropriatory, then there would never be a compensable taking for a public purpose': *Vivendi v Argentina*, ICSID Case No ARB/97/3, Award, 20 August 2007, para 7.5.21.

[74] See Fortier and Drymer, 'Indirect Expropriation' (n 49) 293, 300.

[75] *Patrick Mitchell v The Democratic Republic of Congo*, ICSID Case No ARB/99/7, Decision on the Application for Annulment of the Award, 1 November 2006, para 54:

> In any event, regardless of the various positions adopted in legal doctrine and case law on the question of determining whether the effect should be the sole and unique criterion to be used in assessing an indirect expropriation or a measure tantamount to expropriation, or whether the purpose sought by the State is also to be taken into account, it cannot but be found in the case at hand that the Arbitral Tribunal, in apparently opting for the 'sole effect' doctrine, was merely exercising its freedom of judgment.

[76] This is based on the UNCTAD database of known investment treaty arbitrations. As of October 2017, there were overall 359 cases where an indirect expropriation claim was made: while fifty-three cases out of 359 were still pending, there were fifty-one cases where the investor's indirect expropriation claims had been successful (aside from the question of quantum). That is approximately, one case out of six. See https://investmentpolicy.unctad.org/.

policy purpose in determining the existence (rather than the lawfulness) of an indirect expropriation, found in favour of the investor.[77] For example, while the tribunal in *Deutsche Bank v Sri Lanka* accepted the host States' right to interfere with foreign investments in the exercise of 'legitimate regulatory authority', it nonetheless rejected Sri Lanka's argument, as the taking of Deutsche Bank's rights under the hedging agreement was 'a financially motivated and illegitimate regulatory expropriation by a regulator lacking in independence'.[78]

Similarly, while it eventually found the measures under review amounted to 'an abuse of the Respondent's authority to the degree that they resulted in an indirect expropriation',[79] the tribunal in *Belokon v Venezuela* acknowledged the host States' right to regulate in the public interest as follows:

> The Tribunal naturally accepts that the application of general regulatory powers, such as taxation or determination of bank capitalisation standards, does not in and of itself amount to indirect expropriation. States have considerable policy space to enact the laws and regulations they believe are appropriate.[80]

In *Quirobax v Bolivia*, the tribunal noted that '[f]or an indirect expropriation to exist, it is generally accepted that the State measure must have the effect of substantially depriving the investor of the economic value of its investment [...], the deprivation must be permanent and must not be justified by the police powers doctrine'.[81] The *Quirobax* tribunal found that the termination of the concessions made the claimant's investment 'virtually worthless', and 'the deprivation was permanent and was not justified by the police powers doctrine'.[82]

[77] *Señor Tza Yap Shum v The Republic of Peru*, ICSID Case No ARB/07/6, Award, 7 July 2011; *Les Laboratoires Servier, SAA, Biofarma, SAS, Arts et Techniques du Progres SAS v Republic of Poland*, UNCITRAL, Award, 14 February 2012; *Deutsche Bank AG v Democratic Socialist Republic of Sri Lanka*, ICSID Case No ARB/09/2, Award, 31 October 2012; *Abengoa, SA y COFIDES, SA v United Mexican States*, ICSID Case No ARB(AF)/09/2, Award, 18 April 2013; *Valeri Belokon v Kyrgyzstan*, UNCITRAL, Award, 24 October 2014; *Quiborax SA, Non Metallic Minerals SA and Allan Fosk Kaplún v Plurinational State of Bolivia*, ICSID Case No ARB/06/2, Award, 16 September 2015; *Copper Mesa Mining Corporation v Republic of Ecuador*, PCA No 2012-2, Award, 15 March 2016. It should be noted that some of the decisions reported in the UNCTAD database could not be examined as they are not publicly available or were written in a language other than English, Spanish or French. However, it should be stressed that a finding that no expropriation took place (either because no 'substantial deprivation' was established or because the exercise of police powers was not legitimate) does not always mean that no treaty violation was found. For two recent cases where the tribunal rejected the claim of indirect expropriation (for lack of substantial adverse effect) but found a breach of the FET provision, see *Novenergia II—Energy & Environment (SCA) (Grand Duchy of Luxembourg), SICAR v The Kingdom of Spain*, SCC Case No 2015/063, Final Award, 15 February 2018, paras 759–63 and *Foresight Luxembourg Solar 1 Sàrl et al v Kingdom of Spain*, SCC Case No 2015/150, Final Award, 14 November 2018, paras 423–31.

[78] *Deutsche Bank v Sri Lanka*, Award, 31 October 2012 (n 77), paras 522–4.

[79] *Belokon v Venezuela*, Award, 24 October 2014 (n 77), para 199.

[80] ibid, para 198.

[81] *Quiborax v Bolivia*, Award, 16 September 2015 (n 77), para 238.

[82] ibid, para 239.

It is worth noting that the decisions above (*Deutsche Bank, Belokon* and *Quiborax*), as well as the very few other decisions finding in favour of the investor while recognizing the relevance of the police powers doctrine for purposes of defining an indirect expropriation, have mostly been rendered in the past five years. It is undeniable that, based on a cursory view of all decisions on indirect expropriation rendered in the past few years (whether finding for or against the investor's expropriation claim), the police powers doctrine has grown in relevance and has become more prevalent compared to the sole-effect doctrine.[83]

C. 'Expropriatory Effect': A Concept in Search of a Definition

Whether as the only criterion (pursuant to the 'sole-effect' doctrine) or as one of the relevant criteria (pursuant to the 'police powers' doctrine) employed to determine the existence of an indirect expropriation, the adverse effect of the host State measure under review has been a common feature of practically every indirect expropriation analysis so far carried out by investment treaty tribunals. After twenty years and more than 200 arbitral decisions, the notion of 'effect equivalent to expropriation' or 'expropriatory effect' remains controversial, and thus unclear. However, in line with the similar evolution noted above with regard to the increasing relevance of the public policy objective of the host State's measure under review, investment treaty tribunals seem to have progressively taken a stricter approach with regard to the nature of the required expropriatory effect, if not in form, at least in fact. This section aims to show such evolution by focusing on three key issues inherently linked with the search for expropriatory effect: (1) the 'threshold question' revolves around the issue of the extent of the adverse effect or deprivation; (2) the 'denominator problem' addresses the need to determine what is the overall investment against which a deprivation needs to be measured; and (3) the last issue focuses on the 'object of deprivation'. The order followed here roughly corresponds, in my view, to the chronology with which these issues have surfaced.

[83] This is also in light of the fact that there may be decisions by investment treaty tribunals that, though not referring expressly to the 'police powers' doctrine, clearly identify as similar factors for purposes of an indirect expropriation claim, such as whether the host State's measure at issue is lawful under domestic law, discriminatory, or lacking *bona fides*. See eg *Renta 4 v Russia*, SCC No. 24/2007, Award, 20 July 2012, para 45:

> Indirect expropriation, of course, does not speak its name. It must be deduced from a pattern of conduct, observing its conception, implementation, and effects as such, even if the intention to expropriate is disavowed at every step. The fact that individual measures appear not to be well founded in law, or to be discriminatory, or otherwise to lack bona fides, may be important elements of a finding that there has been the equivalent of an indirect expropriation, an expropriation by other means.

1. The threshold question: substantial versus total deprivation

A first question with regard to the notion of expropriatory effect relates to 'quantum'. Should the adverse effect of the host State's measure under review be 'total' or more simply 'substantial'?[84] As one would expect, claimants/investors tend to argue for the latter, while respondents/host States for the former. In its recent decision on the merits, the tribunal in *Philip Morris v Uruguay* recorded the parties' divergence as to the threshold for finding indirect expropriation as follows: 'the Claimants contending that the interference with the investor's rights, whether regulatory or not, should be such as to substantially deprive the investment of its value, the Respondent holding that such interference must have "rendered *almost without value* the rights remaining with the investor." '[85]

From the very beginning, some tribunals have focused on the government measure's 'total' or 'radical' deprivation of the investment, particularly emphasizing the similar all-encompassing adverse effect of a 'direct' expropriation. For example, as noted above, the tribunal in *Saar Papier v Poland* noted that the 'effect of an expropriation is to take away the entirety of an investment made by an investor' and thus the treaty phrase 'measures tantamount to expropriation' 'must be deemed to be measures that have an economic impact that is comparable to the economic impact of an expropriation'.[86] Since the tribunal found that the host State's conduct had cut off 'the lifeblood of the factory', the tribunal concluded that the conduct under review 'had an effect equivalent to that of an expropriation'.[87] Similarly, the *Tecmed* tribunal asked whether the non-renewal of a permit to operate a waste landfill 'radically deprived [the investor] of the economical use and enjoyment of its investments, as if the rights related thereto [...] had ceased to exist'.[88] More recently, for the purposes of defining a measure equivalent to expropriation, the tribunal in *Venezuela Holdings v Venezuela* emphasized the *totality* of the deprivation. It stated that 'deprivation requires either a total loss of the investment's value or a total loss of control by the investor of its investment, both of a permanent nature'.[89]

84 See Jonathan Bonnitcha, *Substantive Protection under Investment Treaties* (CUP 2014) 255.

85 *Philip Morris Brands Sàrl, Philip Morris Products SA and Abal Hermanos SA v Oriental Republic of Uruguay*, ICSID Case No ARB/10/7, Award, 8 July 2016, para 191 [emphasis original]. Article 5(1) of the Switzerland–Uruguay BIT refers to 'any other measure having the same nature or the same effect' as an expropriation or a nationalization.

86 *Saar Papier v Poland*, Award, 16 October 1995 (n 39), para 84. The tribunal noted that Poland had 'agreed that an expropriation of the main asset of a company would be equivalent to the expropriation of the shares of that company'. Poland had 'also agreed that a prohibition of access to the main asset of a company would be equivalent to the expropriation of that asset and therefore equivalent to an expropriation of the shares of the company': iIbid, para 85.

87 ibid, para 89.

88 *Tecmed v Mexico*, Award, 29 May 2003 (n 63), para 115. See also *Cargill v Mexico*, ICSID Case No. ARB(AF)/05/2, Award, 18 September 2009, para 360.

89 *Venezuela Holdings BV, Mobil Cerro Negro Holding LTD et al v Venezuela*, ICSID Case No. ARB/07/27, Award, 9 October 2014, para 286. See also *Total SA v The Argentine Republic*, Case No ARB/04/01, Decision on Liability, 27 December 2010, para 195 ('Under international law [...] [a]n effective

Nevertheless, other investment treaty tribunals have apparently lowered the threshold to demonstrate the existence of 'expropriatory effect' by referring to the concept of 'substantial' deprivation. The tribunal in *Metalclad* famously emphasized that indirect expropriation existed if the host State interference 'has the effect of depriving the owner, in whole or in significant part, of the use or [. . .] economic benefit of the property'.[90] Similarly, the *Waste Management II* Tribunal noted that in order for a claim of expropriation of contractual rights to succeed, 'it is necessary to show an effective repudiation of the right, unredressed by any remedies available to the Claimant, which has the effect of preventing its exercise entirely or to a substantial extent'.[91]

Despite the fact that references to 'substantial deprivation' have been ubiquitous throughout the investment treaty arbitral practice,[92] there appears to be, in practice, little difference (if any) between 'total' and 'substantial' deprivation. This is for three sets of reasons. First, investment treaty tribunals have resisted providing clear guidance on the level interference that is required to establish 'substantial' deprivation. The tribunal in *Chemtura v Canada* is perhaps the best example of this cautious stance:

> The determination of whether there has been a 'substantial deprivation' is a fact-sensitive exercise to be conducted in the light of the circumstances of each case. [. . .] One important feature of fact-sensitive assessments is that they cannot be conducted on the basis of rigid binary rules. It would make little sense to state a percentage or a threshold that would have to be met for a deprivation to be 'substantial' as such modus operandi may not always be appropriate.[93]

Second, investment treaty tribunals often appear to equate 'substantial deprivation' with total or near-total deprivation. For example, the tribunal in *Sempra v*

deprivation requires, however, a total loss of value of the property such as when the property affected is rendered worthless by the measure').

[90] *Metalclad v Mexico*, Award, 30 August 2000 (n 45), para 103.

[91] *Waste Management v Mexico II*, Award, 30 April 2004 (n 72), para 175. See also the similar language, but in a different context, by the Waste Management tribunal, which had earlier identified the expropriation question before it as 'whether the combined conduct of Mexican public entities had an effect equivalent to the taking of the enterprise, in whole or substantial part': ibid, para 155. See *Gami Investments Inc v Mexico*, UNCITRAL, Final Award, 14 November 2004, para 133, where the tribunal appears, at least implicitly, to admit the possibility of a 'less than total' impact on the investment ('With knowledge of the magnitude of diminution one might be in a position to consider whether a line is to be drawn beyond which the loss is so great as to constitute a taking').

[92] *CMS Gas Transmission Company v The Republic of Argentina*, ICSID Case No ARB/01/8, Award, 12 May 2005, para 262 ('The standard that a number of tribunals have applied in recent cases where indirect expropriation has been contended is that of substantial'). Newcombe and Paradell, *Law and Practice of Investment Treaties* (n 2) 344 ('A substantial deprivation is a necessary *factual* predicate for a determination of *legal* liability for expropriation' [emphasis original]).

[93] *Chemtura Corporation v Government of Canada*, UNCITRAL (formerly *Crompton Corporation v Government of* Canada), Award, 2 August 2010, para 249.

Argentina, first, emphasizes 'substantial deprivation' as being the relevant standard for a finding of indirect expropriation,[94] and immediately after, it states that a 'finding of indirect expropriation would require [. . .] that the value of the business have been virtually annihilated'.[95] Similarly, the tribunal in *Vivendi v Argentina I* seems to eliminate the apparent distinction between 'substantial' and 'complete' deprivation. It noted as follows:

> [. . .] it is not infrequent in cases of indirect expropriation that the investor suffers a substantial deprivation of value of its investment. Numerous tribunals have looked at the diminution of the value of the investment to determine whether the contested measure is expropriatory. The weight of authority (further discussed below) appears to draw a distinction between only a partial deprivation of value (not an expropriation) and a complete or near complete deprivation of value (expropriation).[96]

Similarly, in a recent decision, the tribunal in *Enkev Beheer v Poland* describes the mass of international legal materials (comprising both arbitral decisions and doctrinal writings) on the required level of deprivation for a finding of indirect expropriation as consistent, despite the fact that different terms are employed.[97] In the *Enkev* tribunal's view, these legal materials require the investor to establish the 'substantial, radical, severe, devastating or fundamental deprivation of its rights or their virtual annihilation and effective neutralisation'.[98] Thus, by arguing that 'substantial' deprivation is consistent with 'radical', 'severe', 'devastating' deprivation or 'virtual annihilation', the *Enkev* tribunal appeared to narrow, if not eliminate completely, the apparent distinction between 'substantial' and 'complete' deprivation.

Finally, there seems to be little practical relevance in distinguishing between different thresholds of expropriatory effect, as in many cases the actual finding of deprivation has rested on the tribunal's determination that there was little or no residual value left of the relevant investment. For example, while the *Belokon* tribunal had firmly identified the relevant question as 'whether there has been a substantial deprivation',[99] it quickly concluded that the relevant conduct of the host State (placing the investor's bank under the host State administrative control) had severely affected the bank's profitability and operations 'to the point that even if it were returned to the claimant's control it has little or no residual value'.[100]

[94] *Sempra Energy International v The Argentine Republic*, ICSID Case No AR/02/16, Award, 28 September 2007, para 284.
[95] ibid, para 285.
[96] *Vivendi v Argentina I*, Award, 20 August 2007 (n 73), para 7.5.11.
[97] *Enkev Beheer BV v Republic of Poland*, PCA Case No 2013-01, First Partial Award, 29 April 2014, para 344.
[98] ibid.
[99] *Belokon v Kyrgyzstan*, Award, 24 October 2014 (n 77), para 206.
[100] ibid, para 209.

Similarly, having identified the relevant question as 'whether the revocation of the concessions had the effect of substantially depriving Quiborax of the value of its investment in Bolivia, i.e., of its shares in NMM', the *Quiborax v Bolivia* tribunal 'agrees that, in the absence of the concessions, which were NMM's *raison d'être*, the Claimants' investment in NMM was virtually worthless'.[101]

2. The denominator problem

Any analysis that is premised on establishing a certain level of deprivation (whether substantial or total) requires the determination of what is the overall investment against which a deprivation needs to be measured. In other words, in order to determine whether the host State has caused 'substantial' or 'total' deprivation of the protected investment, a tribunal will need to identify the (contours of the) investment itself. For example, the conduct of the host State under review may have had an adverse impact only on some of the assets making up the investor's larger business (say, for example, the intellectual property rights of a manufacturing business) but not on other assets connected with the same economic operation (say, for example, the land, machineries, licenses, etc). In order to determine whether the impact of the host State's measure is (at least) substantial for purposes of a finding of indirect expropriation, a tribunal may need to determine whether the focus of its analysis should be the entire manufacturing business (ie. all of the assets) or the IP rights, only. In United States law on takings, this is often referred to as the 'denominator problem',[102] and is often linked with the issue of 'partial taking' or 'conceptual severance'.[103]

As noted in the Introduction, investment treaties appear to take a rather broad view of what is the object of an expropriation. As most investment treaties have traditionally used open-ended, asset-based definitions of 'investment', references to 'investments' in the treaty provisions on expropriation can legitimately lead to

[101] *Quiborax v Bolivia*, Award, 16 September 2015 (n 77), para 239. See *RosInvestCo UK Ltd v The Russian Federation*, SCC Case No V079/2005, Final Award, 12 September 2010, para 624:

> in determining whether a measure (or set of measures) is 'equivalent to' expropriation, the Tribunal should evaluate whether the 'net effect' of the measure (or set of measures) is the same as an outright expropriation, i.e., a substantial or total deprivation of the economic value of an asset. The Tribunal agrees with Claimant's submission that the Tribunal need not address this question, because it is confronted with a complete taking of all of the assets of Yukos that amounts to nationalisation or expropriation of RosInvestCo's investment.

[102] John Fee, 'Unearthing the Denominator in Regualtory Taking Claims' (1994) 61 University of Chicago L Rev 1535. See also Alessandra Asteriti, 'Regulatory Expropriation Claims in International Investment Arbitrations: A Bridge Too Far?' in Andrea Bjorklund (ed) *Yearbook of International Investment Law and Policy* (OUP 2012–13) 462.

[103] See Richard Epstein, *Takings: Private Property and the Power of Eminent Domain* (Harvard University Press 1985) 57 et seq; Angela Chang, 'Demystifying Conceptual Severance: A Comparative Study of the United States, Canada, and the European Court of Human Rights' (2013) 98 Cornell L Rev 965.

allowing the concept of 'partial expropriation'. To use the same example above, as intellectual property rights are often expressly included in the list of assets referred to in the treaty provision defining the term 'investment', the protection provided by the treaty vis-à-vis expropriations of investments can be interpreted as protecting the direct and indirect taking of the foreign investor's intellectual property rights, even if that is the only asset that was adversely affected by the host State's conduct. This reading clearly extends the scope of the protection afforded by the expropriation provision. However, it is an interpretation that is arguably in line with the core objectives of investment treaties, which is to encourage foreign investment by safeguarding the foreign investors' assets located in the host State, independently from their connection to a specific enterprise or activity.[104]

Nevertheless, in investment treaty arbitration, the issue of 'partial' expropriation is indeed a controversial one, as some tribunals have expressly denied the very concept of partial expropriation and other tribunals have expressly recognized it.[105] While acknowledging the issue, some investment treaty tribunals have tried to avoid taking a principled approach and suggested adopting a case-by-case approach. The *Chemtura* tribunal, for example, noted as follows:

> For instance, one could think of cases where one specific asset (a building, a piece of land, a line of business) which represents a part of the value of all the different assets held by a foreign investor in the host State has been entirely expropriated. In such case, applying a percentage or threshold approach to the overall assets held by the investor in the host State would preclude the deprivation from being 'substantial', whereas applying the same assessment to the specific asset in question would lead to the opposite conclusion. Given the diversity of situations

[104] UNCTAD, *Scope and Definition: A Sequel* (United Nations 2010) 21–2:

> Protection-oriented instruments seek to safeguard the interests of the investors or, in broader context, to promote foreign investment by safeguarding the investors' property rights, assets and interests. Investment is seen as something that already exists or that will exist, by the time protection becomes necessary. The older terminologies, which referred to 'acquired rights' or to 'foreign property' (OECD Draft Convention on the Protection of Foreign Property 1962) make the context clear. The exact character of the particular assets is not by itself important in this case, since protection is to be extended to assets after their acquisition by the investor, when they form part of the investor's patrimony. Instruments mainly directed at the protection of foreign investment contain definitions of investment that are generally broad and comprehensive. They cover not only the capital (or the resources) that has crossed borders with a view towards the creation of an enterprise or the acquisition of control over an existing one, but also most other kinds of assets of the enterprise or of the investor, such as property and property rights of various kinds, non-equity investment, including several types of loans and portfolio transactions, as well as other contractual rights, including sometimes rights created by administrative action of a host State (licenses, permits, etc.). Such a definition is very common in BITs.

[105] See Ursula Kriebaum, 'Partial Expropriation' (2007) 8 JWIT 69 et seq; Santiago Montt, *State Liability in Investment Treaty Arbitration: Global Constitutional and Administrative Law in the BIT Generation* (Hart 2009) 268.

> that may arise in practice, it is preferable to examine each situation in the light of its own specific circumstances.[106]

Reliance on a case-by-case approach may be (and often is) a code for the recognition that the jurisprudence (in the broad sense of the word) has not yet developed a principled approach with regard to the particular issue.

The complexity of the denominator problem is clearly not a peculiarity stemming out of international investment treaties and arbitration, as the evolution of the law of regulatory taking in the United States clearly shows. In particular, the US case law demonstrates the haphazard, inconsistent, even arbitrary, nature of judicial determinations with regard to the denominator in the regulatory taking 'equation'. A commentator has described the case law as follows:

> To determine the extent of a single parcel, courts have traditionally looked at factors such as whether land is contiguous, held by a common owner, or used for a single purpose, but they have usually made such decisions implicitly—without exploring the basis for their methodology. Courts have also applied these factors inconsistently, making regulatory taking determinations unpredictable and often arbitrary.[107]

However, compared with the chaotic taking jurisprudence in the United States, the level of elaboration of the denominator question so far achieved by investment treaty tribunals is rather underwhelming. The recent decision on the merit of the tribunal in *Philip Morris v Uruguay* perhaps offers a good example. The claimant in *Philip Morris* argued that one of the host State's measures under review, the Single Presentation Regulation (SPR), banned seven of the thirteen variants (within its six brand families), which were manufactured and sold by the investor at the time the SPR measure was imposed and for which the investor owned, or was the licensee of, the relevant trademarks. The investor argued that since each of such 'brand assets' was an investment protected by the BIT, the SPR had indirectly expropriated the seven variants as the ban had rendered them and the associated goodwill 'valueless'.[108]

Having noted the disputed nature of 'whether indirect expropriation may relate to identifiable distinct assets comprising the investment or, rather, is to be determined considering the investment as a whole', the *Philip Morris v Uruguay* tribunal simply noted that 'the answer largely depends on the facts of the individual case'.[109] Interestingly, the tribunal concluded that in order to determine whether the

[106] *Chemtura Corporation v Government of Canada*, Award, 2 August 2010 (n 93), para 249.

[107] Fee, 'Unearthing the Denominator' (n 102) 1535, 1537. For the most recent twist in this saga, see *Murr v Wisconsin*, 137 SCt 1933, 2017.

[108] *Philip Morris v Uruguay*, Award, 8 July 2016 (n 85), para 279.

[109] ibid, para 280.

measure under review had an expropriatory character in this case, the investor's business should be considered as a whole, based on the fact that 'the measure affected its activities in their entirety'.[110] Thus, according to the *Philip Morris* tribunal, it is the scope and impact of *the measure* under review that defines the 'denominator' for purposes of the determination of the expropriatory effect.

Only few academics have ventured to suggest a way to determine when a claim of partial expropriation should be permitted. Professor Kriebaum has proposed to focus on whether the individual right or asset, in addition to being included in the definition of 'investment' in the applicable treaty, 'is capable of economic exploitation independently of the remainder of the investment'.[111] This is a sensible approach and one that appears to have been followed by investment tribunals, at least where the 'self-standing' nature of the investment's various components was relatively evident.[112] However, it is not always clear how one should determine whether or not a particular asset is capable of independent exploitation.[113]

Confusion thus remains a fact in the practice of investment treaty tribunals. For example, the tribunal in *Flamingo v Poland* appears to focus both on specific assets (the lease agreements) and at the same time on the entire investment (airport retail store). Having concluded that 'the Lease Agreements were investments, under Article 1(1)(c) of the Treaty',[114] the tribunal in *Flamingo v Poland* stated as follows:

> In the present case, the Lease Agreements have been annihilated by the acts of PPL, which for purposes of the Treaty are attributable to Respondent. The acts engaged by PPL include: (i) the termination of the Lease Agreements, which in the eyes of the Tribunal was a breach of contract; (ii) the request to the Customs Chamber to seal the premises and the blocking by the authorities of deliveries and BH Travel staff members; and (iii) the order under Polish public law issued by the Governor of Mazovia, upon the request of PPL, to evict BH Travel from Chopin

[110] ibid, para 283. The tribunal continued:

> This is confirmed by the fact that in order to mitigate its effects, Abal resorted to countermeasures involving its business as a whole. Prices were increased initially and then, when its products lost market share, they were lowered in December of 2009, with Abal suffering losses vis-à-vis its competitor Mailhos across its entire portfolio. Prices were then increased again beginning February 2011 with resulting market share decline 'across its portfolio'.

[111] Kriebaum, 'Partial Expropriation' (n 105) 83. See also Montt, *State Liability in Investment Treaty Arbitration* (n 105) 270, according to whom tribunals 'should look for denominators which, properly grounded in the applicable law, represent generally shared business expectations concerning groups of rights that are accepted as autonomous entities'.

[112] See eg *Copper Mesa v Ecuador*, Award, 15 March 2016 (n 77), where the tribunal examined the investor's claim of indirect expropriation of three mining concessions in three separate analyses, concluding that the respondent had expropriated two of them only.

[113] Montt, *State Liability in Investment Treaty Arbitration* (n 105) 273 ('Ultimately, the denominator problem is probably the most difficult normative assessment that decision-makers face in determining whether a state measure effects a full or substantial deprivation').

[114] Article 1(1)(c) reads as follows: 'rights to money or to any performance under contract having a financial value'.

> Airport. These consecutive acts, which were upheld by the Governor of Mazovia's intervention, in addition to the shutdown of the BH Travel shops, deprived Claimant of the benefit of its (indirect) investment in the BH Travel duty-free shops at Chopin Airport.[115]

Furthermore, and crucially, it appears that the (few) investment treaty tribunals that have at least considered the question, have progressively tended to view the entirety of the investment as the relevant 'denominator' for purposes of determining the existence of an expropriatory effect, rather than to focus on its constituent parts.[116] In addition to the decisions in *Chemtura v Canada* and *Philip Morris v Uruguay*, mentioned above, the tribunal in *Grand River v United States* took a very strict approach to the denominator question. It stated as follows:

> The starting point must be the language of Article 1110(1), providing that '[n]o Party may directly or indirectly nationalize or expropriate *an investment* of an investor of another Party in its territory,' unless certain conditions are met (emphasis added). The text speaks of 'an investment,' not 'an investment or some portion thereof.' The most natural reading of the language is that any act of expropriation will affect the totality of an investment. This is in harmony with the conception of expropriation applied in numerous cases—that expropriation involves the deprivation or impairment of all, or a very significant proportion of, an investor's interests.[117]

This appears to be a rather strict interpretation of the term 'investment' included in the expropriation provision in NAFTA, particularly in light of the fact that NAFTA defines 'investment' to mean, in addition to 'an enterprise,' a wide range of different and specific assets (such as tangible and intangible property, debt equity and loan) even if linked to an enterprise or economic activity.[118]

[115] *Flemingo Duty Free Shop Private Limited v the Republic of Poland*, UNCITRAL, Award, 12 August 2016, para 594.

[116] See UNCTAD, *Expropriation* (United Nations 2012) 23, citing *Telenor Mobile Communications AS v Republic of Hungary*, ICSID Case No. ARB/04/15, Award, 13 September 2006, para 67 ('The tribunal considers that, in the present case at least, the investment must be viewed as a whole and that the test the Tribunal has to apply is whether, viewed as a whole, the investment has suffered substantial erosion of value'). See *Merrill & Ring Forestry v Canada*, ICSID Case No. UNCT/07/1, Award, 31 March 2010, para 144; *Grand River Enterprises v USA*, Award, 12 January 2011, para 147. Implicitly, *Windstream Energy LLC v Government of Canada*, PCA Case No 2013-22, Award, 27 September 2016, para 291.

[117] *Grand River Enterprises v USA*, Award, 12 January 2011 (n 116), para 147.

[118] See also *Electrabel v Hungary*, ICSID Case No. ARB/07/19, Decision on Jurisdiction, Applicable Law and Liability, 30 November 2012, para 6.58:

> In this Tribunal's view, it is clear that both in applying the wording of Article 13(1) ECT and under international law, the test for expropriation is applied to the relevant investment as a whole, even if different parts may separately qualify as investments for jurisdictional purposes. Here the investment held by Electrabel as a whole was its aggregate collection of interests in Dunamenti; it was thus one integral investment; and in the context of expropriation it was not a series of separate, individual investments with Dunamenti's PPA as an

These tribunals have, accordingly, denied the existence of an expropriation in cases where the investor was deprived of some rights but retained control over the overall investment.

3. The object of deprivation: property interest, control or value?

The third and final controversial issue with regard to a determination of expropriatory effect relates to the object of the alleged adverse effect or deprivation.[119] So far I have loosely referred to 'indirect expropriation' or 'measures having equivalent effect' as measures that have (at least) an 'adverse effect' on the investment or that 'deprive' the investor of its investment. But what does such expropriatory effect on investment actually entail? Should tribunals determine the existence of the adverse effect on, or deprivation of, the protected investment with reference to the investor's 'property interests' (or 'ownership') in the investment? Should they focus on the investor's 'control over' or 'management of' the investment? Or, more generally, should tribunals focus on the 'benefit' or 'value' of the investment affected by the host State's conduct? In other words, for the purposes of determining the existence of an indirect expropriation, should a tribunal enquire whether the host State's measure under review has deprived the investors of (a) its property interest in the protected investment; (b) its control or management of such investment; or (c) the economic value or benefit of said investment? Are these parameters cumulative or is the existence of any one of them enough to justify a finding of indirect expropriation?

(a) Implications of investment treaties' emphasis on 'effect': substance over form

Ownership, control, value appear, at least in principle, to be different from one another and may lead to different outcomes. Depriving an investor of the ownership of its investment is different from depriving the investor of the control of its investment. Similarly, depriving ownership or control are different from depriving the investor of the value of (or benefit from) its investment. Thus, there may be instances where a host State's measure may entail no deprivation of the ownership of, or control over, the investment but it may lead to the total deprivation of the

autonomous investment set apart from Electrabel's other interests in Dunamenti. In the Tribunal's view, Electrabel's investment was manifestly not confined to the PPA; and the PPA formed an intrinsic and inseparable part of Electrabel's investment as a whole.

See also *Burlington Resources Inc v Republic of Ecuador*, ICSID Case No ARB/08/5, Decision on Liability, 14 December 2012, paras 404, 430 and 456, where a majority of the tribunal noted that the criterion of loss of the economic use or viability of the investment applied to 'the investment as a whole'.

[119] See Bonnitcha, *Substantive Protection* (n 84) 247–55.

value of such investment. Take the example of the foreign investor bringing an expropriation claim following the host State's refusal to renew a radio license previously granted to a locally incorporated company owned and controlled by that foreign investor. One could argue that the refusal to renew the license does not *directly* impact on the investor's ownership or control over its investment. Focusing, for example, on the shareholding in the radio station as the relevant 'investment', the measure under review neither formally transfers the ownership away from the investor (ie formal or direct expropriation) nor does it entail a restriction on the investor's ability to exercise its shareholder's rights, as the measure does not directly address and restrict the investor's right to vote, to receive dividends or to dispose of its shares. Similarly, the host State's measure does not have any direct impact on the investor's control over its shares in the radio station, as the investor remains (at least formally) in control of the relevant shareholding.

However, if the investor is able to show that the refusal to renew the licence has caused the end of the radio station and thus the loss of all (or practically all) of the value of the investment (including the investor's shareholding), an investment treaty tribunal, focusing on the deprivation of the economic value or benefit of the protected investment, may conclude that the host State's refusal constitutes 'a measure having equivalent effect' for the purposes of the applicable treaty.

As noted above, investment treaties are often silent on what should be the object of the relevant deprivation, as they often simply refer to 'expropriation of investments' and 'measures having equivalent effect'.[120] However (and this is the argument being put forward in this section), the emphasis on 'equivalent effect' permits an interpretation of the scope of indirect expropriation that treats the various elements mentioned above (such as ownership, control, value) as autonomous parameters for a determination of equivalent (ie expropriatory) effect. In other words, a showing that the host State has deprived the investor of any of those parameters (thus, including value) is sufficient to justify a finding of expropriatory effect.[121]

If a direct expropriation is one that entails the formal transfer of title away from the investor, with the subsequent complete loss of the investor's investment, a measure having equivalent effect to such expropriation (ie an indirect expropriation) is one that in practice, even if not in form, has a similar effect. Investment treaties' emphasis on the measure's effect justifies relying on substance over form, and thus inevitably relying on the measure's impact on the value of the protected investment.

[120] One should always keep in mind that each treaty should be examined based on its specific wording, but it is safe to say that a great majority of investment treaties focus on these two concepts: 'expropriation of investments' and 'measures having equivalent effect to expropriation'.

[121] For an extensive discussion on the link between the notion of 'investment' and the definition of expropriation in investment treaties, see Zachary Douglas, 'Property, Investment, and the Scope of Investment Protection Obligations' in Zachary Douglas, Joost Pauwelyn and Jorge Vinuales (eds) *The Foundations of International Investment Law: Bringing Theory into Practice* (OUP 2014) 62 et seq.

Ultimately, if the emphasis is on the measure's actual impact on the investment, there is really no difference between a measure that deprives the investor of its ownership rights over the investment and one that entails the total and permanent loss of the investment's value, as the latter will imply the former. In the above-mentioned example about the host State's refusal to renew a radio license, an investor could claim the existence of a measure having equivalent effect to expropriation by arguing that in light of the complete loss of the value of the investor's shareholding, the refusal to renew the licence has had a material (adverse) impact on the investor's rights as owner of the shares: while formally capable of exercising its shareholder's rights, those rights have for all practical purposes disappeared.

This reading is supported by the very few investment treaties (including model treaties) that have elaborated on the notion of indirect expropriation or measures tantamount to expropriation by referring to whether the host State's measure has the effect of depriving the investor of the 'ownership', 'control', 'management', 'benefit' or 'economic value' of its investment. Crucially, while these very few treaties refer to a variety of possible objects of deprivation, the references are neither cumulative nor exhaustive in nature. The most notorious is the 1982 United States Model BIT, which provides the following indicative list of 'measures tantamount to expropriation': 'including the levying of taxation, the compulsory sale of all or part of an investment, or the *impairment or deprivation of its management, control or economic value*'.[122] This language is actually found in only a handful of United States' treaties, such as the 1986 US–Bangladesh BIT.[123]

Similarly, Article 159, paragraph 4, of the 1993 Treaty Establishing the Common Market for Eastern and Southern Africa (COMESA) elaborates on the concept of 'expropriation' by focusing on whether the State measure has 'the effect of depriving an investor of his ownership or control of, or a substantial benefit from his investment'. Article 159.4 also states that expropriation shall include all forms of expropriation, including creeping expropriation in the form of, inter alia, 'measures that frustrate the exercise of the investor's rights to dividends, profits and proceeds or the right to dispose of the investment'.[124]

[122] Art III.1 US Model BIT (1982), reproduced in Kathleen Kunzer 'Developing a Model Bilateral Investment Treaty' (1983) 15 Law & Pol'y Int'l Bus 273, A-1, A-5 [emphasis added]. See the almost identical provision in Article III.1 of the 1986 United States–Egypt BIT. See also UNCTAD, *Taking of Property* (United Nations 2000). The very first US model BIT confirms that the main focus of the expropriation provision in the first forty years of bilateral investment treaties was on the issue of compensation, rather than on defining 'expropriation'; the heading of Article III thereof was 'Compensation for Expropriation'.

[123] Article III.1 reads in part:

> No investment or any Part of an investment of a national or a company of either Party shall be expropriated or nationalized by the other Party or subjected to any other measure or series of measures, direct or indirect tantamount to expropriation (including the levying of taxation, the compulsory sale of all or part of an investment, or the impairment or deprivation of its management, control or economic value) [. . .].

[124] See UNCTAD, *Bilateral Investment Treaties* (n 18) 65–6.

According to these treaties, the concept of indirect expropriation extends to a broad range of measures, including *but not limited to*, the impairment or deprivation of the management, control *or* value of the investment.

(b) Early arbitral practice: a broad view with a few dissenting voices

While the practice of investment treaty tribunals on this issue is neither uniform nor clear, I would argue that, since the very beginning, many arbitral decisions have taken a broad view of indirect expropriation emphasizing, inter alia, whether the host State's measure under review had deprived the investor of the 'use', 'benefit' or 'value' of its investment. For example, as noted in section B, the tribunal in *Goetz v Burundi* found that the government's revocation of the company's duty-free certificate was a 'measure having an effect similar to a measure depriving of or restricting property' pursuant to Article 4 of the 1989 Belgium–Luxembourg–Burundi BIT, as it 'deprived the investment of all of its worth and the investors of the benefit that they could expect from their investments'.[125] Interestingly, the focus was on the measure's (severe) economic impact on the investment, rather than on whether the measure had a direct impact on any of the investors' ownership rights (as the relevant provision may, arguably, have lent itself to).

Similarly, the *Metalclad* tribunal emphasized whether the host State's measure had the effect of depriving the investor of the 'use of property' or the 'reasonably-to-be-expected economic benefit of property'.[126] In *Feldman*, the tribunal noted the many the ways 'in which governmental authorities may force a company out of business, or significantly reduce the economic benefits of its business'.[127]

Several of the early cases referred expressly to interference with, or deprivation of, the value of the investment.[128] For example, having noted that the concepts of 'indirect expropriation' or 'measures having equivalent effect' include measures that have the effect of depriving the investor of 'the use and benefit of

[125] *Goetz and Consorts v Burundi*, Decision on Liability, 2 September 1998 (n 42) at para 124 (note that the 1998 decision is contained in the 29 January 1999 Award embodying the Parties' Settlement Agreement):

> Dès lors que […] la révocation du certificat d'entreprise franche les a contraints à arrêter toute activité […], ce qui a privé de toute utilité les investissements réalisés et dépouillé les investisseurs requérants du bénéfice qu'ils pouvaient attendre de leurs investissements, la mesure litigieuse peut être regardée comme une 'mesure ayant un effet similaire' à une mesure privative ou restrictive de propriété au sens de l'article 4 de la Convention d'investissement.

[126] *Metalclad v Mexico*, Award, 30 August 2000 (n 45) para 103.

[127] *Feldman v Mexico*, Award, 16 December 2002 (n 57), para 103.

[128] See Jan Paulsson and Zachary Douglas, 'Indirect Expropriation in Investment Treaty Arbitration' in N Horn and S Kröll (eds) *Arbitrating Foreign Investment Disputes: Procedural and Substantive Legal Aspects* (Kluwer Law International 2004) 157:

> Where the value of an investment has been *totally* destroyed by *bona fide* regulation in the public interest, it may well be that international law does not allow the Host State to place such a high individual burden on an investor for the pursuit of a regulatory objective for the benefit of the community at large without the payment of compensation.

his investment', the tribunal in *Middle East* added that '[a]s a matter of fact, the investor is deprived by such measures of parts of the value of his investment [and thus] such a taking amounted to an expropriation within the meaning of Art 4 of the BIT'.[129]

Interestingly, the *Tecmed* tribunal adopted a similarly broad view with regard to the object of deprivation by emphasizing the link between loss of value and loss of rights. The tribunal noted that (a first step in) the determination of an indirect expropriation is to ask whether the host State's measure under review has radically deprived the 'economical use and enjoyment of' the investment, 'as if the rights thereto—such as the income or benefits related to the Landfill or to its exploitation—had ceased to exist'. The tribunal explained this with reference to loss of value in the following terms: 'In other words, if due to the actions of the Respondent, the assets involved have lost their value or economic use for their holder and the extent of the loss.'[130] Furthermore, the *Tecmed* tribunal often refers to deprivation of both 'rights' and 'assets' (or 'investment'), confirming a broad view of what the relevant object of the deprivation is.

Equally, in the early days of investment treaty arbitration, there are decisions by arbitral tribunals that appear to take a narrower approach, focusing in particular on whether the host State's measure under review had the effect of depriving the investor of his property rights. The *SD Myers* tribunal for example stated that '[e]xpropriation tend to involve the deprivation of ownership rights'[131] and an 'expropriation usually amounts to a lasting removal of the ability of an owner to make use of its economic rights'.[132]

The tribunal in *Lauder v Czech Republic* offers another very good example. It stated in relevant part as follows:

> 200. […] The concept of indirect (or '*de facto*', or '*creeping*') expropriation is not clearly defined. Indirect expropriation or nationalization is a measure that does not involve an overt taking, but that effectively neutralizes the enjoyment of the

[129] *Middle East Cement Shipping and Handling v Egypt* (n 70), para 107. See *CME Czech Republic BV v Czech Republic*, UNCITRAL, Partial Award, 13 September 2001, para 603:

> Neither the Council's actions in 1996 nor the Council's interference in 1999 were part of proper administrative proceedings. They must be characterized as actions designed to force the foreign investor to contractually agree to the elimination of basic rights for the protection of its investment (in 1996) and as actions (in 1999) supporting the foreign investor's contractual partner in destroying the legal basis for the foreign investor's business in the Czech Republic. The actions and inactions affected the value of CME's shares in ÈNTS, such shares being clearly a 'foreign investment' in accordance with the Treaty.

[130] *Tecmed v Mexico*, Award, 29 May 2003 (n 63), para 115. The *Tecmed* tribunal confirmed the relevance of 'the effects of the actions' of the host State to determine whether the action is expropriatory by pointing to the reference in the relevant expropriation provision to 'effects' ('Section 5(1) of the Agreement confirms the above, as it covers expropriation, nationalization or "[…] any measure with similar characteristics or *effects*"' [original emphasis]). ibid.

[131] *SD Myers v Canada*, Partial Award, 13 November 2000 (52), para 282.

[132] ibid, para 283.

> property. It is generally accepted that a wide variety of measures are susceptible to lead to indirect expropriation, and each case is therefore to be decided on the basis of its attending circumstances (Rudolf Dolzer & Margarete Stevens, *Bilateral Investment Treaties*, p. 98–100 (1995); Giorgio Sacerdoti, *Bilateral Treaties and Multilateral Instruments on Investment Protection*, 379–382 (1997)). The European Court of Human Rights in Mellacher and Others v Austria (1989), held that a '*formal*' expropriation is a measure aimed at a '*transfer of property*', while a '*de facto*' expropriation occurs when a State deprives the owner of his '*right to use, let or sell (his) property*.'
>
> 201. The Arbitral Tribunal holds that the Respondent did not take any measure of, or tantamount to, expropriation of the Claimant's property rights within any of the time periods, since there was no direct or indirect interference by the Czech Republic in the use of Mr. Lauder's property or with the enjoyment of its benefits.
>
> 202. The Claimant has indeed not brought sufficient evidence that any measure or action taken by the Czech Republic would have had the effect of transferring his property or of depriving him of his rights to use his property or even of interfering with his property rights. [. . .][133]

While there is an initial acknowledgment that the concept of indirect expropriation is (at least potentially) broad (one that entails the effective neutralization of the enjoyment of the property), the *Lauder* tribunal's emphasis is on the deprivation of the investor's 'property rights' (including the right to use, let or sell the property), rather than on the deprivation of the 'investment' and the 'value of the investment'.[134]

[133] *Lauder v Czech Republic*, Award, 3 September 2001 (n 68), paras 200–02. It may be worth noting that the Lauder tribunal in an obiter dictum rejected the expropriation claims also because the allegedly expropriatory conduct 'did not benefit the Czech Republic or any person or entity related thereto'. ibid, para 203.

[134] See also *Nykomb v Latvia*, Award, 16 December 2003, section 4.3.1 at page 33:

> The *Arbitral Tribunal* has considered the expert legal opinions and arbitral awards rendered under similar treaties presented in this case by the parties. The Tribunal finds that 'regulatory takings' may under the circumstances amount to expropriation or the equivalent of an expropriation. The decisive factor for drawing the border line towards expropriation must primarily be the degree of possession taking or control over the enterprise the disputed measures entail. In the present case, there is no possession taking of Windau or its assets, no interference with the shareholder's rights or with the management's control over and running of the enterprise—apart from ordinary regulatory provisions laid down in the production licence, the off-take agreement, etc. The Tribunal therefore *concludes* that the withholding of payment at the double tariff does not qualify as an expropriation or the equivalent of an expropriation under the Treaty.

See *Pope & Talbot v Canada*, Interim Award, 26 June 2000 (n 43), where the Tribunal's decision to reject a claim for indirect expropriation seemed to rely principally on the investor retaining control over its investment (para 100). However, the tribunal does also consider the impact of the host State's measure on the profits of the investment, although it confirms its finding based on the conclusion that there is no 'substantial deprivation' on the investment (para 102).

(c) Arbitral practice beyond the early years: conflicting views remain and minority dissenting voices become louder

Even beyond the early years, one can witness the split in the arbitral practice with regard to the relevant object of deprivation for purposes of determining an indirect expropriation.[135]

Many (ie the majority of) investment treaty tribunals continue to rely on the broad approach, focusing on several possible indicators of expropriatory effect, crucially including deprivation of value.[136] In *Biwater v Tanzania*, the tribunal identified the 'relevant standard' when it comes to expropriation or 'measures having effect equivalent to expropriation' in Article 5(1) of the United Kingdom and Tanzania BIT in the following terms:

> This is a broadly framed provision. The Treaty encompasses not only direct expropriation (i.e. a formal Government taking) but also *de facto* or indirect expropriations which do not involve actual takings of title but nonetheless result in the effective loss of management, use or control, or a significant depreciation of the value, of the assets of a foreign investor. This was uncontroversial as between the parties.[137]

The decision of the tribunal in *AES v Hungary* provides an example of a similarly broad approach to the relevant object of deprivation. Having acknowledged that a mere 'negative effect on an investment' cannot automatically be considered an expropriation, the *AES* tribunal stated that for an expropriation to occur, 'it is necessary for the investor to be deprived, in whole or significant part, of the property in or effective control of its investment: or for its investment to be deprived, in whole or significant part, of its value.'[138] The *AES* tribunal rejected the investor's claim, as none of these parameters had been met: first, the host State's measures under review 'did not interfere with the ownership or use of Claimants' property'; second, 'Claimants retained at all times the control of' their investment; and third, 'Claimants continued to receive substantial revenues from their investments during 2006 and 2007, which proves that the value of their investment was not

[135] John G Sprankling, *The International Law of Property* (OUP 2014) 278 et seq.

[136] It should be remembered that the cases considered in the section may either adhere to the so-called 'sole effect' doctrine or the 'police powers' doctrine.

[137] *Biwater Gauff v Tanzania*, ICSID Case No. ARB/05/22, Award, 18 July 2008, para 452. See *Telenor v Hungary*, Award, 13 September 2006 (n 116), paras 64–65 ('The conduct complained of must be such as to have a major adverse impact on the economic value of the investment', as 'substantially to deprive the investor of the economic value, use or enjoyment of its investment'); *Spyridon Roussalis v Romania*, Award, 7 December 2011, paras 327–28.

[138] *AES Summit Generation Limited and AES-Tisza Erömü Kft v The Republic of Hungary*, ICSID Case No AR/07/22, Award, 23 September 2010, para 14.3.1.

substantially diminished and that they were not deprived of the whole or a significant part of the value of their investments.'[139]

Other investment treaty tribunals have focused on the deprivation of control or value, only. The tribunal in *Venezuela Holdings v Venezuela*, for example, put forward its view on the concept of indirect expropriation as follows:

> The Tribunal has to determine whether the measures referred to by the Claimants had an effect equivalent to expropriation within the meaning of Article 6 of the BIT. The Tribunal considers that, under international law, a measure which does not have all the features of a formal expropriation may be equivalent to an expropriation if it gives rise to an effective deprivation of the investment as a whole. Such a deprivation requires either a total loss of the investment's value or a total loss of control by the investor of its investment, both of a permanent nature.[140]

Emphasizing the importance of the loss of economic value or economic viability, the majority of the tribunal in *Burlington v Ecuador* affirmed that a loss of management or control over the investment was not a necessary element of substantial deprivation for purposes of a finding of indirect expropriation. The tribunal explained as follows:

> what appears to be decisive, in assessing whether there is a substantial deprivation, is the loss of the economic value or economic viability of the investment. The loss of viability does not necessarily imply a loss of management or control. What matters is the capacity to earn a commercial return.[141]

Other tribunals have similarly only referred to value as the relevant object of the deprivation. For example, the tribunal in *Total v Argentina*, albeit in an *obiter*

[139] ibid, para 14.3.2-3. See also *AWG v Argentina*, Decision on Liability, 30 July 2010, para 134 ('in applying the provisions of the three BITs applicable to these cases, this Tribunal will have to determine whether they [ie the measures in question] effected a substantial, permanent deprivation of the Claimants' investments or the enjoyment of those investments' economic benefits').

[140] *Venezuela Holdings et al v Venezuela*, Award, 9 October 2014 (n 89), para 286. See *Philip Morris v Uruguay*, Award, 8 July 2016 (n 85), para 192 ('in order to be considered an indirect expropriation, the government's measures interference with the investor's rights must have a major adverse impact on the Claimants' investments. As mentioned by other investment treaty decisions, the State's measures should amount to a "substantial deprivation" of its value, use or enjoyment').

[141] *Burlington Resources Inc v Republic of Ecuador*, Decision on Liability, 14 December 2012 (n 118), para 396. The tribunal in *Inmaris v Ukraine* found that the respondent's travel ban and the cancellation of an entire sailing season caused the claimants' business to suffer substantial harm to the extent that they could not reasonably have been expected to resume operations. The tribunal concluded that the travel ban amounted to an indirect expropriation in that it destroyed the value of the claimants' contractual rights, and that the decrease in value (due to the lasting damage to claimants' business) was, for all intents and purposes, permanent. *Inmaris Perestroika Sailing Maritime Services GmbH and others v Ukraine*, ICSID Case No ARB/08/8, Award, 1 March 2012, paras 300–01.

dictum,[142] stated that under international law a measure is equivalent to an expropriation if it causes an effective deprivation of the investment, that is 'a total loss of value of the property such as when the property affected is rendered worthless by the measure'.[143] Furthermore, the *Total* tribunal noted that such position is 'supported by the general direction of the case law under BITs, other international jurisprudence and scholarly legal opinions'.[144] Interestingly, however, the tribunal included in the accompanying footnote references to arbitral decisions taking different views on the relevant object of deprivation.[145]

Some investment treaty tribunals have emphasized the link between the impact on the investor's rights and the impact on the investment's value. For example, the tribunal in *Glamis Gold v USA* noted, first, that in the case of an indirect (or regulatory) taking 'the threshold examination is an inquiry as to the degree of the interference with the property right' and, second, that this inquiry 'involves two questions: the severity of the economic impact and the duration of that impact'.[146] In other words, in order to determine the existence of a sufficiently high degree

[142] Since the expropriation clause in the applicable France and Argentina BIT refers to 'any other equivalent measures having a similar effect of dispossession', the *Total* tribunal rejected claimant's indirect expropriation argument based on the existence of a substantial deprivation of the value of the investment, noting the difference between the wording in the applicable treaty and the standard reference to 'measures having equivalent effect to expropriation': *Total v Argentina*, Award, 21 December 2010 (n 89), para 193.

[143] ibid, para 195.

[144] ibid. See also *Electrabel v Hungary*, Decision on Jurisdiction, Applicable Law and Liability, 30 November 2012 (n 118), para 6.53:

> As regards indirect expropriation, the Tribunal considers that the wording of Article 13(1) ECT requires Electrabel to establish that the effect of the PPA's termination by Hungary was materially the same as if its investment in Dunamenti had been nationalised or directly expropriated by Hungary. In other words, Electrabel must prove, on the facts of this case, that its investment lost all significant economic value with the PPA's early termination.

[145] On the one hand, the *Total* tribunal cites in the relevant footnote the decision in *Sempra Energy International v Argentina*, Award, 28 September 2007 (n 94), para 285, which takes a broad approach ('a finding of indirect expropriation would require more than adverse effect. It would require that the investor no longer be in control of its business operation, or that the value of the business have been virtually annihilated'). On the other hand, it cites the decision in *Enron Corporation and Ponderosa Assets, LP v Argentine Republic*, ICSID Case No ARB/01/3, Award, 22 May 2007, para 245, which focuses exclusively on whether the measure under review had deprived the investor of its 'control' or 'management' of its investment. See *Total v Argentina*, Award, 21 December 2010 (n 89), para 195, footnote 227 (the list also contains references to the following decisions: *Tecmed v Mexico*, Award, 29 May 2003 (n 63), para 115; *CME Czech Republic BV v Czech Republic*, Partial Award, 13 September 2001 (n 129), para 604 and *Goetz and Consorts v Burundi*, ICSID Case No. ARB/95/3, Award, 10 February 1999, para 124).

[146] *Glamis Gold v USA*, Award, 8 June 2009, para 356. This is the relevant section of the paragraph in full:

> There is for all expropriations, however, the foundational threshold inquiry of whether the property or property right was in fact taken. This threshold question is relatively straightforward in the case of a direct taking, for example, by nationalization. In the case of an indirect taking or an act tantamount to expropriation such as by a regulatory taking, however, the threshold examination is an inquiry as to the degree of the interference with the property right. This often dispositive inquiry involves two questions: the severity of the economic impact and the duration of that impact.

of interference with the investor's property rights, the *Glamis Gold* tribunal relied heavily on *the economic impact* of the host State's measure *on the investment.*[147]

However, several investment treaty tribunals have continued to adopt a narrower approach, focusing more on whether the host State measure under review had deprived the investor of the 'ownership', 'use' or 'control', without including an examination of the impact on the value of the investment. Many of the early decisions involving the measures taken by Argentina to address the economic crisis of 2000–01 provide good examples of the narrower approach. While it referred to *Metalclad* and the concept of 'substantial deprivation', the tribunal in *CMS v Argentina* rejected the investor's regulatory expropriation claim based on the fact that 'the investor has full ownership and control of the investment'.[148] Having similarly relied on whether the host State had deprived the investor of the control over, or management of, the investment, the *Sempra v Argentina* tribunal added that the key standard is whether the measures under review had 'as a result a substantial deprivation of rights'.[149]

Unsurprisingly, there are also cases where it is not clear which approach is being adopted by the investment treaty tribunal, as there are references to 'ownership and control', on the one hand, and to 'value' on the other, without any clarification on the relationship between the two.[150]

[147] ibid, para 358:

> To determine whether Claimant's investment in the Imperial Project has been so radically deprived of its economic value to Claimant as to potentially constitute an expropriation and violation of Article 1110 of the NAFTA, the Tribunal must assess the impact of the complained of measures on the value of the Project.

ibid, para 536:

> In light of this significantly positive valuation, the Tribunal holds that the first factor in any expropriation analysis is not met: the complained of measures did not cause a sufficient economic impact to the Imperial Project to effect an expropriation of Claimant's investment. The Tribunal thus holds that Claimant's claim under Article 1110 fails.

[148] *CMS v Argentina*, Award, 12 May 2005 (n 92), paras 263–64. See *Enron Corporation and Ponderosa Assets, LP v Argentine Republic*, ICSID Case No ARB/01/3, Award, 22 May 2007, paras 245–46.

[149] *Sempra v Argentina*, Award, 28 September 2007 (n 94), para 284. One should note that the *CMS*, *Enron* and *Sempra* tribunals were all chaired by the same arbitrator, Professor Orrego Vicuna. For a broader approach that includes an assessment of the measure's impact on the investment economic value, see *LG&E Energy Corporation, LG&E Capital Corporation and LG&E International Inc v Argentine Republic*, ICSID Case No ARB/02/1, Decision on Liability, 3 October 2006, paras 190–91:

> In evaluating the degree of the measure's interference with the investor's right of ownership, one must analyze the measure's economic impact—its interference with the investor's reasonable expectations—and the measure's duration. In considering the severity of the economic impact, the analysis focuses on whether the economic impact unleashed by the measure adopted by the host State was sufficiently severe as to generate the need for compensation due to expropriation. In many arbitral decisions, the compensation has been denied when it has not affected all or almost all the investment's economic value. Interference with the investment's ability to carry on its business is not satisfied where the investment continues to operate, even if profits are diminished. The impact must be substantial in order that compensation may be claimed for the expropriation.

[150] See *BG v Argentina*, Award, 24 December 2007, where the tribunal stated as follows:

More importantly, there is a growing number of tribunals that, in order to establish an indirect expropriation, expressly require a focus on the deprivation of the essential components or attributes of the property rights and thus resist the proposition that loss of value is sufficient to establish expropriatory effect. The tribunal in *El Paso v Argentina* is a good example. First, the tribunal 'considers that at least one of the essential components of the property rights must have disappeared for an expropriation to have occurred'. In its view, the 'removal of the ability of an owner to make use of its economic rights' is key.[151] Second, the *El Paso* tribunal affirms repeatedly that 'a mere loss in value of the investment, even if important, is not an indirect expropriation'.[152]

The *El Paso* tribunal is, moreover, interesting, as it tries to argue that its view (according to which 'a mere, but important, loss of value' is insufficient for a finding of indirect expropriation) is in fact in line with the several decisions that are often cited (by claimants) to justify a broader view of an indirect expropriation (including *Middle East Cement, Goetz and Others, Metalclad, Tecmed, LG&E*).[153]

In our view, the *El Paso* tribunal's attempt is nevertheless unsuccessful, as it appears to (a) ignore certain express references in those earlier decisions (eg 'the investor is deprived by such measures of parts of the value of its investment' in *Middle East Cement*);[154] (b) miss the link that often inevitably exists between loss of value and loss of use or enjoyment (with regard to the *Goetz and Others* decision, 'there is a reference to the deprivation of the expected benefit, but this was a result of the cancellation by the State of a free-zone certificate which prevented

> 266. Most recently, the tribunal in *LG&E Energy Corp., LG&E Capital Corp., LG&E International Corp. v The Argentine Republic* summarized as follows the requirements for establishing indirect expropriation under the Argentina–U.S. BIT as follows: 'Generally, the expression "equivalent to expropriation" or "tantamount to expropriation" found in most bilateral treaties, may refer both, to the so-called "creeping expropriation" and to the de facto expropriation. Their common point rests in the fact that the host State's actions or conduct do not involve "overt taking" but the taking occurs when governmental measures have "effectively neutralize[d] the benefit of property of the foreign owner." Ownership or enjoyment can be said to be "neutralized" where a party no longer is in control of the investment, or where it cannot direct the day–today operations of the investment.' [. . .]
>
> 269. Having considered the foregoing, the Tribunal concludes that Argentina has not violated Article 5 of the BIT, as it did not expropriate BG's investment.
>
> 270. Specifically, the impact of Argentina's measures has not been permanent on the value of BG's shareholding in MetroGAS. It might well be that the measures adopted by Argentina were severe causing a fluctuation of BG's investment during the crisis. However, MetroGAS' business never halted, continues to operate, and has an asset base which is recovering.

---

[151] *El Paso Energy International Company v The Argentine Republic*, ICSID Case No ARB/03/15, Award, 31 October 2011, para 245.

[152] ibid, paras 249 (there is even a section of the tribunal's analysis that is entitled in that way) and 256.

[153] ibid, paras 250–55:

> The Tribunal is, of course, aware of some cases or general dicta that might seem to support the idea that a substantial deprivation of the value of an investment can also be viewed as an expropriation. But a careful scrutiny of those cases, some of which were cited by the Claimant, does not support such a conclusion, as will be shown now.

[154] ibid, para 250.

the investor from continuing any economic activity, which is indeed a situation where it can be said that the investor was expropriated as it completely lost the use of its property');[155] and (c) confuse the question of the 'object' of deprivation with the 'quantum' of deprivation ('In *LG&E*, for example, although according to the claimant the value of LG&E's holdings in the licenses had been reduced by more than 90% as a result of Respondent's abrogation of the principal guarantees of the tariff system, the tribunal did not find an expropriation as the measures themselves did not interfere "with the investment's ability to carry on its business." ')[156]

In its recent decision, the tribunal in *Mamidoil v Albania* takes a similar strict view on what is the object of deprivation for the purposes of a finding of indirect expropriation. Expressly relying on the *El Paso* tribunal's 'careful analysis' of *Tecmed, Goetz* and *Middle East Cement*, the *Mamidoil* tribunal agrees that in all of these awards, in addition to the fact that the investment lost value and the investor was deprived of benefits, the emphasis was crucially also on the fact that 'these effects resulted from a loss of one or several attributes of ownership'.[157] The *Mamidoil* tribunal elaborates further as follows:

> In its literal translation, expropriation describes a specific effect on property itself and not a damage inflicted to property. The effect can be a direct taking as it can be an indirect deprivation of one or several of its essential characteristics. These are traditionally defined by its use and enjoyment, control and possession, and disposal and alienation. If one of these attributes is affected, the resulting loss of value and/or benefit may lead to a claim for expropriation.[158]

Accordingly, in the view of the *Mamidoil* tribunal, in order to find an indirect expropriation, the claimant needs to show both an adverse effect on one of the 'attributes of property' and the ensuing loss of 'value' or 'benefit'.

Interestingly, the *Mamidoil* tribunal justifies its focus on 'the substance and attributes of property' on the basis that the contrary approach (based exclusively on loss of value and profitability) would deprive the expropriation claim of 'its distinct nature and amalgamate it with other claims'.[159] This is unfortunately unclear, as it does not appear that there are any other investment treaty standards, apart from

[155] ibid, para 251.
[156] ibid, para 255.
[157] *Mamidoil Jetoil Greek Petroleum Products Societé SA v Republic of Albania*, ICSID Case No ARB/11/24, Award, 30 March 2015, para 568.
[158] ibid, para 569.
[159] ibid, para 570:

> Thus, a mere loss of value or a loss of benefits that is [not] connected to and caused by the dissolution of at least one attribute of property, does not constitute indirect expropriation. The contrary approach would not only contradict the literal meaning of the term 'expropriation,' but would also be inconsistent with the clear intention of State parties when they entered into the BIT and the ECT and provided for separate standards of protection.

the indirect expropriation one, that are exclusively based on the host State's causing loss of value or profitability. Nevertheless, it is clear that like the *El Paso* tribunal, the *Mamidoil* tribunal stands for the proposition that a necessary condition for a finding of indirect expropriation is whether the host State's conduct will affect the substance and attributes of property, including use and enjoyment, control and possession, and disposal and alienation.[160]

The *Mamidoil* tribunal's reasoning is also unclear with regard to the extent of the adverse effect on the attributes of property. In order to find support for the proposition that the 'decisive criterion' for a finding of expropriation 'is not the fact of having incurred a damage or the loss of value as such', the *Mamidoil* tribunal refers directly to both *Santa Elena v Costa Rica* and *El Paso v Argentina*.[161] While in the latter, as noted above, the tribunal emphasized that 'at least one of the essential components of the property rights must have disappeared', in the former the tribunal described expropriation as when 'the owner has truly lost all the attributes of ownership'. A legitimate question would then be whether, in the view of the *Mamidoil* tribunal, a finding of indirect expropriation req uires the deprivation of *all* the attributes of ownership, or the deprivation of one such attributes is sufficient (as long as the loss of value or benefit is at least substantial).

D. Recent Treaty Practice

Following the initial wave of arbitral decisions, several States have started re-evaluating their international investment policy focusing, inter alia, on the kind of expropriation provisions that had been included in their existing treaties as well as the kind of expropriation provisions that should be included in their future ones.[162] A survey conducted by UNCTAD on investment treaties concluded between 2011 and 2016 (107) shows that approximately two-thirds of them contain a 'clarification of what does and does not constitute an indirect expropriation'.[163] Often such clarification takes inspiration from the approach initially put forward by the United States and Canada in their 2004 model BITs.

The novel approach with regard to the expropriation provision is as follows: while the expropriation provision in the body of the treaty remains practically unchanged, a footnote to, or additional paragraph in, that provision refers to a more detailed interpretation provided in an annex to the treaty. Accordingly, while the main expropriation provision still refers to 'indirect expropriation' and

[160] ibid, para 571.
[161] ibid, para 566.
[162] Karl Sauvant and Federico Ortino, *Improving the International Investment Law and Policy Regime: Options for the Future* (Ministry for Foreign Affairs of Finland 2013).
[163] UNCTAD, 'Taking Stock of IIA Reform' Issues Note (United Nations 2016) 15–19 and UNCTAD, *World Investment Report* (United Nations 2017) 121.

'measures equivalent to expropriation', the Annex on Expropriation contains a more detailed definition of the concept of 'indirect expropriation'. The Annex B on Expropriation in the 2004 United States model BIT reads as follows:

> 1. Article 6 [Expropriation and Compensation] is intended to reflect customary international law concerning the obligation of States with respect to expropriation.
> 2. An action or a series of actions by a Party cannot constitute an expropriation unless it interferes with a tangible or intangible property right or property interest in an investment.
> 3. Article 6 [Expropriation and Compensation] addresses two situations. The first is direct expropriation, where an investment is nationalized or otherwise directly expropriated through formal transfer of title or outright seizure.
> 4. The second situation addressed by Article 6 [Expropriation and Compensation] is indirect expropriation, where an action or series of actions by a Party has an effect equivalent to direct expropriation without formal transfer of title or outright seizure.
>   (a) The determination of whether an action or series of actions by a Party, in a specific fact situation, constitutes an indirect expropriation, requires a case-by-case, fact-based inquiry that considers, among other factors:
>   (i) the economic impact of the government action, although the fact that an action or series of actions by a Party has an adverse effect on the economic value of an investment, standing alone, does not establish that an indirect expropriation has occurred;
>   (ii) the extent to which the government action interferes with distinct, reasonable investment-backed expectations; and
>   (iii) the character of the government action.
>   (b) Except in rare circumstances, non-discriminatory regulatory actions by a Party that are designed and applied to protect legitimate public welfare objectives, such as public health, safety, and the environment, do not constitute indirect expropriations.[164]

While it is beyond the scope of this contribution to examine the specific reasons behind the changes introduced,[165] it is fair to say that a key part of the strategy was to bring about clarity with regard to the notion of 'indirect expropriation'. More importantly, clarifying the notion of indirect expropriation through an annex

[164] The Annex on Expropriation of the 2012 United States model BIT is for all practical purposes identical to the 2004 one.

[165] For a detailed discussion of the 2004 and 2012 US model treaties, see Andrea Menaker, 'Benefitting from Experience: Developments in the United States' Most Recent Investment Agreements' (2005) 12 UC Davis J Int'l L & Pol'y 121 and Lee Caplan and Jeremy Sharpe, 'United States' in Chester Brown (ed) *Commentaries on Selected Model Investment Treaties* (OUP 2013) 755 et seq, respectively.

appended to the new (model) treaty has one key advantage: it strengthens the continuity with past treaty practice. Moreover, the approach based on keeping the original language in the basic provision on expropriation but adding a clarification in an annex to the treaty may have the additional effect of influencing how investment tribunals would interpret *existing* investment treaties, which do not include such an annex.[166]

In addition to bringing about additional clarity, there is no doubt that the language in the annex has also narrowed the scope of the concept of indirect expropriation. There are at least three reasons for this. First, anchoring the expropriation provision in the treaty to customary international law (paragraph 1) has the likely effect of limiting an expansive reading of the protection afforded by the treaty provision.

Second, paragraph 2 requires that, in order to constitute an expropriation, an action of the host State has to interfere with a tangible or intangible property right or property interest in an investment. This could justify the argument according to which the host State's measure under review needs to have a direct (adverse) impact on the 'property right or interest' rather than a mere (adverse) impact on the investment. This clarification appears to relate to one of the controversial issues concerning the determination of expropriatory effect, particularly the object of the deprivation, discussed in section C. Accordingly, the requirement of an interference with property rights may thus exclude simply relying on the measure's impact on the value of the investment. This appears to be confirmed by paragraph 4(a)(i) of the Annex, which states that 'the fact that an action or series of actions by a Party has an adverse effect on the economic value of an investment, standing alone, does not establish that an indirect expropriation has occurred'.

The recent EU–Canada CETA appears to have followed a similar path, aimed at limiting the 'object of deprivation' for purposes of determining an indirect expropriation. Annex 8A on Expropriation clarifies that:

> indirect expropriation occurs if a measure or series of measures of a Party has an effect equivalent to direct expropriation, in that it substantially deprives the investor of the fundamental attributes of property in its investment, including the right to use, enjoy and dispose of its investment, without formal transfer of title or outright seizure.

The reference to deprivation of 'the fundamental attributes of property' in the CETA Annex on Expropriation reminds (at least in part) to those dissenting voices

[166] The decision of the tribunal in *Methanex v United States*, Award, 7 August 2005, may provide the best evidence for such additional impact: issued just after the adoption (by the United States and Canada) of their new model BITs (which included in respective annexes the narrower definition of an indirect expropriation), the *Methanex* tribunal adopted the police powers doctrine to interpret Article 1110 NAFTA.

in existing investment arbitral practice that argued for a more limited understanding of the relevant 'object' of deprivation. The decisions of the *El Paso* and *Maminoil* tribunals examined above referred to 'essential components of property rights', 'attributes of ownership', or 'essential characteristics or attributes' and pointed to the 'use and enjoyment, control and possession, and disposal and alienation'. To confirm the link, the Annex does specify that 'the right to use, enjoy and dispose of its investment' are examples of such fundamental attributes. At the international level, one can find references to similar concepts in decisions by the Iran–US Tribunal. For example in *Tippets*, the Iran–US Tribunal stated that a taking of property includes the case where 'the owner was deprived of fundamental rights of ownership'.[167] At the domestic level, some French scholars identify the right to use, benefit and dispose of the property as the three '*attributs du droit de propriété*' (to be distinguished from the '*caractères du droit de propriété*', ie that the right is absolute, exclusive and perpetual).[168]

However, as the list in the CETA Annex appears to be indicative, it is not clear whether there exist other fundamental attributes of property beyond the three expressly mentioned. For example, is the investor's right to the 'value' of its investment a fundamental attribute of property? And even if that were not the case, could an investor claim that a substantial reduction of the value of its investment (due to the host State's conduct) is enough to demonstrate a 'substantial deprivation' of its right to use or enjoy, or even dispose of its investment? Would a tribunal require a stronger link between the host State's conduct and the fundamental attribute of property being affected?

There is a third and final reason justifying the conclusion that the annex on expropriation in recent treaties has dramatically limited the scope of protection afforded by the expropriation provision. In fact, my argument is that the Annex on Expropriation in the 2004 United States model (as well as those of Canada and the EU) has not just limited the scope of the expropriation provision, but it has modified the very nature of such provision (at least compared with traditional investment treaties). By referring to the public policy objectives of the host State's measure under review as part of the 'case-by-case fact-based inquiry' pursuant to paragraph 4(a) and the general presumption with regard to non-discriminatory regulatory actions pursuant to paragraph 4(b), the Annex has embraced a different understanding of indirect expropriation compared to the one found in most

[167] *Tippets, Abbett, McCarthy, Stratton v TAMS–AFFA Consulting Engineers of Iran*, Iran-US Claims Tribunal, 22 June 1984, 6 Iran–US CTR 219, 225. See also the reference to 'fundamental right of ownership' in *Mezzanine v Hungary*, ICSID Case No. ARB/12/3, Award, 17 April 2015, para 178.

[168] Pierre Voirin and Gilles Goubeaux, *Doit Civil—Tome 1* (LGDJ 2013) 255 et seq. See also the request to the Constitutional Council relating to its Decision 85-189 DC, 17 July 1985, where the right to dispose is referred to as an '*attribut fundamental*', '*attribut essentiel*', and '*attribut capital*' of property. (I am indebted to Dr Florian Grisel for this reference.) See also the reference to the concept of 'fundamental attributes of property ownership' in United States takings law, such as in *Guimont v Clarke* 121 Wn.2d 586 (1993) 854 P.2d 1.

modern investment treaties: rather than focusing exclusively on the measure's substantial deprivation of the investment (in line with the 'sole-effect' doctrine), a finding of indirect expropriation now revolves principally around the soundness and legitimacy of the allegedly expropriatory measure, according to the 'police powers' doctrine.[169]

In one of the very first cases where the applicable investment treaty contains an annex on expropriation, the *Bear Creek v Peru* tribunal's interpretation makes the point very clearly. The case revolved around a silver mine near Peru's border with Bolivia acquired by a Canadian investor, Bear Creek, following an express authorization by Peruvian authorities. Following violent protests from the local communities, the Peruvian government revoked the relevant authorization, effectively bringing to a halt the project. Bear Creek brought a claim before the International Centre for Settlement of Investment Disputes (ICSID) based on the 2008 Canada–Peru FTA, alleging inter alia indirect expropriation. The *Bear Creek* tribunal considered the three factors identified in the relevant annex (which are the same to the ones in the US model BIT) as part of the case-by-case, fact-based inquiry: (a) the measure's economic impact; (b) the measure's interference with distinct, reasonable investment-backed expectations; and (c) the character of the measure. The point worth highlighting here is that the bulk of the tribunal's decision on indirect expropriation focuses on whether the Peruvian government's revocation was justified. The *Bear Creek* tribunal in fact, quickly found that (a) 'there is an "economic impact" as [the measure at issue] has an adverse effect on the economic value of Claimant's investment'; and (b) the measure at issue 'interferes with Claimant's distinct, reasonable investment-backed expectations'.[170] The tribunal then spends the next twenty pages determining whether the reasons advanced by the respondent could legitimately justify the revocation of the relevant authorizations. The *Bear Creek* tribunal concluded that the revocation under review was indeed an indirect expropriation as in the tribunal's view, Peru's measure 'was based on reasons which

[169] Andrew T Guzman and Jan H Dalhuisen, 'Expropriatory and Non-Expropriatory Takings under International Investment Law' (2012) UC Berkeley Public Law Research Paper 5:

> It is our view that a taking that is more than *de minimis* is non-expropriatory if it belongs in either of two categories: (i) takings that promote public welfare (also referred to as 'super' public purpose), a category that includes health, safety, and security; and (ii) takings that are incidental to legitimate, ordinary government action.

[170] *Bear Creek Mining Corporation v Republic of Peru*, ICSID Case No ARB/14/21, Award, 30 November 2017, paras 375–76 and 415. On the second point, the tribunal noted as follows (ibid, para 376):

> As Claimant points out and as is obvious to the Tribunal, Claimant relied on the express governmental authorization by Supreme Decree 083, when it exercised its options to acquire the Karina Mining Concessions in December 2007. Without these authorizations, Claimant could not have been expected to invest the amounts it undisputedly invested between 2007 and 2011.

have been found to be illegal according to Peruvian law and do not justify a breach of the FTA'.[171]

A brief mention needs to be made here of the approach recently put forward by Brazil with regard to expropriation in its recent Cooperation and Facilitation Investment Agreement (CFIA) model. While Brazil's model is very different from traditional investment treaties, it does include some of the traditional investment protection guarantees such as non-discrimination, transparency and expropriation. Interestingly, with regard to the latter provision, Brazil's model as well as the few bilateral agreements signed by Brazil in the past three years on that basis,[172] explicitly acknowledges that only direct expropriation (that is, where an investment is nationalized or otherwise directly expropriated through formal transfer of title or ownership rights) is covered.[173]

Preliminary Conclusions

This chapter's main findings have been the following. First, there is evidence that the original aim of the expropriation provision in modern investment treaties was to afford foreign investors protection vis-à-vis the host State's conduct that entirely deprived the investor of the value of its investments. This conclusion stemmed in particular from two key aspects of investment treaties. First, most investment treaties expressly defined the scope of expropriation on the basis of the concepts of 'indirect expropriation' and 'measures having equivalent effect'. Second, from the very beginning, investment treaties lacked any visible attempt to limit the protection afforded by the expropriation provision on the basis of the host State's right to regulate in the public interest, as it was (and has been ever since) under both customary international law and the constitutional laws of many countries. Accordingly, based on the expropriation provision in traditional investment treaties, a showing that the host State has entirely deprived the investor of the value of its investment appeared to be in principle sufficient to justify a finding of compensable expropriation.

[171] ibid, para 415.

[172] In 2015, Brazil signed six treaties named 'Cooperation and Investment Facilitation Agreement' (CIFA), with Angola, Chile, Colombia, Malawi, Mexico and Mozambique. A further agreement was signed with Peru in 2016. For the text of the CIFAs, see http://www.mdic.gov.br/comercio-exterior/negociacoes-internacionais/218-negociacoes-internacionais-de-investimentos/1949-nii-acfi accessed 20 May 2019.

[173] See Geraldo Vidigal and Beatriz Stevens, 'Brazil's New Model of Dispute Settlement for Investment: Return to the Past or Alternative for the Future?' (2018) 19 JWIT 475; Natali Cinelli Moreira, 'Cooperation and Facilitation Investment Agreements in Brazil: The Path for Host State Development' (Kluwer Arbitration Blog, 13 September 2018) http://arbitrationblog.kluwerarbitration.com/2018/09/13/cooperation-and-facilitation-investment-agreements-in-brazil-the-path-for-host-state-development/ accessed 20 May 2019.

Second, arbitral practice registered early on a split in how to define the concept of indirect expropriation, with a majority of tribunals relying exclusively upon the adverse effect of the host measure under review (according to the so-called 'sole-effect' doctrine) and a minority considering, in addition to the adverse effect on the protected investment, the measure's public policy purpose (according to the so-called 'police powers' doctrine). While the split continues today, the tables have turned as today's prevalent approach in the arbitral practice with regard to the definition of an indirect expropriation appears to be one that gives relevance to the public policy purpose of the allegedly expropriatory measure.

Third, after twenty years and more than 200 arbitral decisions, the notion of 'effect equivalent to expropriation' or 'expropriatory effect' remains controversial and thus unclear. However, in line with the increasing relevance of the so-called 'police powers' doctrine, investment treaty tribunals seem to have progressively taken a stricter approach with regard to the nature of the required expropriatory effect, if not in form, at least in fact. This is evidenced in particular by the way several investment tribunals have addressed (a) the issue of the extent of the adverse effect or deprivation (ie the 'threshold question'); (b) the determination of the overall investment against which a deprivation needs to be measured (the 'denominator problem'); and (c) the 'object of deprivation'.

Three preliminary reflections are advanced. First, the fact that traditional investment treaties favour a definition of expropriation that appears to focus exclusively on the adverse effect of the host State's allegedly expropriatory conduct confirms the conclusion that the aim of these treaties was to provide a remarkably broad level of protection to foreign investments. Accordingly, an indirect expropriation will be found (and thus will be compensable) if the investor successfully demonstrates that the host State's conduct has at least substantially deprived the investor of its investment.

Second, despite investment treaties' apparent exclusive reliance on expropriatory effect in order to define the scope of an indirect expropriation, at least some investment tribunals showed early on a willingness to 'choose' an interpretation of the treaty provision on expropriation that was more deferential to the host State's right to regulate. In addition to the host State measure's adverse impact on the investment, these tribunals took into account the public policy rationale of the measure under review in order to determine the existence of an indirect expropriation. Defining indirect expropriation according to the 'police powers' doctrine limits the protection offered by the treaty provision on expropriation. Unsurprisingly, in most of the cases where the tribunal has adopted an interpretation of indirect expropriation based on (a version of) the police powers doctrine, the investor's expropriation claim has not been successful.[174]

[174] As noted in section B, only a handful of arbitral decisions where the tribunal, having clearly endorsed the relevance of the public policy purpose in determining the existence (rather than the lawfulness) of an indirect expropriation, found in favour of the investor. See cases cited at n 77.

Third, while the preference for the police powers doctrine has recently grown in the arbitral practice (in part supported by a similar endorsement in recent investment treaties), there still remains today a clear split in the way investment tribunals define indirect expropriation for purposes of investment treaty protection: some rely exclusively on the adverse impact of the host State's conduct on the investment, while others include in their expropriation analysis the public policy objective of the host State's measure under review. In other words, investment tribunals' approach with regard to the definition of an indirect expropriation remains inconsistent. However, inconsistency can also be found with regard to the way investment tribunals have examined 'expropriatory effect' (whether as the only relevant criterion, or as one of the criteria to determine the existence of an indirect expropriation). As investment tribunals have adopted different (and often unclear) positions with regard to the so-called 'threshold question', 'denominator problem' and 'object of deprivation', the level of overall uncertainty with regard to the law on expropriation remains frustratingly high.

III
Ensuring Reasonableness in the Conduct of Host States

The Origin and Evolution of Investment Treaty Standards. Federico Ortino, Oxford University Press (2019).
DOI: 10.1093/oso/9780198842637.001.0004

Introduction

Reasonableness represents a very useful tool in understanding investment treaty standards. While it is a notoriously ubiquitous concept (employed in a multitude of legal systems and areas of law),[1] reasonableness is well known as a ground for the judicial review of a State's conduct in domestic legal systems,[2] in particular the conduct of the administration[3] and the legislature.[4] The world of domestic judicial review shares many similarities with the world of international investment treaties.[5]

However, as a ground of judicial review, 'reasonableness' remains an imprecise and contested concept. The reason I use 'reasonableness' in the context of this book is principally to contrast it with the two other guarantees that have been examined in chapters I and II (that is, the guarantee of legal stability and the guarantee against substantial deprivation of the value of the investment). Accordingly, for the purposes of the analysis carried out in this chapter, I use reasonableness in a broad sense. First, reasonableness is understood both as a procedural standard, which focuses on the *process* leading up to the adoption of the relevant State's conduct under review (procedural reasonableness),[6] and as a substantive standard, which focuses on the *content* of such conduct (substantive reasonableness).

Second, and more fundamentally, when one focuses on its substantive version, a review based on reasonableness is understood here to entail, at a minimum, consideration of the policy justification underlying the public conduct at issue,[7] though a variety of other factors may also play a role, such as factual circumstances,

[1] Frederic G Sourgens, 'Reason and Reasonableness: The Necessary Diversity of the Common law' (2014) 67 Maine L Rev 73. See Andreas Lowenfeld, *International Litigation and the Quest for Reasonableness* (OUP 1996).

[2] Valentina Vadi, *Proportionality, Reasonableness and Standards of Review in International Investment Law and Arbitration* (Edward Elgar 2018) 134; Jan Wouters and Sanderijn Duquet, 'The Principle of Reasonableness in Global Administrative Law' (2013) Jean Monet Working Paper 12/13.

[3] TR Hickman, 'The Reasonableness Principle: Reassessing its Place in the Public Sphere' (2004) 63 Cambridge L J 166.

[4] Andrea Morrone, 'Constitutional Adjudication and the Principle of Reasonableness' in G Bongiovanni, G Sartor and C Valentini (eds) *Reasonableness and the Law* (Springer, 2009) 215.

[5] Federico Ortino, 'The Investment Treaty System as Judicial Review' (2013) 24 Am Rev Int'l Arb 437, 438.

[6] In this sense, procedural reasonableness is synonymous with 'procedural fairness'. On 'procedural fairness' as a ground of review in English law, see Harry Woolf, Jeffrey Jowell and Andrew Le Sueur, *De Smith's Judicial Review* (7th edn, Sweet & Maxwell 2013) chapters 6–10. Cf Tor-Inge Harbo, 'Introducing Procedural Proportionality Review in European Law' (2017) 30 LJIL 25.

[7] Substantive reasonableness assumes 'a sufficient causal link between the legitimate objective sought, and the behaviour that one seeks to establish as reasonable': Olivier Corten, 'The Notion of "Reasonable" in International Law: Legal Discourse, Reason and Contradictions' (1999) 48 ICLQ 613, 623.

the law of the host State and the interests of the investor.[8] Accordingly, under this broad understanding, substantive reasonableness covers several legal concepts, principles and tests that are often employed by investment tribunals to review host States' conduct pursuant to investment treaties.[9] It covers, for example, the notion of 'arbitrariness' that focuses on the absence of any plausible reason, which could justify the conduct at issue.[10] It covers the three prongs of the proportionality principle: (a) 'means–ends rationality' (or 'suitability'), which focuses on whether the 'means' employed by the host State are rationally related to (or suitable to achieve) the 'ends' pursued by the host State; (b) 'least restrictive means' (or necessity), which focuses on whether the governmental conduct under review is the least restrictive (or most cost-effective) means reasonably available in order to achieve its purported aim; and (c) 'proportionality balancing' (or proportionality in the strict sense), which focuses on whether the governmental measure under review has an excessive (or disproportionate) impact on the investor's interests.[11] Finally, for the purposes of this analysis, reasonableness is also understood to include the protection of legitimate expectations, which, in its orthodox understanding, is subject to a balancing exercise involving consideration of any overriding public interests.[12]

Crucially, a broad understanding of 'reasonableness' (including the above-mentioned variety of standards of review) leaves open the question of 'deference' which, in the words of Professor Schill, 'is a parameter of the relationship between international and domestic law and protects a state's domestic policy space against control by international law and international tribunals'.[13] It is important

[8] ICJ, *Interpretation of the Agreement of 25 March 1951 between the WHO and Egypt*, ICJ Reports 1980, 73, para 49 ('what is reasonable and equitable in any given case must depend on its particular circumstances'). See Sourgens, 'Reasons and Reasonableness' (n 1) 75:

> reasonableness recognizes that there is not one absolute rule of conduct premised upon moral or religious command. Instead, law depends upon the reciprocal regard for the interests of others—even and particularly those others holding different moral, religious and political points of view. What this reciprocal regard legally requires of us is determined by a balancing test governed by the reasonableness standard.

[9] In a domestic law context, one would usually refer to these as the 'grounds for review'. See Woolf et al, *Judicial Review* (n 6). See further Joel Trachtman, 'Trade and ... Problems, Cost–Benefit Analysis and Subsidiarity' (1998) 9 EJIL 32, 35 (referring to 'trade-off devices').

[10] See *Elettronica Sicula SpA (ELSI) (United States of America v Italy)*, Judgment of 20 July 1989, [1989] ICJ Rep 15, at 76, para 128.

[11] On the proportionality principle, see Alec Stone Sweet and Jud Mathews, 'Proportionality Balancing and Global Constitutionalism' (2008) 47 Columbia J Transn'l L 73; Jurgen Schwarze, *European Administrative Law* (Sweet & Maxwell 2006); Evelyn Ellis (ed), *The Principle of Proportionality in the Laws of Europe* (OUP 1999); Nicholas Emiliou, *The Principle of Proportionality in European Law: A Comparative Study* (Kluwer 1996); Marta Cartabia, 'I principi di ragionevolezza e proporzionalità nella giurisprudenza costituzionale italiana', *Conferenza trilaterale delle Corti Costituzionali italiana, portoghese e spagnola*, Rome, Palazzo della Consulta, 24–26 ottobre 2013 (emphasizing how the Italian Constitutional Court employs the various proportionality prongs under its reasonableness review without, however, a clear orderly systematization) https://www.cortecostituzionale.it/documenti/convegni_seminari/RI_Cartabia_Roma2013.pdf accessed 20 May 2019.

[12] Søren Schønberg, *Legitimate Expectations in Administrative Law* (Oxford University Press 2000); Paul Craig, *EU Administrative Law* (OUP, 2012) ch 18.

[13] Stephan Schill, 'Deference in Investment Treaty Arbitration: Reconceptualizing the Standard of Review Through Comparative Public Law' (2012) 3 J Int'l Dispute Settlement 577, 583.

to emphasize that the various tests or standards of review (falling under a broad understanding of reasonableness) imply a different level of scrutiny of, and thus deference towards, the host State's exercise of regulatory powers. Let us compare for example, 'means–ends rationality' with 'proportionality balancing'. The former test is said to be a more deferential test, as it merely focuses on establishing a reasonable link between the host State's conduct under review and a legitimate public policy. Crucially, means–ends rationality takes as given the policy objective(s) pursued by the public authority (say environmental protection), including the specific level(s) of protection chosen by that public authority (say zero pollution). On the other hand, the proportionality balancing test is a more intrusive review, as the adjudicator will need to balance the various interests at issue in order to determine whether the host State's conduct has a disproportionate impact on the investor's interests. Crucially, under this test, the very policy objective, and in particular the specific level of protection, pursued by the host State will be subject to scrutiny.[14]

The aim of the chapter is twofold. First, it investigates the extent to which investment treaties include a guarantee of 'substantive reasonableness' as one of the key protections granted to foreign investments. Second, it attempts to identify the type of test or standard of review that has been employed by investment tribunals in assessing the lawfulness of host States' conduct. The analysis focuses in particular on the following treaty provisions: (a) full protection and security; (b) non-impairment through arbitrary or unjustifiable measures; and (c) fair and equitable treatment. This chapter also examines the application by investment tribunals of the so-called 'police powers' doctrine in defining an indirect expropriation.

Four main findings stem from the present analysis. First, many of the investment treaty provisions referring to broad, open-ended standards (such as full protection and security (FPS), fair and equitable treatment (FET) and non-impairment clauses) appear to have originally shared the two distinctive features of 'reasonableness-based provisions', that is, (a) focus on the merit or soundness of the host State's conduct; and (b) consideration of a variety of factors, depending on the circumstances of the specific case. Second, while investment treaty tribunals have (at least for the most part) applied 'full protection and security', 'non-impairment through arbitrary or unjustifiable measures' and 'fair and equitable treatment' as reasonableness-based provisions, tribunals have differed with regard to the specific reasonableness test that they have employed in order to review the lawfulness of the host State conduct. Third, while a growing number of investment tribunals have, contrary to its apparent original nature, interpreted the provision

[14] See further Caroline Henckels, *Proportionality and Deference in Investor–State Arbitration: Balancing Investment Protection and Regulatory Autonomy* (OUP 2015). In the WTO context, see Don Regan, 'The Meaning of 'Necessary' in GATT Article XX and GATS Article XIV: The Myth of Cost–Benefit Balancing' (2007) 6 World Trade Rev 347; Filippo Fontanelli, 'Necessity Killed the GATT—Art XX GATT and the Misleading Rhetoric about "Weighing and Balancing"' (2012/13) 5 Eur J Legal Studies 36.

on indirect expropriation as a reasonableness-based provision, tribunals have shown a similar ambivalence in defining the 'legitimacy' of the exercise of the host State's so-called 'police powers'. Finally, while the evolution of treaty practice seems recently to have given preference to protection based on reasonableness, many of these recent treaties remain unclear with regard to the specific reasonableness test being chosen.

This chapter starts with the analysis of the origin of the three key standards of protection provisions in investment treaties (FPS, FET and non-impairment) (section A). It then examines the way investment tribunals have applied the 'full protection and security' provision (section B), the 'fair and equitable treatment' and 'non-impairment' provisions (section C), and the expropriation provision according to the police powers doctrine (section D). Finally, the chapter examines recent treaty practice with regard to the above-mentioned provisions (section E).

A. The Origin of Reasonableness-Based Provisions in Modern Investment Treaties

This section examines the origin of some of the key standards regularly found in modern investment treaties: FPS, non-impairment through arbitrary or unjustifiable measures (non-impairment), and FET, by focusing on the broader context at the time when the first bilateral investment treaties (late 1950s) were concluded.

These section puts forward two basic arguments. First, there is evidence showing that many of the investment treaty provisions referring to broad, open-ended standards were aiming to provide extensive protections to foreign capital. Second, these various treaty standards share the two distinctive features of what we have referred to as 'reasonableness-based provisions' in that they (a) focus on whether or not the host State's conduct affecting the foreign investment is justified by a legitimate public policy; and (b) entail the consideration (and balance) of a variety of factors depending on the circumstances of the specific case.

1. Express references in early investment protection instruments to 'standards'

There are plenty of references to various open-ended standards in several relevant investment instruments in the immediate aftermath of the Second World War. In order to protect (and encourage the flow of) foreign capital, these instruments prohibited in particular 'discriminatory', 'unreasonable' or 'unjustified' measures or required (or envisaged) 'fair', 'just' or 'equitable' treatment of, or 'most constant protection and security' to the property of foreign nationals.

The 1948 Havana Charter for an International Trade Organization (Havana Charter)[15] is a first example. Having recognized that adequate supplies of capital funds, materials, modern equipment and technology and technical and managerial skills (so-called 'facilities') are required in order to promote economic development and reconstruction, Article 11.1 of the Havana Charter imposed, inter alia, two requirements with regard to 'unreasonable or unjustifiable' measures, one on capital exporting countries and one on capital importing countries. They read as follows:

> (a) [...] Members shall not impose unreasonable or unjustifiable impediments that would prevent other Members from obtaining on equitable terms any such facilities for their economic development or, in the case of Member countries whose economies have been devastated by war, for their reconstruction;
> (b) no Member shall take unreasonable or unjustifiable action within its territory injurious to the rights or interests of nationals of other Members in the enterprise, skills, capital, arts or technology which they have supplied.

Along the same lines, but in positive terms, Article 12.1(c) of the Havana Charter recognizes that 'without prejudice to existing international agreements to which Members are parties, a Member has the right [...] (iv) to prescribe and give effect to other reasonable requirements with respect to existing and future investments'.

Article 11.2 of the Havana Charter envisaged future bilateral or multilateral agreements aimed to ensure 'just and equitable treatment for the enterprise, skills, capital, arts and technology brought from one Member country to another'.

The States parties to the Economic Agreement of Bogota,[16] which was adopted in 1948 (only a few months after the signature of the Havana Charter) but never entered into force, referred to similar standards. Article 22 stated, in relevant part, that (a) '[f]oreign capital shall receive equitable treatment'; (b) State parties 'agree not to take unjustified, unreasonable or discriminatory measures that would impair the legally-acquired rights or interests of nationals of other countries in the enterprise, capital, skills, arts or technology they have supplied'; and (c) 'agree not to set up within their respective territories unreasonable or unjustifiable impediments that would prevent other States from obtaining on equitable terms the capital, skills, and technology needed for their economic development'.

The United States focused on similar language in particular to afford protection to foreign capital in its post-war Friendship, Commerce and Navigation (FCN) treaties. For example, the 1950 United States FCN treaty with Ireland included the following provision:

[15] *Havana Charter for an International Trade Organization*, 24 March 1948, United Nations Conference on Trade and Employment, UN Doc E/CONF.2/78, Sales No 1948.II.D.4.

[16] *Economic Agreement of Bogota*, Organization of American States Treaty Series No 21.

> Each Party shall at all times accord equitable treatment to the capital of nationals and companies of the other Party. Neither Party shall take unreasonable or discriminatory measures that would impair the legally acquired rights or interests of nationals and companies of the other Party in the enterprises which they have established or in the capital, skills, arts or technology which they have supplied.[17]

Subsequent US FCNs refer to 'fair and equitable' rather than simply 'equitable' treatment.[18] Unsurprisingly, that wording (together with the 'unreasonable and discriminatory' one) also feature in the 1955 Standard Draft United States FCN Treaty.[19]

Another common feature of US FCN treaties was the 'most constant protection and security', which nationals of either party, as well as their property, shall receive within the territory of the other party.[20] At a minimum, this standard reflected the obligation under customary law of due diligence to accord physical protection and security to foreign nationals and their property.[21]

Similar language may be found in the two investment promotion instruments that have greatly influenced modern bilateral investment treaties. Article I of the 1959 Abs-Shawcross Draft Convention provides as follows:

> Each Party shall at all times ensure fair and equitable treatment to the property of the nationals of the other Parties. Such property shall be accorded the most constant protection and security within the territories of the other Parties and the management, use, and enjoyment thereof shall not in any way be impaired by unreasonable or discriminatory measures.[22]

Article 1 on Treatment of Foreign Property of the 1967 Organisation for Economic Co-operation and Development (OECD) Draft Convention on the Protection of Foreign Property reads almost verbatim to Article I of the Abs-Shawcross Draft Convention.[23]

[17] See Article V of 1950 Ireland–United States FCN. Cf Kenneth Vandevelde, *Bilateral Investment Treaties: History, Policy, and Interpretation* (OUP 2010) 215 et seq.

[18] See eg Article I of the 1954 United States FCN Treaty with Germany.

[19] Article VI.1 reads in relevant part as follows: 'Neither Party shall take unreasonable or discriminatory measures that would impair the legally acquired rights or interests within its territories of nationals and companies of the other Party in the enterprises which they have established, in their capital, or in the skills, arts or technology which they have supplied.'

[20] See Article II.1 and Article VIII.2 of the United States–Ireland FCN, respectively.

[21] See Articles 10–12 of the 1929 Harvard Law School, The Law of Responsibility of States for Damages Done in their Territory to the Person or Property of Foreigners. For a historical and broad view of the standard, see Todd Weiler, *The Interpretation of International Investment Law: Equality, Discrimination and Minimum Standards of Treatment in Historical Context* (Martinus Nijhoff 2013) chapter 3.

[22] Georg Schwarzenberger, 'The Abs-Shawcross Draft Convention on Investments Abroad: A Critical Commentary' (1960) 9 J Pub L 147 .

[23] OECD, *Draft Convention on the Protection of Foreign Property and Resolution of the Council of the OECD on the Draft Convention* (OECD 1967):

While the very first modern bilateral investment treaty (BIT) (1959 Germany–Pakistan) did not contain a provision requiring 'fair and equitable' treatment or prohibiting 'unjustifiable' or 'arbitrary' measures,[24] soon thereafter these clauses became standard in the more than 3000 international investment treaties that have been signed since.[25]

2. What is the 'original' meaning of 'fair', 'equitable', 'unreasonable', 'arbitrary', 'discriminatory'? Clues pointing to extensive protection

Extensive scholarly work has recently gone on (and is still underway) to shed light on the 'original' meaning of some of the key investment protection standards, particularly 'fair and equitable treatment' and 'most constant (or full) protection and security'.[26] This work shows the complexity of the issues at hand and, unsurprisingly, the disagreement among legal historians. While the question about the original meaning remains disputed, this section highlights three related (and rather uncontroversial) clues that point to one simple conclusion: these various standards were aimed at providing *extensive* protections to foreign capital.

(a) No clear link between investment treaty standards and customary law

The first clue is the lack of a clear link between the investment treaty standards at issue and the (narrowly construed) minimum standard of treatment in customary law. One of the bones of contention in the current scholarly debate is the extent to which investment treaty standards (signed since 1959) were meant to codify customary international law or go beyond it. The assumption behind this question is that investment treaty standards, if 'understood and applied independently and autonomously', appear to offer a (much?) wider protection compared to that provided for by the customary minimum standard of treatment of aliens (including investors).[27] This may be made particularly evident by highlighting the rather

> Each Party shall at all times ensure fair and equitable treatment to the property of the nationals of the other Parties. It shall accord within its territory the most constant protection and security to such property and shall not in any way impair the management, maintenance, use, enjoyment or disposal thereof by unreasonable or discriminatory measures.

---

[24] The 1959 German–Pakistan BIT did contain a prohibition of 'discriminatory' measures, as well as the 'protection and security' standard: see Articles 2 and 3, respectively.

[25] The first German BIT that included 'fair and equitable treatment', 'full protection and security' and the prohibition of 'unreasonable and discriminatory measures' was with Bolivia in 1986.

[26] See Ioana Tudor, *The Fair and Equitable Treatment Standard in the International Law of Foreign Investment* (OUP 2008); Martins Paparinskis, *The International Minimum Standard and Fair and Equitable Treatment* (OUP 2013); Todd Weiler, *The Interpretation of International Investment Law* (n 21); Mona Pinchis, 'Fair and Equitable Treatment in International Trade and Investment Law: 1918–1956' (Phd dissertation, King's College London 2017); Kenneth J Vandevelde, *The First Bilateral Investment Treaties: US Postwar Friendship, Commerce, and Navigation Treaties* (OUP 2017).

[27] FA Mann, 'British Treaties for the Promotion and Protection of Investments' (1981) BYIL 241, 244.

narrow language used in the landmark *Neer Claims* decision to articulate the customary minimum standard of treatment:

> the propriety of governmental acts should be put to the test of international standards [...] the treatment of an alien, in order to constitute an international delinquency should amount to an outrage, to bad faith, to wilful neglect of duty, or to an insufficiency of governmental action so far short of international standards that every reasonable and impartial man would readily recognize its insufficiency.[28]

As it was in the case of the definition of expropriation analysed in chapter II, there is little in the very text of investment treaties that clearly shows an intention to codify the customary minimum standard of protection. For example, while a few treaties do expressly link some of the investment protection standards to 'customary international law' (or more generally to 'international law'),[29] the vast majority (at least up until the twenty-first century) do not.[30]

Similarly, there is practically no evidence in the text of investment treaties that points to an understanding of the protection offered to foreign investment through the various open-ended provisions that is as narrow as the protection provided under (what appears to be) the customary minimum standard of treatment. In other words, investment treaties do not expressly require that state conduct must be 'egregious' or 'manifest' (ie 'this is conduct that shocks the conscience'),[31] in

[28] *LFH Neer and Pauline Neer (USA) v United Mexican States*, United Nations, Reports of International Arbitral Awards, 1926, IV, 60ff. See Edwin Borchard, 'The "Minimum Standard" of the Treatment of Aliens' (1940) 3 Mich L Rev 445, 455 ('The more extreme denials of justice will be judged international delinquencies without reference to the question of equality'); and Louis Sohn and RR Baxter, 'Responsibility of States for Injuries to the Economic Interests of Aliens' (1961) 55 AJIL 545, 547 ('International scrutiny should be allowed only in case of a manifest misapplication of law on the national level').

[29] See UNCTAD database, 'Mapping of IIA Content' https://investmentpolicy.unctad.org/international-investment-agreements/iia-mapping accessed 20 May 2019.

[30] See OECD, 'Fair and Equitable Treatment Standard in International Law' (2004) OECD Working Papers on International Investment, 2004/03, 9–10, referring to Sacerdoti's explanation that the lack of any reference to international standard was '... possibly a way of avoiding the divergence surrounding the latter and in order to give to it a direct content'. See Giorgio Sacerdoti, 'Bilateral Treaties and Multilateral Instruments on Investment Protection' (1997) Recueil des Cours, Tome 269, 347.

[31] See *Rochin v California*, 342 US 165 (1952) 173:

> What the majority hold is that the Due Process Clause empowers this Court to nullify any state law if its application 'shocks the conscience,' offends 'a sense of justice,' or runs counter to the 'decencies of civilized conduct.' The majority emphasize that these statements do not refer to their own consciences, or to their senses of justice and decency. For we are told that 'we may not draw on our merely personal and private notions'; our judgment must be grounded on 'considerations deeply rooted in reason and in the compelling traditions of the legal profession.' We are further admonished to measure the validity of state practices not by our reason or by the traditions of the legal profession, but by 'the community's sense of fair play and decency'; by the 'traditions and conscience of our people'; or by 'those canons

order to fail the various investment protection standards. The treatment required by investment treaties is 'simply' 'fair and equitable', and host State's measures that are prohibited by investment treaties are 'simply' 'unreasonable', 'unjustifiable', 'arbitrary' or 'discriminatory'.

However, one does find some evidence of the existence of a link between the treaty standards and general international law (including both custom and general principles of law) in some of the official commentaries annexed to the early, influential, international investment instruments, mentioned above. The authors of the Abs-Shawcross Draft Convention, for example, emphasized in a general comment that the draft convention 'restates what are believed to be fundamental principles of international law regarding the treatment of the property, rights, and interests of aliens […] though in the last few decades in some countries there has been a tendency to disregard them'.[32] Specifically with regard to 'Fair and Equitable Treatment, Protection and Security' in Article I, the authors noted, first, that the 'exclusion of "unreasonable" conduct merely gives clear expression to a concept inherent in any system of law and which […] has been affirmed in general terms by the ICJ [International Court of Justice] in, for example, the advisory opinion on *Conditions of Admission of a State to Membership in the United Nations*' and, second, that the 'prohibition of measures of discrimination is in close accord with the principle laid down by the PCIJ [Permanent Court of International Justice] in the *Case of Certain German Interests in Polish Upper Silesia*'.

Similar language can be found in the Notes and Comments to the OECD Draft Convention on the Protection of Foreign Property. According to the official commentary, each of the three rules in Article 1—'fair and equitable treatment', 'most constant protection and security' and 'exclusion of unreasonable and discriminatory measures'—stems from the 'well-established general principle of international law that a State is bound to respect and protect the property of nationals of other States'.[33] Moreover, according to the official commentary, the fair and equitable treatment standard required in Article 1 'conforms in effect to the "minimum standard" which forms part of customary international law'.[34]

However, these statements may be seen more as an attempt to strengthen the legitimacy of the two draft conventions (or the scope of the protection provided by customary law), rather than as codifying uncontroversial general international law. Commenting on the substantive provisions in the Abs-Shawcross Draft

of decency and fairness which express the notions of justice of English-speaking peoples' [ibid 175–6].

See Rosalie B Levinson, 'Time to Bury the Shocks the Conscience Test' (2010) 13 Chap L Rev 307.

[32] The Preamble also refers to the convention as 'a restatement of principles of conduct relating to foreign investments' but without clearly specifying 'whether these principles of conduct are supposed to be restatements of principles of business practice, ethical imperatives, or rules of international law': Schwarzenberger, 'The Abs-Shawcross Draft Convention on Investments Abroad' (n 22) 147, 149.

[33] See Notes and Comments to Article 1, para (a), subpara 1.

[34] See ibid, subpara 4(a).

Convention, Professor Metzger, former Assistant Legal Advisor at the United States State Department, confirmed the extensive protections provided to foreign capital therein, stating as follows:

> if the Draft Convention were widely adopted by both capital-exporting and capital-importing countries, it would create a regime far more 'protective' of private foreign investment than that created by (a) existing international law; (b) existing domestic law of most countries, including the United States; or (c) existing bilateral treaties such as the friendship, commerce, and navigation treaties of the United States.[35]

One further corroborating clue may be found, for example, in an internal study on United States FCN treaty practice produced in 1971 by the US States Department. Commenting on the 'most constant protection and security' clause (often featuring in US FCN treaties), Charles Sullivan, the study's author, expressly acknowledged that, while broadly expressive of the applicable principles of international law, the 'protection and security' provision 'actually goes beyond the international law standard'.[36]

(b) Overlapping nature of investment treaty standards

A second clue showing that standards such as fair and equitable treatment, full protection and security and the prohibition of unreasonable/arbitration/discriminatory measures were aimed at providing extensive protection to foreign capital, can be found in the often 'overlapping' nature of these standards.[37]

For example, having provided that 'foreign capital shall receive equitable treatment', Article 22 of the 1948 Economic Agreement of Bogota states that 'States therefore agree not to take unjustified, unreasonable or discriminatory measures.'

[35] Stanley Metzger, 'Multilateral Conventions for the Protection of Private Foreign Investment' (1960) 9 J Pub L 133, 133–4.

[36] Charles Sullivan, 'Treaty of Friendship, Commerce and Navigation: Standard Draft' (Unpublished: United States Department of State, 1971) 112. Sullivan further noted with regard to Article VI(1) as follows: '[The Legal Adviser's Office] considered the treaty provisions stronger than any universally accepted international law rule, and the international law reference [which had been included in early FCN treaties] might open the way to a claim that Article VI is merely declaratory of a weaker principle of international law.' See Weiler, *The Interpretation of International Investment Law* (n 21) 163. See further UNCTAD, *Fair and Equitable Treatment* (United Nations, 1999) 40:

> These considerations point ultimately towards fair and equitable treatment not being synonymous with the international minimum standard. Both standards may overlap significantly with respect to issues such as arbitrary treatment, discrimination and unreasonableness, but the presence of a provision assuring fair and equitable treatment in an investment instrument does not automatically incorporate the international minimum standard for foreign investors. Where the fair and equitable standard is invoked, the central issue remains simply whether the actions in question are in all the circumstances fair and equitable or unfair and inequitable.

[37] See Vandevelde, *Bilateral Investment Treaties* (n 17) 202.

It has been noted that by using the word 'therefore', the Economic Agreement of Bogota seemed to associate 'fair and equitable treatment' with 'reasonable and non-discriminatory treatment'.[38]

Commenting on Article I of the Abs-Shawcross Draft Convention, which combined 'fair and equitable treatment', 'most constant protection and security' and the prohibition of 'unreasonable or discriminatory measures', Schwarzenberger noted how the provision presented 'an imaginative attempt to combine the minimum standard with the standard of equitable treatment'.[39]

In its Notes and Comments to the concept of 'unreasonable measures' in Article 1, the drafters of the 1967 OECD Draft Convention note that 'in many cases such a measure will also violate the standard of "fair and equitable treatment" '.

In his 1971 study on US FCN treaties, Sullivan noted the multiple role of the 'equitable treatment' clause as follows:

> This Article is intended to establish a general outlook or approach to the treaty as a whole. It is a statement of general principle rather than a tight legal rule, and its placement makes it a link of agreed principle between the Preamble and the body of the treaty. Article I, however, also provides a basis for making representations against actions detrimental to United States interests that may not be covered by any specific legal rule in the treaty, as, for example, a measure that is superficially non-discriminatory but is so framed as to harm only some United States interest.[40]

Accordingly, Sullivan's comment appears to highlight the (at least partial) overlap between the fair and equitable treatment standard and other standards, in particular the prohibition of discriminatory measures.[41]

While it certainly contributed to the complexity in identifying the 'original' meaning of investment treaty standards, the apparent intent to allow for the scope of the various treaty standards to overlap with one another may show a willingness to afford a rather broad protection to foreign investments. In other words, the aim

[38] ibid, 195.

[39] Schwarzenberger, 'The Abs-Shawcross Draft Convention on Investments Abroad' (n 22) 152.

[40] Sullivan, 'Treaty of Friendship, Commerce and Navigation' (n 36) 67. See further Pinchis, 'Fair and Equitable Treatment' (n 26).

[41] In 1984, the OECD Committee on International Investment and Multinational Enterprise concluded that the fair and equitable treatment standard added a substantive legal standard referring to general principles of international law, rather than merely affirmed other obligations in the BIT: OECD, *Intergovernmental Agreements Relating to Investment in Developing Countries* (OECD 1984). See Vandevelde, *Bilateral Investment Treaties* (n 17) 201; UNCTAD, *Fair and Equitable Treatment* (n 36) 37:

> Nevertheless, although some instances of practice support the notion that the fair and equitable treatment encompasses the other treatment standards in most investment instruments, this is the minority position. [...] Still with reference to plain meaning, however, if there is discrimination on arbitrary grounds, or if the investment has been subject to arbitrary or capricious treatment by the host State, the fair and equitable standard has been violated.

behind inserting these various (even partially overlapping) standards in the treaty was to make sure that one would provide the necessary protection. Or to use an English proverb, 'throw enough mud at the wall and some of it will stick'.

(c) Open-ended nature of investment treaty standards

The third and final clue is in the 'open-ended' nature of the investment protection standards at issue (particularly, fair and equitable treatment). In the above-quoted passage from the Sullivan's study, it is clear how one of the specific functions of the 'equitable treatment' clause was to provide protection for actions detrimental to United States interests that were not subject to any other specific rule in the treaty.[42] Having outlined the guarantees vis-à-vis expropriation, discrimination, unreasonableness and lack of due process in post-war United States FCN Treaties, Professor Vandevelde describes the 'fair and equitable treatment' provision as follows:

> The fair and equitable treatment provision embodied all of these principles, but was intended to impose an independent standard applicable to situations where fair and equitable treatment was denied, even though the host state's action did not violate any of the other provisions of the treaty. When the State Department discussed the kinds of host state conduct to which this provision would apply, it most often referred to conduct that was unreasonable or discriminatory, although, as will be seen below, this did not exhaust the meaning of the provision.[43]

In today's debate, this function is often referred to as the 'gap-filling' function of FET.[44]

Similarly, Pinchis has shown how the 'equitable treatment' clause was elaborated by the League of Nations during the interwar period as a broad and flexible method that could address unanticipated measures that impair States' reasonable expectations.[45] Pinchis states as follows:

> Negotiated *ex ante*, the 'equitable treatment' clause established a remedy to rebalance the economic opportunities created by international commercial treaties by addressing unforeseen forms of 'indirect', 'disguised', or 'administrative' protectionism.[46]

[42] See further Vandevelde, *The First Bilateral Investment Treaties* (n 26) ch 8; Pinchis, 'Fair and Equitable Treatment' (n 26) ch 3.

[43] Vandevelde, *The First Bilateral Investment Treaties* (n 26) 384.

[44] Rudolf Dolzer, 'Fair and Equitable Treatment: A Key Standard in Investment Treaties' (2005) 39 Int'l Lawyer 87, 90 ('Essentially, the purpose of the clause as used in BIT practice is to fill gaps which may be left by the more specific standards, in order to obtain the level of investor protection intended by the treaties').

[45] Mona Pinchis, 'The Ancestry of "Equitable Treatment" in Trade: Lessons from the League of Nations during the Inter-War Period' (2014) 15 JWIT 13.

[46] ibid. It should be stressed that, for the League, the relevant context was 'international commerce', and thus it is unclear whether this would have applied to movement of ideas and capital. With regard to

Commenting on the equitable treatment standard reflected in Article I of the Abs-Shawcross draft convention, Schwarzenberger highlighted its 'commendable elasticity', even if at the cost of 'a corresponding measure of vagueness and subjectivity'.[47]

3. Investment treaty standards (such as fair and equitable treatment, full protection and security, non-impairment through arbitrary, unreasonable or discriminatory measures) as reasonableness-based standards

An examination of the early, formative years of modern investment treaties can also provide some clues with regard to the content of the standards of 'fair and equitable treatment', 'full protection and security', 'non-impairment through unreasonable, arbitrary and discriminatory measures'. This section argues that the various treaty standards at issue share some basic, distinctive features. In line with the broad definition of 'reasonableness' adopted for the purposes of this chapter, these standards appear to focus on the merit of the state's conduct and entail the consideration (and balance) of a variety of factors, depending on the circumstances of the specific case.

(a) Focus on the merit or soundness of the host State's conduct

Contrary to other provisions focusing on the impact of the State's conduct on the foreign investment or on the State's respect of an undertaking given to the foreign investor, the requirements of 'fair and equitable treatment' or 'full protection and security' and the prohibition of 'unreasonable, arbitrary or discriminatory' measures seem to focus on the merit (ie the soundness) of the State's conduct affecting the foreign investment. Often this focus requires an examination of whether the State's conduct at issue is indeed 'justified'; that is, taken for a reason. In the context of explaining the prohibition of 'unreasonable' measures both the Abs-Shawcross and OECD draft conventions refer to Judge Azvedo's individual opinion in *Admission of a State to the United Nations*, where it was highlighted that 'the right in question must be exercised in accordance with standards of what is normal, having in view the social purpose of the law' and that there exist 'restrictions on arbitrary decision'.[48]

In international law, a reference to 'arbitrary' conduct is often made to highlight the (complete) lack of a reason justifying that very conduct. In the *ELSI Case*, the ICJ rejected the United States' claim of arbitrary or unreasonable exercise of

the pre-Second World War period, see further Paparinskis, *The International Minimum Standard* (n 26) 84–9.

[47] Schwarzenberger (n 22) 153.

[48] ICJ Reports, 1947–48, 57, at 80.

authority by the Mayor of Palermo, based on the prohibition of 'arbitrary or discriminatory measures' in the 1948 United States–Italy FCN Treaty, in part because it found that the concern underlying the requisition by the Mayor of Palermo was indeed a very real and legitimate one. The ICJ found that it 'cannot be said to have been unreasonable or merely capricious for the Mayor to seek to use the powers conferred on him by the law in an attempt to do something about a difficult and distressing situation'.[49]

Paragraph 7(c) of the 1967 OECD Draft Convention commentary links an unreasonable (and arbitrary) measure to the concepts of 'abuse or misuse of a right', which is said to include the exercise of a right for an end different from that for which the right was created[50] or 'when the need is plainly not one of a public character'.[51]

Pargraph 8(d) of the same official commentary of the 1967 OECD Draft Convention explains 'discriminatory measures' for the purposes of Article 1 in terms of lack of justification: 'The essence of discrimination, from the point of view of Article 1, is differentiation introduced in the treatment of property as a result of the measures in question, which is not justified by legitimate considerations.'

(b) Focus on a variety of factors

A second, related, feature common to the various treaty standards here at issue is the relevance of an examination of a variety of factors to be determined on a 'case-by-case' basis. This can be seen, for example, in the way the principle of 'due diligence' under the 'most constant protection and security' was defined in the 1929 Harvard Draft Convention. Having established a State's responsibility for its failure to exercise due diligence to prevent the injury to the alien, Article 10 states that the 'diligence required may vary with the private or public character of the alien and the circumstances of the case'.[52]

Similarly, the Notes and Comments to Article 1 of the 1967 OECD Draft Convention explain that a measure taken in the exercise of sovereign powers may

[49] See *Elettronica Sicula SpA (ELSI) (United States of America v Italy)*, Judgment of 20 July 1989 (n 10), at 76, para 129:

> United States counsel felt able to describe the requisition generally as being an 'unreasonable or capricious exercise of authority.' Yet one must remember the situation in Palermo at the moment of the requisition, with the threatened sudden unemployment of some 800 workers at one factory. It cannot be said to have been unreasonable or merely capricious for the Mayor to seek to use the powers conferred on him by the law in an attempt to do something about a difficult and distressing situation.

[50] Alexandre Kiss, 'Abuse of Rights' in Rudiger Wolfrung (ed) *The Max Planck Encyclopedia of Public International Law* (OUP 2010) https://opil.ouplaw.com/ accessed 20 May 2019.

[51] See Bin Cheng, *General Principles of Law as Applied by International Courts and Tribunals* (Cambridge, CUP 1953) 133 (interestingly, Cheng refers to the same opinion of Judge Azevedo when examining the theory of abuse of rights and the concept of 'abuse of discretion').

[52] 'Harvard Draft Convention on the Responsibility of States for Damage Done in Their Territory to the Person or Property of Foreigner' (1929) 23 AJIL Special Supplement 133.

be considered ‘unreasonable’ and thus unlawful under the draft convention ‘in view of the manner or circumstances in which the power has been exercised’.[53] Linking ‘unreasonable’ measures to ‘arbitrary’ conduct, the commentary finds support in Judge Azvedo’s individual opinion in *Admission of a State to the United Nations*. Interestingly, Judge Azvedo noted the difficulty of fixing a priori the limits of a non-arbitrary exercise of a right and thus implicitly recognized the need to consider the specific circumstances of each case.[54]

The link made in the OECD Draft Convention commentary between an unreasonable (and arbitrary) measure and the concepts of ‘abuse or misuse of a right’[55] may also emphasize the need to consider a variety of factors to be determined on a case-by-case basis. For example, in explaining the concept of ‘abuse of discretion’ as part of the principles of good faith and abuse of rights, Cheng makes this very point:

> Whenever, therefore, the owner of a right enjoys a certain discretionary power, this must be exercised in good faith, which means that it must be exercised reasonably, honestly, in conformity with the spirit of the law and with due regard to the interests of others. But since discretion implies subjective judgment, it is often difficult to determine categorically that the discretion has been abused. Each case must be judged according to its particular circumstances by looking either at the intention or motive of the doer or the objective result of the act, in light of international practice and human experience. When either an unlawful intention or design can be established, or the act is clearly unreasonable, there is an abuse prohibited by law.[56]

An analysis involving all the circumstances of the case is very much the position that FA Mann puts forward in his 1981 brief note with regard to the meaning of ‘fair and equitable treatment’ in investment treaties. Having affirmed that the treaty standard ‘goes far beyond’ the customary minimum standard of treatment, Mann emphasized the need to consider a variety of factors as follows:

> A tribunal would not be concerned with a minimum, maximum or average standard. It will have to decide whether in all the circumstances the conduct in issue is fair and equitable or unfair and inequitable.[57]

53 Paragraph 7(b).
54 ICJ Reports, 1947–48, 57, at 80.
55 Paragraph 7(c).
56 Cheng, *General Principles of Law* (n 51) 133–4.
57 Mann, ‘British Treaties’ (n 27) 241, 244. Interestingly, taking the factual matrix of the famous *Barcelona Traction* case to create an hypothetical dispute between a British investor and the Philippines, Mann concluded as follows (ibid): ‘Whether or no such treatment would be lawful under the law of the Philippines, it should not be open to doubt that it is neither fair nor equitable nor reasonable and would, therefore, attract the liability of the Philippines.’ See UNCTAD, *Fair and Equitable Treatment* (n 36) 39.

(c) Focus on balancing different interests

There is one final aspect that should at least be mentioned here. In addition to taking into account a variety of factors, some of the scholarly commentaries (particularly on the fair and equitable treatment standard) seem to emphasize the ability of fair and equitable treatment to *balance* between different interests. For example, Schwarzenberger praises the 'fair and equitable treatment' language in the Abs-Shawcross Draft Convention because the standard of equitable treatment is capable of balancing the interests of investors and the host State as well as the interests of different States.

> The experiences of the last forty years suggest that whenever, in fact, an agreed settlement has been reached, the creditors have consented to temper the application of the minimum standard by the introduction of an equitable element in the form of considerable concessions on their part. Thus, it appears wise to anticipate—and limit—such contingencies. Moreover, in relations between heterogeneous communities—in varying stages of technological advancement, social structure, and political organisation—and in an age of rapid change, the standard of equitable treatment provides equality on a footing of commendable elasticity.[58]

While noting the imprecise and unpredictable content of 'equity' and 'equitable principles' inherent in fair and equitable treatment, Lauterpacht stressed nonetheless its positive implications because of its compromising or balancing abilities:

> the very fact that States are prepared to have recourse to equity in a particular situation [...] represents a deliberate attempt to solve a problem by blunting the sharp edges of the controversy, albeit in what the outside observer may identify as an inadequate manner.[59]

B. Full Protection and Security and Due Diligence

A first example of a reasonableness-based provision in international investment treaties is the 'full protection and security' provision.

The obligation to ensure 'full protection and security' has one main and undisputed scope of application: it requires the contracting parties to exert due diligence in order to protect the physical safety of persons and installations connected with

[58] Schwarzenberger, 'The Abs-Shawcross Draft Convention on Invesetments Abroad' (n 22) 152–3.

[59] Elihu Lauterpacht, *Aspects of the Administration of International Justice* (Grotius Publications, 1991) 122, cited in Weiler, *The Interpretation of International Investment Law* (n 21) 217–18.

the protected investment from acts of private parties.[60] Such requirement includes the State's duty to prevent acts of private parties that may harm the physical security of the protected investment and the duty to apprehend and bring to justice those responsible for such injuries.[61] Accordingly, the main focus of the obligation to ensure full protection and security is with the State's alleged *failure* to prevent the act of a third party causing harm and/or to apprehend and punish those third parties responsible for such acts. However, and crucially, such failure will constitute a breach of the obligation to ensure full protection and security only if the host State fails to exercise the diligence due to ensure the safety of the protected investments.

In general international law, due diligence is an obligation of conduct, as opposed to an obligation of result. Accordingly, a State is not responsible for the mere occurrence of harm to the alien (as it would be the case under a rule of 'strict liability') but for failing to take the necessary, diligent or reasonable steps to prevent (and punish) such harm.[62]

While international tribunals, including investment treaty ones, have often referred to the duty of due diligence (or the duty of vigilance or of care), their decisions usually lack extensive elaboration on the meaning of such standard, particularly in the context of the 'full protection and security'. In one of the early investment treaty arbitrations, the *AMT v Zaire* tribunal, asked what are the means by which to ascertain whether there has been a breach of the obligation of vigilance to ensure the protection and security of the American investment in Zaire. The tribunal raised the following further questions:

> What then is the practical criterion to determine the level of the precautionary measure to be taken by the receiving State consistent with the minimum standard recognized by international law? More particularly, what are the appropriate measures to be adopted by the Republic of Zaire in the circumstances to protect the security of the investment of AMT? Has Zaire taken any of these measures?[63]

In finding that Zaire had breached the treaty, the *AMT* tribunal, however, did not answer any of these questions and simply noted that Zaire had 'tak[en] no measure whatever that would serve to ensure the protection and security of the investment

[60] Giuditta Cordero Moss, 'Full Protection and Security' in August Reinisch (ed) *Standards of Investment Protection* (OUP 2008) 138.

[61] Eric de Brabandere, 'Host States' Due Diligence Obligations in International Investment Law' (2015) 42 Syracuse J Int'l L & Com 319, 325.

[62] Timo Koivurova, 'Due Diligence' in Rudiger Wolfrung (ed) *The Max Planck Encyclopedia of Public International Law* (OUP 2010). See further the two reports produced by the International Law Association (ILA) Study Group on Due Diligence in International Law published respectively in (2014) 76 Int'l L Ass'n Rep Conf 947 and (2016) 77 Int'l L Ass'n Rep Conf 1062.

ILA Study Group on Due Diligence in International Law Second Report July 2016 Tim Stephens (Rapporteur) and Duncan French (Chair).

[63] *American Manufacturing & Trading, Inc (AMT) v Republic of Zaire*, ICSID Case No ARB/93/1, Award, 21 February 1997, para 6.07.

in question'[64] and failed to 'take every measure necessary to protect and ensure the security of the investment made by AMT in its territory'.[65]

While this section shows that investment tribunals have (at least for the most part) applied 'full protection and security' as a reasonableness-based provision, it also highlights that, in assessing whether host States have exercised 'due diligence', investment tribunals have adopted different approaches (sometimes deferential and other times more demanding) when it comes to the standard of review.

1. The very first case: *AAPL v Sri Lanka*

The *AAPL v Sri Lanka* arbitration,[66] the very first investor–State arbitration based on a modern investment treaty, shows some of the complexities (and divergences) in defining and applying the duty of due diligence in the context of an FPS claim.

In *AAPL*, following the destruction of a shrimp farm and the killing of several staff members of that farm during a military operation between Sri Lankan military forces and Tamil rebels, the investor brought a claim under the United Kingdom–Sri Lanka BIT. Having rejected the claimant's argument that the treaty obligation to ensure full protection and security created a strict liability on the part of the host State, the tribunal's description of the standard of due diligence emphasizes whether the host State's conduct had been 'reasonable under the circumstances'. For example, the *AAPL* tribunal referred to various arbitral decisions that had elaborated on the traditional rule of due diligence in international law, including two in particular. First, the *AAPL* tribunal referred to Max Huber's report in the 1923 *Spanish Zone of Morocco* claims, highlighting that the degree of vigilance required in proving the necessary protection and security would differ according to the circumstances.[67] Second, the *AAPL* tribunal also cited the Mexico/USA General Claim Commission in the 1926 *Home Insurance Company* case, emphasizing the importance of the 'duty to protect', which required undertaking all 'means reasonably necessary to accomplish that end'.[68]

However, some of the references used by the *AAPL* tribunal show a certain ambivalence with regard to the contour and details of the due diligence standard. For example, the *AAPL* tribunal referred to Professor Freeman's 1957 Lectures at the Hague Academy of International Law, who seemed to hint at a rather demanding standard by noting that due diligence 'is nothing more nor less than the reasonable measures of prevention which a well-administered government could be expected

[64] ibid, para 6.08.
[65] ibid, para 6.11.
[66] *Asian Agricultural Products Ltd (AAPL) v Republic of Sri Lanka*, ICSID Case No ARB/87/3, 27 June 1990.
[67] ibid, para 73.
[68] ibid, para 75.

to exercise under similar circumstances'.[69] On the other hand, the *AAPL* tribunal also highlighted Professor Brownlie's apparently more deferential view that responsibility for damage to foreign property exists in the case of '[s]ubstantial negligence to take reasonable precautionary and preventive action'.[70]

Nevertheless, the members of the *AAPL* tribunal disagreed on the actual application of the due diligence standard to the specific facts of the case at hand. Having examined all the available evidence, a majority of the *AAPL* tribunal concluded that Sri Lanka had violated its due diligence obligation, as it did not undertake 'all possible measures that could be reasonably expected to prevent the eventual occurrence of killings and property destruction'. While it found no conclusive evidence as to whether the destruction of the farm and the killing of the staff members had actually been perpetrated by the government forces or the rebels, the majority of the *AAPL* tribunal did find that the governmental forces were capable, under the prevailing circumstances, of providing adequate protection that could have at least minimized the risks of killings and destruction when planning to undertake a vast military counterinsurgency operation. In particular, the tribunal majority concluded that 'reasonably the Government should have at least tried to use such peaceful available high level channel of communication in order to get any suspect elements excluded from the farm's staff'.[71]

The majority's willingness to delve into the existence of an alternative, more peaceful (ie less destructive) course of action, which was reasonably available to the Sri Lankan military forces, is paired with the majority's willingness to review the factual basis of the explanation provided by the host State. The Sri Lankan government had in fact submitted military reports prepared after the military operation, pointing to alleged 'heavy firing coming from the direction of the farm' and that the farm had become a 'terrorist facility' which 'resisted the security forces during a period over two hours'. However, the majority of the *AAPL* tribunal found such a version of the events lacking, and that they were contradicted by eyewitness accounts that the taking over of the farm by the security forces faced no resistance and there was no destruction at that time. Thus, the officers' version of the events could not justify the government's inability to prevent the destruction and killings and, in the view of the majority, was simply 'intended to cover up their inability to prevent the destruction of the farm'.[72]

[69] ibid, para 77. Interestingly, the *AAPL* tribunal used Professor Freedman's statement to emphasize (ibid):

> the 'sliding scale,' from the old 'subjective' criteria that takes into consideration the relatively limited existing possibilities of local authorities in a given context, towards an 'objective' standard of vigilance in assessing the required degree of protection and security with regard to what should be legitimately expected to be secured for foreign investors by a reasonably well organized modern State.

[70] ibid, para 76.

[71] ibid, para 85, 562.

[72] ibid, para 85, 563.

The opinion of the dissenting arbitrator highlights the difficulty of applying the standard of due diligence, as such application relies heavily on an appreciation of the factual circumstances of the case at hand. First, according to the dissenting arbitrator, in a situation of national emergency involving military operation, a due diligence review should afford a wide margin of discretion to the host State. In the dissenting arbitrator's view, the majority's application of due diligence 'fails to take into account the national emergency and extraordinary conditions under which the Government mounted a strategic and highly sensitive security operation to regain its sovereign control of the area of insurgency [. . .] the timing and modalities of the security operation must surely fall within its exclusive discretion'.[73]

Second, the dissenting arbitrator argued that, in any event, the majority's conclusion with regard to the existence of an alternative, more peaceful, course of action (so-called 'precautionary measures') failed to assess the reality of the situation on the ground[74] and appreciate the extraordinary nature of the situation under review.[75] In the dissenting arbitrator's opinion, these conditions of civil war 'constituted an extraordinary situation which did not admit of reliance on the type of leisurely police precautionary measures envisaged by the Tribunal'.[76] In other words, even if the tribunal should have reviewed the timing and modalities of the military operation, the dissenting arbitrator believed that the more peaceful course of action was in fact not an available alternative, and for this reason alone, the tribunal should have rejected any finding of negligence or lack of due diligence against the respondent.

2. Subsequent arbitral practice and divergent application of the 'due diligence' standard

In applying the FPS standard in cases of physical harm caused by private parties, subsequent investment tribunals have regularly relied either expressly or implicitly

[73] *Asian Agricultural Products Ltd (AAPL) v Republic of Sri Lanka*, ICSID Case No ARB/87/3, 27 June 1990, Dissenting Opinion, 593.

[74] ibid, 594:

> The control exercised by the insurgents over the whole area, the previous acts of property destruction and theft, and even murder committed on the farm by the insurgents and the firm management's nervous attempts to secure a peaceful haven for its operations all ruled out any meaningful prospect of the farm management securing the removal of 'suspect rebels' from the farm by peaceful means.

[75] ibid, 594:

> It has to be stressed also that the security forces did not single out the Serendib farm for special treatment. 'Operation Day-Break' was a major, comprehensive military operation that was designed to regain government control over the entire Manmunai area. [. . .] The majority opinion hardly adverts to the fact that the insurrection had developed into a full-scale civil war with tragic loss of life on both rides.

[76] ibid, 594.

on the obligation of the host State to exercise due diligence as reasonable under the circumstances.[77] Linking the FPS provision in the applicable treaty to the general duty under customary international law, the tribunal in *Noble Ventures*, for example, expressly excluded the existence of a 'strict standard' and referred instead to the State's obligation to exercise due diligence.[78]

Even if not expressly mentioned, arbitral tribunals appear to focus their inquiry on whether, under the circumstances, the host State could have reasonably prevented the harm suffered by the investment, rather than whether the investment had suffered any harm. For example, in *Parkerings*, the tribunal rejected the investor's claim that the host State had not guaranteed the physical protection of the investment because 'Claimant does not show that such vandalism would have been prevented if the authorities had acted differently'.[79] In the *ELSI* case, the ICJ rejected the claim that the Italian authorities had failed to prevent 'some occupation of the plant by the workers after the requisition' based on an assessment of the Italian authorities' conduct under the circumstances. Having noted that the workers' occupation had been 'peaceful', the ICJ noted the following:

> The reference in Article V to the provision of 'constant protection and security' cannot be construed as the giving of a warranty that property shall never in any circumstances be occupied or disturbed. The dismissal of some 800 workers could not reasonably be expected to pass without some protest. Indeed, the management of ELSI seems to have been very much aware that the closure of the plant and dismissal of the workforce could not be expected to pass without disturbance.[80]

However, there appear to be differences in the way the due diligence standard have been applied by investment tribunals in specific circumstances. In line with the

[77] De Brabandere, 'Due Diligence' (n 61) 338–9:

> Investment law cases over the past decade confirm not only the existence of the due diligence standard to test State's behavior, but also the principle mentioned above, that the State is not responsible for the acts of individuals as such, but only for having failed to exercise due diligence in preventing harm caused by the act in question.

[78] *Noble Ventures, Inc v Romania*, ICSID Case No ARB/01/11, Award, 12 October 2005, para 164. See also *Bernhard von Pezold and others v Republic of Zimbabwe*, ICSID Case No ARB/10/15, Award, 2015, para 596 ('The Parties agree that the FPS standard is not a strict liability test, but is an "all reasonable measures" (i.e., a due diligence) standard').

[79] *Parkerings-Compagniet AS v Republic of Lithuania*, ICSID Case No ARB/05/8, Award, 11 September 2007, para 356.

[80] *Elettronica Sicula SpA (ELSI) (United States of America v Italy)*, Judgment of 20 July 1989 (n 10), para 108. In any event, the ICJ also noted that it was not altogether clear that the occupation had actually caused harm to the company (ibid, para 107–08):

> It is difficult to accept that the occupation seriously harmed the interests of ELSI in view of the evidence produced by Italy that measures taken by the Mayor of Palermo for the temporary management of the plant permitted the continuation and completion of work in progress in the months following the requisition.

dissenting arbitrator in *AAPL*, several investment tribunals appear to set the bar rather high for a violation of the FPS obligation. Based on its assessment of the *ELSI* decision, the *Noble Venture* tribunal, for example, noted that violations of the protection standard 'are not easily to be established'.[81] A high bar may sometimes be inferred from the fact that tribunals often reject the FPS claim by pointing to the lack of evidence. In *Tecmed v Mexico*, the investor had claimed that the Mexican authorities had violated the FPS standard by not acting 'as quickly, efficiently and thoroughly as they should have' to avoid, prevent or put an end to the adverse social demonstrations expressed through disturbances in the operation of, and access to, the Landfill and the personal security of the investment staff.[82] The tribunal rejected the investor's claim based on the lack of sufficient evidence supporting the allegation that the Mexican authorities had 'not reacted reasonably, in accordance with the parameters inherent in a democratic state, to the direct action movements conducted by those who were against the Landfill'.[83]

Even when the tribunal has accepted the investor's claim, it often follows a finding that the host State has taken no action whether to prevent the harm, to stop the harmful conduct or to apprehend and punish those responsible. In *Wena v Egypt*, for example, the tribunal concluded that the respondent had failed to accord the foreign investment FPS (as well as FET) as Egypt took no action to prevent the seizure of the investor's hotels (despite Egypt being aware of the intentions to seize the hotels), it took no immediate action to restore the hotels promptly to the investor's control and it never imposed substantial sanctions on those responsible for the seizure.[84]

A high bar may also be evinced with tribunals' willingness to take into account the level of development and stability of the host State as relevant circumstances in determining whether or not the host State has exercised due diligence. In *Pantechniki v Albania*, the tribunal was confronted with the investor's claim that riots had caused damage to its investment and that the host State's due diligence obligation embodied in the treaty standard of FPS required Albania to actively protect the claimant's investment from the looting and to take precautionary measures to prevent it from occurring. The sole arbitrator rejected the investor's FPS claim as he concluded that Albanian authorities (the police, in particular) were 'powerless in the face of social unrest of this magnitude'.[85] The sole arbitrator's decision relied

[81] *Noble Ventures, Inc v Romania* (n 78), para 165. See Cordero Moss, 'Protection and Security' (n 60) 142 citing the decision in *The Channel Tunnel Group Limited, France-Manche SA v United Kingdom and France* (*Eurotunnel*) for the proposition that 'the limits of sovereign appreciation are exceeded only when the State's failure to maintain the public order becomes intolerable'.

[82] *Técnicas Medioambi entales Tecmed, SA v The United Mexican States*, ICSID Case No ARB (AF)/00/2, Award, 29 May 2003, para 175.

[83] ibid.

[84] *Wena Hotels Ltd v Arab Republic of Egypt*, ICSID Case No ARB/98/4, Award, 8 December 2000, para 84.

[85] *Pantechniki SA Contractors & Engineers (Greece) v The Republic of Albania*, ICSID Case No ARB/07/21, Award, 30 July 2009, para 82.

on the view that the standard of due diligence is 'that of a host state in the circumstances and with the resources of the state in question'.[86]

On the other side, there have been a few decisions that seem to have followed the stricter approach similar to the one adopted by the majority in *AAPL*. In *von Pezold v Zimbabwe*, the tribunal found that the respondent had breached the FPS standard in relation to the failure of police to protect the investors' properties from occupation (or to remove the occupants) and in relation to the non-responsiveness of police to various violent incidents that had occurred, as detailed by the claimants in their witness statements.[87] The respondent had submitted in its defence that the Zimbabwean police force was 'overwhelmed' by the spontaneous occupations across the country and its intervention would have required 'disproportionate force'.[88] However, the tribunal, without much elaboration, simply found such defences 'unconvincing'.[89]

An apparently strict approach seems to have been adopted by the tribunal in *Ampal v Egypt*, where the investors had argued that Egypt had violated the FPS standard by not acting diligently in preventing the several attacks on the Trans-Sinai gas pipeline between February 2011 and May 2012. While the tribunal acknowledged the difficult circumstances in Egypt in the wake of the Arab Spring Revolution,[90] it concluded that the failure by the Egyptian authorities 'to take any concrete steps' to protect the claimants' investment from damage in reaction to third-party attacks on the pipeline constitutes a breach of the obligation of due diligence that Egypt was required to exercise in ensuring the FPS of the claimants' investment.[91] In particular, based on the detailed factual record that had been established in the context of an earlier arbitration between the same disputing parties, the tribunal emphasized the insufficiency of the reaction by the Egyptian authorities in the following terms:

[86] ibid, para 81 citing Andrew Newcombe and Luis Paradell, *Law and Practice of Investment Treaties: Standards of Treatment* (Wolters Kluwer Law and Business 2009) 310. See Koivurova, 'Due Diligence'(n 62) para 40 referring to the ICJ Judgement in the *Nicaragua Case* ('figuring prominently in the ICJ's assessment that Nicaragua had not failed to act diligently was the traditional criterion of due diligence whereby developing States with their less developed economy and human and material resources cannot be expected to uphold the same degree of diligence as their developed counterparts'). In support of a more subjective view, see De Brabandere, 'Due Diligence' (n 61) 357:

> Despite these ambiguities, the preferable standard is without doubt *diligentia quam in suis*, when one deals with due diligence in relation to physical protection and security. As noted earlier, the application of due diligence in other fields of international law, notably environmental law, allows taking into account the economic and other capabilities of a State.

[87] *Bernhard von Pezold and others v Republic of Zimbabwe*, Award, 28 July 2015 (n 78), para 597.

[88] ibid, para 589.

[89] ibid, para 598.

[90] *Ampal-American Israel Corporation and others v Arab Republic of Egypt*, ICSID Case No ARB/12/11, Decision on Liability, 21 February 2017, para 284.

[91] ibid, para 290.

> It is apparent to the Tribunal that, when considering the totality of these attacks, a certain pattern emerges: an attack is perpetrated, to which GASCO reacts months later and then adopts some measures to heighten the security of the pipeline, those measures are seldom implemented (or there is no evidence on the record that they were), another attack happens, and so on.[92]

The *Ampal* decision highlights the importance of the tribunal's assessment of the factual circumstances in determining whether a breach of the duty of due diligence has indeed occurred. More fundamentally, the *Ampal* decision also shows the difficulty in evaluating whether the tribunal has adopted a strict or deferential standard of review in applying the duty of due diligence. On the one hand, the tribunal's reliance on a 'pattern' of failing to properly respond to the attacks may be interpreted as meeting an even more deferential due diligence standard. On the other hand, the tribunal's apparent disregard of the overall political and security context affecting Egypt during the Arab Spring Revolution may justify describing the decision as adopting a stricter due diligence standard.[93]

3. What standard when assessing acts of State organs causing harm to the investment?

There is more controversy over whether the duty of due diligence is the correct parameter when assessing acts of States which have caused harm to the investment. Some tribunals have applied the due diligence standard to review both acts of third parties and the State.[94]

[92] ibid, para 287. The tribunal highlights in particular the report of the Egyptian authorities with regard to the fifth attack on the pipeline (ibid, para 288):

> the report describes how, as the attack was unfolding, EGAS personnel made contact with an Egyptian army patrol and asked them to stop saboteurs from laying explosives on the pipeline at a facility just 1.5 kilometers away from where the patrol was stationed. The Egyptian security forces refused to mobilize. Some 40 minutes later, the explosives were detonated. 275 Gas supply to EMG was cut-off for almost three months thereafter.

See the dictum in *Eureko v Poland*, Partial Award, 19 August 2005, para 237, regarding the relevance of repeated actions for purposes of determining violation of the full protection and security ('If such actions were to be repeated and sustained, it may be that the responsibility of the Government of Poland would be incurred by a failure to prevent them').

[93] As part of the factual record established in a previous arbitration between the disputing parties, the tribunal had noted the following (*Ampal v Egypt* (n 90), para 603):

> With the eruption of the popular uprising that toppled President Mubarak in January 2011, Sinai's Bedouin seized the opportunity to shrug off Egypt's internal security yoke and push for communal empowerment. Militants grew strong and lawless, and their violence against the police led Egypt's State police to abandon the area. A security vacuum resulted.

[94] *Waguih Elie George Siag and Clorinda Vecchi v The Arab Republic of Egypt*, ICSID Case No ARB/05/15, Award, 1 June 2009, where the claimants' investment was expropriated by force and in opposition to explicit pleas for protection and, while the Egyptian courts on several subsequent occasions

However, several other tribunals seem to have rejected, at least implicitly, such application. For example, there are some investment tribunals that seem to have excluded, a priori, the application of the FPS standard in the case of acts of the State or State organs causing harm to the investment.[95] Second, even if full protection and security has been said to be in principle applicable to both acts of private parties and the State, some investment tribunals have not made any reference to the due diligence standard when considering State conduct involving physical violence.[96] De Brabandere has argued that when it is the State itself that impairs the physical security of foreign investors and investments, the due diligence standard should not apply.[97]

However, even if not employing the concept of due diligence to review acts of the State or State organs that have directly impaired the investment's physical protection and security, investment tribunals crucially seem to focus on an assessment of whether those acts were reasonable and justified under the circumstances.[98] The *Biwater* tribunal, for example, concluded that even if no force had been used in removing the management from the offices or in the seizure of the investor's premises, these acts were 'unnecessary and abusive' and amounted to a violation of the obligation to ensure FPS.[99]

Similarly, the *Siag* tribunal concluded that the conduct of Egypt 'fell well below the standard of protection that the investors could reasonably have expected', and in particular Egypt's failure to return the investment following repeated rulings of Egypt's own courts that the expropriation was illegal was 'indeed the most egregious element in the whole affairs'.[100]

The *Tulip* tribunal rejected the investor's claim of violation of the FPS based on an examination of all the circumstances of the case and in particular the following: the

cancelled the Resolutions or decrees that purported to give legitimacy to the expropriation, yet the claimants' investment was not returned to them in the twelve years following expropriation.

---

[95] *El Paso Energy International Company v The Argentine Republic*, ICSID Case No ARB/03/15, Award, 31 October 2011, para 524:

> In the present case, none of the measures challenged by El Paso were taken by a third party; they all emanated from the State itself. Consequently, these measures should only be assessed in the light of the other BIT standards and cannot be examined from the angle of full protection and security.

See also *Oxus Gold v Republic of Uzbekistan*, UNCITRAL, Award, 17 December 2015, paras 834–36.

[96] *Biwater Gauff (Tanzania) Ltd v United Republic of Tanzania*, ICSID Case No ARB/05/22, Award, 24 July 2008, para 731; *Eureko v Poland*, Partial Award, 19 August 2005 (n 92), paras 236–37; *Tulip Real Estate and Development Netherlands BV v Republic of Turkey*, ICSID Case No ARB/11/28, Award, 10 March 2014, para 433.

[97] De Brabandere, 'Due Diligence' (n 61) 334–7.

[98] Christoph Schreuer, 'Full Protection and Security' (2010) J Int'l Dispute Settlement 353, 359 ('The cases summarized above indicate that unjustified coercive measures taken by organs of the host State against the investor and his property constitute violations of the "protection and security" standard if they prejudice the investor to a material degree').

[99] *Biwater v Tanzania*, Award, 24 July 2008 (n 96), para 731.

[100] *Siag v Egypt*, Award, 1 June 2009 (n 94), para 448.

State (assuming that Emlak were an emanation of the State) did not plan to engage in an unlawful seizure of the investor's property, Emlak's attempt to repossess the site did not involve substantial violence, the Turkish police did not assist Emlak through use of force or being inactive, and, most significantly, the State took action against Emlak representatives for improperly using force.[101]

Interestingly, in the context of reviewing (physically violent) conduct of the host State, investment tribunals have highlighted the overlap between 'full protection and security' and the standard of 'fair and equitable treatment' and the prohibition of arbitrary and discriminatory measures impairing the investment.[102]

C. Fair and Equitable Treatment (and Non-Impairment) Standards: Good Faith, Arbitrariness and Legitimate Expectations

The objective of this section is twofold. First, it aims to show whether investment tribunals have interpreted the provisions on FET standard (as well as the so-called 'non-impairment' clause) as reasonableness-based provisions, in particular focusing on a review of the substantive soundness of the host State's conduct.[103] Second, it aims to identify the different standards of review (or reasonableness tests), which investment tribunals have referred to, or have employed, in order to carry out such assessment.

This section focuses on three concepts that are often employed by investment tribunals in order to apply the FET (and the non-impairment) provisions: (i) the principle of good faith; (ii) the prohibition of arbitrary (or unjustifiable or unreasonable) conduct; and (iii) the protection of legitimate expectations. The section argues, first of all, that there is little doubt that by focusing on these three concepts, arbitral tribunals have applied the FET (and the non-impairment) provisions (at least in substantial part) as reasonableness-based standards. In particular, and in line with the definition of a reasonableness-based provision adopted in this work, the following analysis finds that: (a) the common underlying factor in determining a claim of violation of the FET standard for lack of *good faith* is whether or not the host State's conduct was justified by a legitimate concern or policy; (b) a review

[101] *Tulip v Turkey*, Award, 10 March 2014 (n 96), paras 430–36.

[102] *The Rompetrol Group NV v Romania*, ICSID Case No ARB/06/3, Award, 6 May 2013, para 197:

> As to the parallel guarantees of 'non-impairment' and 'full protection and security,' the Claimant does not appear to argue that, in the concrete circumstances of this case, they cover any situation which is not already covered by its claims under the guarantee of fair and equitable treatment. The Tribunal will accordingly consider the application of all of these standards of protection together, against the Claimant's allegations of breach.

[103] Both provisions have also been applied to impose 'procedural' requirements. See Rudolf Dolzer and Christoph Schreuer, *Principles of International Investment Law* (2nd edn, OUP 2012) 154–6, 191–7.

about *arbitrariness* (or *unreasonableness*) involves at a minimum a determination of whether or not there exists a legitimate interest underlying the host State's measure at issue;[104] and (c) many investment tribunals have recognized a role for the host State's right to regulate in the public interest in the application of the doctrine of *legitimate expectations* as part of FET.

Second, this section highlights, however, that there is inconsistency (and sometimes also uncertainty) as to the standard of review that investment tribunals apply, particularly in the context of a claim of arbitrary conduct or frustration of legitimate expectations. For example, while most tribunals have set a high threshold for a finding of *arbitrariness*, some tribunals (appear to) have given the concept a broader (more intrusive) reach by carrying out a review based on 'means–ends rationality' or even 'proportionality balancing'. Similarly, in applying the concept of legitimate expectations as part of the FET provision, investment tribunals have so far failed to adopt a clear and consistent approach with regard to the balancing exercise between the protection of investors' legitimate expectations and the host State's right to regulate in the public interest.

1. Good faith

In international law, one of the functions of the principle of good faith is to control the exercise of rights by States.[105] According to Cheng, the principle of good faith prohibits (a) the malicious exercise of a right (ie for the sole purpose of causing injury to another); (b) the fictitious exercise of a right (ie for the purpose of evading either a rule of law or a contractual obligation); and (c) abuse of discretion (ie when a discretionary power is not exercised reasonably, honestly, in conformity with the spirit of the law and with due regard to the interests of others).[106] According to Cheng, beyond the prohibition of abuses, the importance of the principle of good faith is in recognizing the interdependence of rights and obligations. In other words, good faith 'reconciles conflicting interests, establishes the proper limits of rights, and secures harmony in the legal order'.[107]

While its presence cannot generally be found in investment treaties, the principle of good faith has very quickly gained a role in the application of investment treaty standards, in particular with regard to the standard of FET.[108] According to the *Tecmed* tribunal, for example, the treaty obligation to provide FET to foreign

[104] In this minimum understanding, arbitrariness is very close (if not synonymous) to lack of good faith.

[105] Cheng, *General Principles of Law* (n 51) 121 et seq.

[106] ibid.

[107] ibid, 136 ('By infusing such qualities as honesty, sincerity, reasonableness and moderation into the exercise of rights, it promotes the smooth and proper functioning of the legal system').

[108] Dolzer and Schreuer, *Principles of International Investment Law* (n 103) 156–8; José E Ponce and Ricardo Cevallos, 'Good Faith in Investment Arbitration' (2016) 13 TDM 5.

investments 'is an expression and part of the *bona fide* principle recognized in international law'.[109] More specifically, the *Waste Management II* tribunal interpreted the customary minimum standard of treatment in Article 1105 of the North American Free Trade Agreement (NAFTA) as including the obligation 'to act in good faith'.[110]

As one of the principles of the FET standard, good faith has been applied in connection with a variety of alleged abuses by the host State. In its broadest application, the obligation to act in good faith overlaps with other principles of FET, such as the prohibition of arbitrary, unreasonable or discriminatory conduct. In *Saluka*, for example, the tribunal explained that the protection afforded by the FET standard includes the requirement that the host State 'implements its policies *bona fide* by conduct that is, as far as it affects the [foreign investment], reasonably justifiable by public polices' and that it 'does not manifestly violate the requirements of consistency, transparency, even-handedness and non-discrimination'.[111]

Despite its potentially broad scope, good faith appears to have mostly been employed in the context of investors' claims of malicious or fictitious exercises of host States' rights, to use Cheng's dichotomy.[112] More fundamentally, the point that I would like to emphasize in this section is that the common underlying factor in determining a claim of violation of the FET standard for lack of good faith is whether or not the host State's conduct was justified by a legitimate concern or policy in line with my understanding of a reasonableness-based standard. Three examples follow.

In *Waste Management II*, for example, the claimant alleged that various Mexican agencies had conspired together to frustrate the concession in violation of Article 1105 NAFTA (an alleged malicious exercise of a right). The *Waste Management II* tribunal recognized that a deliberate conspiracy—that is a conscious combination of various agencies without justification to defeat the purposes of an investment agreement—would constitute a breach of Article 1105 NAFTA, as the latter requires the State to act in good faith and 'not deliberately to set out to destroy or frustrate the investment by improper means'.[113] The *Waste Management II* tribunal eventually rejected the investor's claim as the investor had failed to prove its

[109] *Tecmed v Mexico*, Award, 29 May 2003 (n 82), para 153, quoting I Brownlie, *Principles of Public International Law* (OUP 1989) 19. See also *Sempra Energy International v The Argentine Republic*, ICSID Case No ARB/02/16, Award, 28 September 2007, paras 298–99.

[110] *Waste Management, Inc v United Mexican States ('Number 2')*, ICSID Case No ARB(AF)/00/3, Award, 30 April 2004, para 138.

[111] *Saluka Investments BV v The Czech Republic*, UNCITRAL, Partial Award, 17 March 2006, para 307.

[112] See Deyan Draguiev, 'Bad Faith Conduct of States in Violation of the "Fair and Equitable Treatment" Standard in International Investment Law and Arbitration' (2014) 5 J Intn'l Dispute Settlement 273.

[113] *Waste Management II*, Award, 30 April 2004 (n 110) para 138.

allegation and the tribunal believed that there were instead 'sufficient reasons to explain the collapse of the concession [without the] need to resort to conspiracy theories, unsupported by solid evidence'.[114]

In *Bayindir v Pakistan*, the investor, a Turkish construction company, brought an FET claim when the host State had terminated the contract to construct a highway in Pakistan for lack of performance. The claimant had alleged that the termination was unrelated to its performance of the contract but was instead linked to conspiracy, improper motivation and bad faith on the part of Pakistan (an alleged fictitious exercise of a right). While acknowledging that, if proven, such allegations would be capable of founding a FET claim under the BIT, the *Bayindir* tribunal eventually rejected the investor's claim as 'the Pakistani authorities' concerns about Bayindir's performance must be deemed founded'.[115]

In *Frontier Petroleum v Czech Republic*, the claimant asserted that its investment in the aviation industry in the Czech Republic was mistreated as a result of inaction of the Czech courts and officials, malfeasance by Czech bankruptcy trustees and through the manifest inadequacy of the legal system of the Czech Republic. In particular, the claimant argued that 'from the fair and equitable treatment standard flows a duty of fidelity to the principle of good faith' and thus foreign investors hold a legitimate expectation that the State 'is prepared to take reasonable steps to ensure that its officials exercise any discretion delegated to them in good faith and in a reasonable and fair-minded manner'.[116] The investor's claim is a reminder of the third (and broadest) application of the good faith principle identified by Cheng, that is 'abuse of discretion'. While it recognized that 'action in good faith' is one of the concrete principles of the fair and equitable treatment standard,[117] the *Frontier* tribunal linked the obligation to act in good faith under FET with the following, non-exhaustive, examples of 'bad faith action' by the host State:

(a) the use of legal instruments for purposes other than those for which they were created,
(b) a conspiracy by state organs to inflict damage upon or to defeat the investment,
(c) the termination of the investment for reasons other than the one put forth by the government, and expulsion of an investment based on local favouritism,

[114] ibid, para 139. See *GAMI Investments Inc v Mexico*, UNCITRAL, Final Award, 15 November 2004, para 97, where the tribunal, as part of its inquiry under Article 1105 NAFTA of the manner in which Mexico had applied its laws, pointed to the fact that '[p]roof of a good faith effort by the Government to achieve the objectives of its laws and regulations may counter-balance instances of disregard of legal or regulatory requirements'.

[115] *Bayindir v Pakistan*, Award, 2009, para 314. C McLachlan, L Shore and M Weiniger, *International Investment Arbitration: Substantive Principles* (2nd edn, OUP 2017) at 275 ('An international tribunal should give particular weight to government regulatory decisions taken in good faith in the interests of public morals, health or the environment').

[116] *Frontier v Czech Republic*, Award, 12 November 2010, para 275.

[117] ibid, para 284.

(d) reliance by a government on its internal structures to excuse non-compliance with contractual obligations would also be contrary to good faith.[118]

While the *Frontier* tribunal eventually rejected all of the investor's claims, it is interesting to note how the tribunal seems to focus on the more conspicuous cases of lack of good faith or, to use Cheng's dichotomy, the malicious and fictitious exercise of a right. Nevertheless, the above list confirms the underlying point that the obligation to act in good faith under the FET standard requires the host State to act in the pursuit of a legitimate policy objective.[119]

The focus on the more conspicuous cases of lack of good faith also explains why there are only a handful of decisions rendered in favour of the investor.[120] One such case is *Railroad Development Corporation (RDC) v Guatemala*, where the investor claimed violation of the FET standard pursuant to Article 10.5 CAFTA (which adopts the approach taken by the NAFTA contracting parties in their 2001 interpretation of the minimum standard of treatment in Article 1105 NAFTA) inter alia because the host State had failed to act in good faith towards RDC and its

[118] ibid, para 300. See also *Siemens AG v The Argentine Republic*, ICSID Case No. ARB/05/15, Award, 6 February 2007, para 308:

> The Tribunal also finds that when a government awards a contract, which includes among its critical provisions an undertaking of that government to conclude agreements with its provinces, the same government cannot argue that the structure of the State does not permit it to fulfil such undertaking. This runs counter to the principle of good faith underlying fair and equitable treatment.

[119] See *Chemtura v Canada*, UNCITRAL (formerly *Crompton Corporation v Government of* Canada), Award, 2 June 2010, where the tribunal concluded that there was no evidence in the record that the measures under review (including a special review of lindane and the denial of a phase-out) were conducted unfairly or in bad faith. On the contrary, the tribunal found (paras 147 and 184) that 'there is ample evidence that the use of lindane caused genuine concerns, both in Canada and abroad'.

[120] See *Compania de Aguas del Aconquija and Vivendi Universal v Argentina*, Case No ARB/97/3, Award, 20 August 2007, where claimants had argued that, having been invited by the Province and the National Government to engage in a third round of renegotiations in early 1997; they were entitled to expect that the Province would act in good faith in those negotiations. However, according to the claimants, the submission of the unilaterally amended version of the agreement to the Legislature, and further unilateral amendments made by the Legislature, violated not only transparency, stability and the claimants' legitimate expectations, but also the elemental requirement of good faith dealings. In particular, the manner in which the amendments were made—unilaterally and without any attempt at notification or consultation with claimants—is impossible to reconcile with any notion of good faith (para 5.2.14). The tribunal accepted the investors' claim (and violation of the FET) as (para 7.4.19):

> [o]n the facts before us, it is only possible to conclude that the Bussi government, improperly and without justification, mounted an illegitimate 'campaign' against the concession, the Concession Agreement, and the 'foreign' concessionaire from the moment it took office, aimed either at reversing the privatisation or forcing the concessionaire to renegotiate (and lower) CAA's tariffs.

Similarly, the *Saluka* tribunal accepted the investor's claims that the host State had refused to negotiate in good faith in order to find a solution to the investment's financial problems, although the tribunal did not expressly mention lack of good faith, rather lack of consistency, transparency and adequate communication: *Saluka v Czech Republic*, Partial Award, 17 March 2006 (n 111) paras 361, 417–32.

investment by terminating a contract to operate the railway system in Guatemala. While formally the termination was due to certain legal defects in the contract, the claimant alleged that the true motive behind the termination was to coerce the investor to renegotiate and surrender its rights under the contract.[121] While it rejected the allegation of bad faith, the respondent accepted that the obligation to act in good faith is one of the obligations comprised in the minimum standard of treatment. Interestingly, the respondent pointed to two elements of acting in good faith (stemming from the relevant description in *Waste Management II*): the first element, whether the State acted 'improperly' or 'without justification', is a requirement that the State act rationally in accordance with its own laws; the second element requires that the State acted 'deliberately' or 'consciously' in order to destroy the relevant investment.[122]

After a detailed examination of the evidence, the *RDC* tribunal found a violation of the minimum standard of treatment. While expressly only referring to 'bad faith' as treatment in principle amounting to an international delinquency according to the *Neer* case,[123] the tribunal appears to base its findings of violation on the host State's failure to act in good faith, and in particular on a malicious (or at least fictitious) exercise of governmental powers. The *RDC* tribunal stated as follows:

> In the circumstances of this case, the *lesivo* remedy has been used under a cloak of formal correctness allegedly in defense of the rule of law, in fact for exacting concessions unrelated to the finding of lesivo. [. . .] In the Tribunal's view, the manner in which and the grounds on which Respondent applied the *lesivo* remedy in the circumstances of this case constituted a breach of the minimum standard of treatment in Article 10.5 of CAFTA by being, in the words of *Waste Management II*, 'arbitrary, grossly unfair, [and] unjust.'[124]

2. Arbitrary (or unjustifiable or unreasonable) conduct

The prohibition of arbitrary conduct is a principle of the international law for the protection of foreign nationals, including investors. It finds recognition in customary law as part of the 'minimum standard of treatment' and in conventional law in several standards, including in particular the guarantee against impairment of investments by arbitrary measures (so-called 'non-impairment' clause or

[121] *Railroad Development Corporation v Republic of Guatemala*, ICSID Case No ARB/07/23, Award, 29 June 2012, paras 64 and 157.
[122] ibid, para 163.
[123] ibid, para 216.
[124] ibid, paras 234–35.

standard) and the FET standard, which are found in several post-Second-World-War FCN treaties[125] and modern investment treaties.

The guarantee against arbitrary impairment is often included in the same clause providing for FET (and FPS). For example, having provided for FET and FPS in sub-paragraph a, Article II.2 of the 1991 Argentina–United States BIT states in sub-paragraph b, that 'Neither Party shall in any way impair by arbitrary or discriminatory measures the management, operation, maintenance, use, enjoyment, acquisition, expansion, or disposal of investments.'[126] Other treaties refer to 'unreasonable'[127] or 'unjustified'[128] or 'unfair'[129] instead of 'arbitrary'.[130]

Unsurprisingly, many investment tribunals have analysed the investor's claim of arbitrary conduct without distinguishing between the 'non-impairment' clause and the FET standard (including when linked to the customary minimum standard of treatment).[131] Given the potential overlap between the various standards, recent investment treaties have omitted the non-impairment clause and/or elaborated specific elements of FET, including 'manifest arbitrariness'.[132]

Whether under the FET provision or under the non-impairment clause, investment tribunals have applied the prohibition of arbitrary or unjustifiable or unreasonable conduct as a reasonableness-based standard, including a review of whether there exists a legitimate interest or concern underlying the host State's measure at issue. While most tribunals have set a high threshold for a finding of arbitrariness, some have given the concept a broader (more intrusive) reach.

[125] See Article I of the Supplementary Agreement to the 1948 Italy–United States FCN Treaty (404 UNTS 326):

> The nationals, corporations and associations of either High Contracting Party shall not be subjected to arbitrary or discriminatory measures within the territories of the other High Contracting Party resulting particularly in: (a) preventing their effective control and management of enterprises which they have been permitted to establish or acquire therein; or, (b) impairing their other legally acquired rights and interests in such enterprises or in the investments which they have made [. . .].

[126] See also Article 3.1 of the 1996 Latvia–Lithuania BIT at issue in *UAB E energija (Lithuania) v Republic of Latvia*, ICSID Case No ARB/12/33.

[127] See Article 2.2 of the 2004 Cyprus–Libya BIT at issue in *Olin Holdings Limited v Libya*, ICC Case No 20355/MCP; Article III(2) of the 1994 Bolivia–Chile BIT at issue in *Quiborax SA Non Metallic Minerals, SA and Allan Fosk Kaplin v Pharmaceutical State of Bolivia*, ICSID Case No ARB/06/2; Article 2(2) of the 1990 United Kingdom–Argentina BIT at issue in *National Grid plc v Argentina*, UNCITRAL, Award, 3 November 2008.

[128] See Article III(1) of the 1991 Argentina–Spain BIT at issue in *Teinver SA, Transportes de Cercanías SA and Autobuses Urbanos del Sur SA v The Argentine Republic* (*Teinver v Argentina*), ICSID Case No ARB/09/1.

[129] See Article 3.2 of the 1992 Hungary–Portugal BIT at issue in *Dan Cake v Hungary*, ICSID Case No ARB/12/9.

[130] See treaties concluded by the Netherlands and the United Kingdom and Newcombe and Paradell, *Standards of Treatment* (n 86) 298–300.

[131] Dolzer and Schreuer, *Principles of International Investment Law* (n 103) 194 and cases cited therein. See recently, *Olin Holdings Limited v Libya*, ICC Case No 20355/MCP, Final Award, 25 May 2018, paras 376–77.

[132] See the treaties signed recently by the European Union, including the 2016 Comprehensive Economic and Trade Agreement ('CETA') with Canada, Article 8.10(2).

(a) Arbitrariness and the 'high threshold' approach

When it comes to defining the concept of arbitrary conduct, a regular starting point is dictionary definitions, which however, include a range of meanings, from the neutral 'relating to, or dependent on, the discretion of an arbiter, arbitrator, or other legally-recognized authority', to the more reproachable 'derived from mere opinion or preference; not based on the nature of things; hence, capricious, uncertain, varying', to the abusive 'unrestrained in the exercise of will; of uncontrolled power or authority, absolute; hence, despotic, tyrannical'.[133]

A second regular starting point is the passage in the *ELSI* judgment by the ICJ: 'Arbitrariness is not so much something opposed to a rule of law, as something opposed to the rule of law. [. . .] It is a wilful disregard of due process of law, an act which shocks, or at least surprises, a sense of juridical propriety.'[134]

The *ELSI* judgment provides useful elements both in terms of 'relevant indicators' and 'required threshold' of arbitrariness. First, the ICJ set the bar for responsibility rather high by emphasizing that arbitrariness is 'something opposed to the rule of law' and 'an act which shocks, or at least surprises, a sense of juridical propriety'.[135] Second, the ICJ emphasized that, while unlawfulness under municipal law may be relevant to support a finding of arbitrariness in international law, 'by itself, and without more, unlawfulness cannot be said to amount to arbitrariness'.[136] Third, in the view of the ICJ, the fact that the conduct under review (the mayor's requisition of the foreign-owned company) was not capable in practice of achieving its intended purpose (ie to address the company's difficulties) was not sufficient to demonstrate arbitrariness or unreasonableness where (a) the concern underlying the measure at issue was indeed a very real one (ie a public order issue linked with 'the threatened sudden unemployment of some 800 workers at one factory'); and (b) the act under review came within the powers attributed to the mayor under municipal law (even if those powers had been misapplied) and was subject to 'appropriate remedies of appeal'.[137] In other words, a host State conduct is arbitrary if there is no plausible reason justifying it or if the measure is taken *ultra vires* and no judicial remedies are available.[138]

The existence of substantive and procedural elements in the ICJ definition of arbitrariness in *ELSI* is in line with the Court's own statements about the insufficiency of a finding of lawfulness or illegality under municipal law and the need

[133] Jacob Stone, 'Arbitrariness, the Fair and Equitable Treatment Standard, and the International Law of Investment' (2012) 25 LJIL 77, 85 quoting the Oxford English Dictionary. See *Ronald S Lauder v Czech Republic*, UNCITRAL, Award, 3 September 2001, para 221 (citing the Black's Law Dictionary).

[134] See *Elettronica Sicula SpA (ELSI) (United States of America v Italy)*, Judgment of 20 July 1989 (n 10), 76, para 128.

[135] ibid, para 128.

[136] ibid, para 124.

[137] ibid, para 129.

[138] See Christoph Schreuer, 'Protection against Arbitrary or Discriminatory Measures' in Catherine A Rogers and Roger P Alford (eds) *The Future of Investment Arbitration* (OUP 2009) 188.

for the conduct under review to shock or at least surprise a sense of juridical propriety.[139] Most investment tribunals (whether applying the stand-alone arbitrary impairment clause, FET or the customary minimum standard of treatment) have reiterated that mere illegality is not enough for a finding of arbitrariness[140] and focused on an inquiry of substantive and procedural arbitrariness, de facto setting a high threshold of arbitrariness.[141]

With regard to procedural arbitrariness, the *Waste Management v Mexico* tribunal noted that a mere contractual breach (such as the failure to pay) does not amount to an arbitrary act in violation of the customary minimum standard of treatment (incorporated in Article 1105 NAFTA) 'provided that it does not amount to an outright and unjustified repudiation of the transaction and provided that some remedy is open to the creditor to address the problem'.[142] The tribunal in *Noble Ventures v Romania* rejected the claim that the judicial reorganization proceedings violated the arbitrary impairment clause because such proceedings 'were initiated and conducted according to the law and not against it'.[143]

Most investment tribunals have focused on an inquiry of substantive arbitrariness. A majority of tribunals appears to require a high threshold for a finding of arbitrariness (and this does not seem to depend on whether the tribunal is applying the customary minimum standard of treatment or the treaty prohibition of arbitrary impairment).[144] Rather than requiring a rational relationship between the measure at issue and its underlying policy, the aim of these tribunals is, more simply, to determine whether or not there exists a legitimate interest or concern underlying the measure under review.[145] In the words of Endicott, 'arbitrariness is lack of reason'.[146]

For example, in the context of applying the arbitrary impairment clause, the tribunal in *Genin* rejected the investor's claim as the tribunal accepted the respondent's explanation that the decision to annul the investor's banking license

[139] See Newcombe and Paradell, *Standards of Treatment* (n 86) 250–1 referring to substantive and procedural arbitrariness in the context of the customary minimum standard of treatment.

[140] See *ADF v United States*, ICSID Case No. ARB (AF)/00/1, Award, 9 January 2003, para 43 ('something more than simple illegality or lack of authority under the domestic law of a State is necessary to render an act or measure inconsistent with the customary international law requirements'). See further Patrick Dumberry, 'The Prohibition against Arbitrary Conduct and the Fair and Equitable Treatment Standard under NAFTA Article 1105' (2014) 15 JWIT 117.

[141] Most tribunals applying the prohibition of arbitrary conduct expressed by the customary minimum standard of treatment (MST) (particularly in the context of NAFTA article 1105) have clearly emphasized the existence of a high threshold. See Dumberry, 'The Prohibition against Arbitrary Conduct' (n 140) 145.

[142] *Waste Management II*, Award, 30 April 2004 (n 110) para 115. See *Glamis Gold v United States*, Award, 8 June 2009, para 771 ('If there was a procedural error, it was corrected quickly and effectively through domestic channels, a process that does not evince "a complete lack of due process" ').

[143] *Noble Ventures, Inc v Romania* (n 78) para 178.

[144] Stone, 'Arbitrariness, the Fair and Equitable Treatment Standard' (n 133) 93.

[145] Veijo Heiskanen, 'Arbitrary and Unreasonable Measures' in August Reinisch (ed) *Standards of Investment Protection* (OUP 2008) 104.

[146] Timothy Endicott, 'Arbitrariness' (2014) XXVII J L Jurisprudence 49, 49.

had been taken in the course of exercising its statutory obligations to regulate the Estonian banking sector. The tribunal also accepted the respondent's explanation that the circumstances of political and economic transition prevailing in Estonia at the time justified heightened scrutiny of the banking sector, thus concluding that such state regulation 'reflects a clear and legitimate public purpose'.[147] Similarly, the tribunal in *Lauder v Czech Republic* determined that the acts of the Czech Republic's Media Council were arbitrary because they were 'not founded on reason or fact, nor on the law which expressly accepted "applications from companies with foreign equity participation," but on mere fear reflecting national preference'.[148]

The *Noble Venture v Romania* tribunal found that the judicial reorganization proceedings initiated with regard to the investment were not arbitrary (in violation of the non-impairment clause) because they were justified by the undisputed socio-economic circumstances of the investment. The tribunal emphasized (a) the factual insolvency of the steel mill; (b) no prospect of the budgetary creditors rescheduling debts on a short-term basis; (c) no prospect of the claimant making further investments; and (d) the desperate situation for the approximately 4000 employees, as well as for the whole region.[149] In *Enron v Argentina*, the investor's claim of arbitrariness (in violation of the non-impairment clause in the United States–Argentina BIT) was based on the argument that Argentina's emergency legislation of 2001 'destroyed the rights and reasonable expectations of the claimants, lacked proportionality and were in violation of the law'.[150] The tribunal rejected the investor's arbitrariness claims, adopting a clearly high threshold for a finding of arbitrary conduct. The *Enron* tribunal noted as follows:

[147] *Alex Genin v Estonia*, ICSID Case No. ARB/99/2, Award, 25 June 2001, para 370. The *Genin* tribunal's reference to 'bad faith' in the determination of arbitrariness confirms the nature and intensity of the review, as bad faith constitutes evidence of the lack of any legitimate justification for the conduct under review. Contrary to what is sometimes said about the *Genin* decision, bad faith is not a necessary requirement for a finding of arbitrariness, but certainly a sufficient one. See *Siemens v Argentina*, Award, 6 February 2007 (n 118) para 318, where the tribunal appears to read the decision in *Genin* as 'requiring' bad faith for a violation of arbitrariness.

[148] *Lauder v Czech Republic*, Award, 3 September 2001 (n 133) para 232 (tribunal was applying the prohibition of impairment by arbitrary and discriminatory measures in Article II(2)(b) of the United States–Czech Republic BIT).

[149] *Noble Ventures, Inc v Romania* (n 78) para 177. Having noted that FET is broader than any of the other non-contingent standards (non-impairment, FPS and umbrella clauses), the tribunal also rejected the investor's FET claim based on an apparently more intense scrutiny involving an assessment of any alternative option and the extent of the (employees') interests at stake (ibid, para 182):

> As described above with regard to alleged arbitrariness, the situation of the Claimant, CSR and its employees was such that the judicial proceedings seemed to be the only solution to an otherwise insoluble situation. Bearing in mind the interests of the approximately 4,000 employees who depended on CSR and their prospects at that time, the initiation of the proceedings was neither unfair nor inequitable.

[150] *Enron Corporation and Ponderosa Assets, LP v Argentine Republic*, ICSID Case No ARB/01/3, Award, 22 May 2007, para 278.

> The measures adopted might have been good or bad, a matter which is not for the Tribunal to judge, and as concluded they were not consistent with the domestic and the Treaty legal framework, but they were not arbitrary in that they were what the Government believed and understood was the best response to the unfolding crisis. Irrespective of the question of intention, a finding of arbitrariness requires that some important measure of impropriety is manifest, and this is not found in a process which although far from desirable is nonetheless not entirely surprising in the context it took place.[151]

Similarly, in *National Grid v Argentina*, the claimant had argued that the emergency measures adopted by Argentina to address the economic crisis violated the 'no unreasonable impairment' clause in the United Kingdom–Argentina BIT because (a) they dismantled the entire remuneration regime in the electricity transmission industry; (b) they were contrary to its legitimate expectations; (c) they were not a legitimate and proportionate attempt at fair burden sharing.[152] The tribunal found, first of all, that the plain meaning of the terms 'unreasonable' and 'arbitrary' to be substantially the same in the sense of 'something done capriciously, without reason'.[153] Second, the tribunal summarily rejected the investor's claim based on the 'no unreasonable impairment' clause on the fact that Argentina's measures were taken 'in the context of an unfolding crisis' and, while they may have contradicted commitments made to the claimant, each one of the measures under review 'provided the reasons why it was taken'.[154]

In the context of applying the prohibition of arbitrary conduct as part of the customary minimum standard of treatment pursuant to Article 1105 NAFTA, the tribunal in *Glamis Gold v United States* rejected the investor's claims of arbitrariness on the basis that the various measures under review could be justified at least to some extent in order to address legitimate concerns. For example, the tribunal found that the Senate Bill 22 requiring mandatory complete backfilling of open-pit metallic mines was not arbitrary inter alia because 'it is clear from the record that the bill addresses some, if not all, of the harms caused to Native American sacred sites by open-pit mining'.[155]

(b) Arbitrariness and the broader (more intrusive) reach

Over the years, however, some investment tribunals appear to have given a broader reading of the prohibition of arbitrary conduct, whether as part of the customary minimum standard of treatment, the non-impairment clause, or the FET standard. For example, while referring to some of the above-mentioned 'precedents' (like

[151] ibid, para 281.
[152] *National Grid plc v Argentina*, Award, 3 November 2008 (n 127), para 191.
[153] ibid, para 197.
[154] ibid, para 198.
[155] *Glamis Gold Ltd v United States*, Award, 8 June 2009 (n 142) paras 804–05.

ELSI and *Genin*), the tribunal in *LG&E v Argentina* described the 'no arbitrary impairment' clause in the 1991 United States–Argentina BIT as requiring a more demanding obligation, which would even include proportionality balancing. The *LG&E* tribunal noted that the clause requires contracting parties to engage 'in a rational decision-making process [which] would include a consideration of the effect of a measure on foreign investment and a balance of the interests of the State with any burden imposed on such investment'.[156]

In *Merrill & Ring*, the tribunal affirmed that the customary minimum standard of treatment referred to in Article 1105 NAFTA includes a prohibition of arbitrary conduct, but disagreed with earlier NAFTA tribunals with regard to the correct threshold for determining a finding of arbitrariness. The *Merrill & Ring* tribunal noted that 'today's minimum standard is broader than that defined in the *Neer* case and its progeny' and that the 'standard provides for the fair and equitable treatment of alien investors within the confines of reasonableness'.[157]

In *Teinver v Argentina*,[158] the tribunal was confronted with Article III(1) of the Argentina–Spain BIT prohibiting the impairment of the investment through 'unjustified' (and discriminatory) measures. The tribunal first noted that the disputing parties agreed that 'unjustified' measures are equivalent to 'arbitrary' measures. Second, with regard to the notion of 'arbitrary' or 'arbitrariness', the tribunal found more persuasive the broader interpretation put forward by the claimant, noting that '[s]ince the *ELSI* decision, several tribunals have gone beyond the limited notion of arbitrariness set out in that case and, relying on the ordinary meaning of the term, have articulated a broader notion of arbitrary treatment'.[159] Interestingly, as the tribunal had already found that certain of the measures at issue were 'arbitrary' in violation of the FET standard, it then concluded that '[f]or the same reasons, [...] the conduct in question also amounts to unjustified measures under Article III(1) of the Treaty'.[160]

The tribunal in *AES Summit Generation v Hungary* was confronted with a claim of violation of Article 10(1) Energy Charter Treaty (ECT), which focused on both the FET standard and the prohibition to impair foreign investments by 'unreasonable' (and discriminatory) measures. The *AES* tribunal seems to equate (albeit not expressly) 'unreasonable' with 'arbitrary' for the purposes of the non-impairment clause, as it eventually concluded that Hungary's decision to introduce an administrative pricing scheme for energy generators was 'not an arbitrary or unreasonable

[156] *LG&E Energy Corporation, LG&E Capital Corporation and LG&E International, Inc v Argentine Republic*, ICSID Case No ARB/02/1, Decision on Liability, 3 October 2006, para 158.

[157] *Merrill & Ring Forestry LP v Canada*, ICSID Case No UNCT/07/1, Award, 31 March 2010, para 213. See also *Bilcon of Delaware et al v Government of Canada*, PCA Case No 2009-04, Award on Jurisdiction and Liability, 17 March 2015, paras 433–44.

[158] *Teinver v Argentina* (n 128).

[159] ibid, para 923.

[160] ibid, para 925.

measure'.[161] The *AES* tribunal also relied on its findings with regard to the non-impairment clause to conclude that there was nothing 'so irrational or otherwise unreasonable' as would constitute a breach of the FET standard.[162] Interestingly, in order to determine whether a State's act is unreasonable, the *AES* tribunal seems to put forward a more demanding two-step test involving a determination of the existence of a rational policy and the reasonableness of the act of the State in relation to the policy.[163] The tribunal noted as follows:

> A rational policy is taken by a state following a logical (good sense) explanation and with the aim of addressing a public interest matter. [. . .] A challenged measure must also be reasonable. That is, there needs to be an appropriate correlation between the state's public policy objective and the measure adopted to achieve it. This has to do with the nature of the measure and the way it is implemented.[164]

With regard to the first part of the test, Hungary had advanced three main concerns underlying the Parliamentary act and implementing decrees: these concerns were related to (a) the generators' failure to negotiate a price reduction; (b) compatibility with EU state aid law; and (c) excessive profit levels enjoyed by some generators.[165] While it rejected (by majority) the first two concerns, the *AES* tribunal accepted the third one as 'a perfectly valid and rational policy objective'.[166] Interestingly, having noted that the level of generators' returns had become a public issue and something of a political lighting rod in the face of upcoming elections, the tribunal stated that 'the fact that an issue becomes a political matter [. . .] does not mean that the existence of a rational policy is erased'.[167]

With regard to the second part of the test (the existence of a reasonable correlation between the state's policy objective and the measure adopted to achieve it), the tribunal found that the measures were 'reasonable, proportionate and consistent' with the relevant public policy, as the Hungarian Parliament considered the reintroduction of administrative pricing to be 'the best option at the moment'.[168] The tribunal also reviewed whether the generators were still going to receive a 'reasonable return' and it concluded that the prices fixed for the investor pursuant to

[161] *AES Summit Generation Limited and AES-Tisza Erömü Kft v The Republic of Hungary*, ICSID Case No ARB/07/22, Award, 23 September 2010, para 10.3.37.

[162] ibid, para 9.3.37. The *AES* tribunal would also find no violation of the requirement to protect investor's legitimate expectations, to provide stable legal framework and to comply with transparency and due process under the FET standard: ibid, paras 9.3.26, 9.3.35 and 9.3.73.

[163] ibid, para 10.3.7.

[164] ibid, para 10.3.8.

[165] ibid, para 10.2.3.

[166] ibid, para 10.3.34.

[167] ibid, paras 10.3.21–22.

[168] ibid, paras 10.3.35–36. The tribunal relied on its conclusions in the context of the non-impairment clause to conclude that the measures under review did not violate the fair and equitable treatment standard: ibid, para 9.3.37.

the legislation and decrees were indeed reasonable, taking into account their consistency with the original returns the investor earned at the time of the original investment.[169]

The *AES* two-step approach was also followed by the *Micula* tribunal in order to determine whether the measure under review (Romania's repeal of certain incentives) was 'substantively improper' because it was 'arbitrary, unreasonable, discriminatory or in bad faith'.[170] Having specifically referred to the two-step test adopted in *AES*, the *Micula* tribunal appears to emphasize the more demanding nature of that test compared to that adopted for example in *ELSI* or *Lauder*. The *Micula* tribunal noted as follows:

> In other words, for a state's conduct to be reasonable, it is not sufficient that it be related to a rational policy; it is also necessary that, in the implementation of that policy, the state's acts have been appropriately tailored to the pursuit of that rational policy with due regard for the consequences imposed on investors.[171]

(c) Arbitrariness and investment tribunals' ambivalent approach

In addition to distinguishing between the more and less deferential approaches adopted by investment tribunals with regard to the definition of arbitrary conduct, it is worth emphasizing a certain amount of ambivalence about the notion of arbitrariness, which characterizes certain arbitral decisions. And this ambivalence goes in both directions.

First of all, despite referring to broader, more intrusive definitions of what constitutes arbitrary (or unjustified or unreasonable) conduct noted above in section C.2, some tribunals do not seem to actually carry out a more stringent review of the specific measure at issue. For example, despite the apparent suggestion of a cost–benefit analysis, the *LG&E* tribunal rejected the investor's claim of arbitrary conduct on what appears to be a narrower (ie more lenient) test. The *LG&E* tribunal stated as follows:

> Even though the measures adopted by Argentina may not have been the best, they were not taken lightly, without due consideration. This is particularly reflected in the PPI adjustments which, before deciding on their postponement, Argentina

[169] ibid, paras 10.3.37 and 10.3.44.

[170] *Ioan Micula, Viorel Micula, SC European Food SA, SC Starmill SRL and SC Multipack SRL v Romania*, ICSID Case No ARB/05/20, Award, 11 December 2013, para 520. The tribunal had decided to use the distinction introduced by the respondent between (a) conduct that is substantively improper; (b) conduct that violates the investor's legitimate expectations; and (c) conduct that is procedurally improper. While the tribunal's analysis mainly focused on the FET standard, the tribunal did not seem to exclude (at least partial) overlap between FET and the prohibition of unreasonable impairment in the Sweden–Romania BIT (both found in Article 2(3)). See ibid, para 728 ('When discussing unreasonableness in the context of fair and equitable treatment, the Tribunal will thus refer to the arguments made by the Claimants on that issue in the context of the impairment clause').

[171] ibid, para 525.

> negotiated with the investors. The Tribunal concludes that the charges imposed by Argentina to Claimants' investment, though unfair and inequitable, were the result of reasoned judgment rather than simple disregard of the rule of law.[172]

At times, however, the reverse may be true, where a tribunal seems at first to adopt a narrow, more deferential, definition of 'arbitrary' only to then apply a broader, more stringent, review of the specific measure. For example, in its analysis of the non-impairment clause in the United States–Ecuador BIT, the *Occidental v Ecuador I* tribunal initially referred to the narrow, dictionary definition given by the *Lauder* tribunal whereby arbitrary means 'depending on individual discretion; [...] founded on prejudice or preference rather than on reason or fact'. However, while the tribunal believed that the conduct of the Ecuadorian tax authorities at issue was not found on prejudice or preference, it nonetheless found a violation of the non-impairment clause because the confusion and lack of clarity attributable to the Ecuadorian tax authority with regard to the question of VAT 'resulted in some form of arbitrariness, even if not intended'.[173]

Similarly, having adopted the narrow definition given by the ICJ in the *ELSI* case ('wilful disregard of due process of law, an act which shocks, or at least surprises, a sense of juridical propriety'), the *Philip Morris v Uruguay* tribunal appears to subject (at least one of) Uruguay's measures aimed at curbing smoking and protecting public health to a more demanding review, including, possibly, proportionality balancing. In its lengthy analysis of the single presentation requirement (SPR), for example, a majority of the *Philip Morris* tribunal rejected the investor's claim as it believed that the SPR:

> was an attempt to address a real public health concern, that the measure taken was not disproportionate to that concern and that it was adopted in good faith. [...] [i]n short, the SPR was a reasonable measure, not an arbitrary, grossly unfair, unjust, discriminatory, or a disproportionate measure, and this is especially so considering its relatively minor impact on [the investment].[174]

[172] *LG&E v Argentina* (n 156), para 162. The tribunal had already found that Argentina's abrogation of certain specific guarantees given to the investor had violated the stability and predictability underlying the standard of fair and equitable treatment: ibid, para 133.

[173] *Occidental Exploration and Production Company v The Republic of Ecuador* (*Occidental v Ecuador I*), LCIA Case No. UN3467, Final Award, 1 July 2004, para 163.

[174] *Philip Morris Brans Sàrl, Philip Morris Products SA and Abal Hermanos SA v Oriental Republic of Uruguay*, ICSIC Case No ARB/10/7, Award, 8 July 2016, para 409–10. See also the decision in *UAB v Latvia*, where the tribunal first defines 'arbitrary' based exclusively on the narrow *Lauder* and *ELSI* language, but then appears to subject at least some of the various measures at issue to a broader (ie more stringent) review, including whether the measures 'bear any reasonable relationship to some rational policy' and whether 'other actions by the Municipality would have been more reasonable or appropriate under the circumstances': *UAB E energija (Lithuania) v Latvia*, Award, 22 December 2017 (n 126), paras 841, 911 and 961.

By linking the conclusion that the measure was not disproportionate to the measure's impact on the investment, the majority seems to rely on some form of proportionality balancing.[175]

However, the *Philip Morris* tribunal's stance regarding what constitutes arbitrary conduct in violation of the FET standard remains somewhat unclear, as the tribunal seems to take a more lenient approach in its review of the second measure at issue, the 80% limit. The tribunal notes, first, that the present dispute concerns a legislative policy decision taken against the background of a strong scientific consensus as to the lethal effects of tobacco. It then recognizes that substantial deference is due to national authorities' decisions as to the measures that should be taken to address an acknowledged and major public health problem. Finally, the tribunal identifies as the relevant question whether the 80% limit was entirely lacking in justification or wholly disproportionate, due account being taken of the legitimate underlying aim.[176]

Another example of a somewhat ambivalent approach with regard to the notion of arbitrary/unreasonable is the recent decision in *Antaris v Czech Republic.* At issue in that dispute was the Solar Levy, a tax designed to reduce excessive profits in the photovoltaic sector and to shelter consumers from excessive electricity price rises. The *Antaris* tribunal rejected the investor's arbitrary impairment claim, apparently adopting a deferential approach. The tribunal found that the tax measure under review 'was specifically targeted at those solar installations that received a [feed-in-tariff] FiT which was excessive' and it expressly agreed with the respondent's argument that 'for purposes of the reasonableness analysis, it does not matter whether a tribunal believes that a particular course of action is "good" or "bad," that a different solution might have been "better," or that a State could have done "more," or that other States took different measures'.[177] However,

[175] See also eg *Bilcon of Delaware v Canada* (n 157), where, while the tribunal emphasized the 'high threshold' of the minimum standard of treatment under Article 1105 NAFTA, a majority, nonetheless, found that the host State's environmental impact assessment of the investor's project for a quarry and marine terminal violated Article 1105 as it was, inter alia, 'arbitrary' because it apparently had been carried out in violation of domestic law. The majority of the *Bilcon* tribunal found that Canada's joint review panel (JRP) 'effectively created, without legal authority or fair notice to Bilcon, a new standard of assessment rather than fully carrying out the mandate defined by the applicable law' (ibid, para 591). On the other hand, the dissenting arbitrator noted how 'a potential breach of Canadian law does not meet the high threshold of the *Waste Management* standard': *Bilcon of Delaware et al v Government of Canada*, PCA Case No 2009-04, Dissenting Opinion, 10 March 2015, para 36.

[176] *Philip Morris v Uruguay*, Award, 8 July 2016 (n 174) paras 418–19. See further Tania Voon, '*Philip Morris v Uruguay*: Implications for Public Health' (2017) 18 JWIT 320, 330 ('This dispute epitomises the uncertainty and debate surrounding the scope and content of the FET obligation').

[177] *Antaris Solar GmbH and Dr Michael Göde v Czech Republic*, PCA Case No 2014-01, Award, 2 May 2018, paras 443–44:

> The Tribunal accepts that the Respondent had the rational objective of reducing excessive profits and sheltering consumers from excessive electricity price rises, and that its actions were not arbitrary or irrational. There was an appropriate correlation between the Respondent's objectives and the measures it took. There is nothing irrational or unreasonable about the imposition of a charge to regulate what the Respondent reasonably regarded as windfall profits and to reduce the impact on consumers [. . .].

and perhaps to address an argument advanced by the claimants,[178] the *Antaris* tribunal also added a finding that the measures under review were 'proportionate', and based that finding on the extent of the reduction in profits that the measures had on the claimants' investment.[179]

3. The protection of legitimate expectations

If there is no doubt that the FET standard represents today the most important substantive protection guaranteed by investment treaties, there is equally no doubt that the concept of legitimate expectations represents the cornerstone of that protection.

While the concept of legitimate expectations may be found in many legal systems (including England, Germany, India, Canada, Australia, the European Union), its precise legal content varies according to the specific legal system at issue. For example, many of the domestic legal systems that do recognize and protect legitimate expectations do so only with regard to the more 'procedural' variety of the concept of legitimate expectations (ie an expectation to be consulted or to a fair hearing).[180] This is the case, for example, in Australia, Canada and India.[181] And this was traditionally also the case in English law,[182] at least until the Court of Appeal in *Coughlan* expanded the concept to include 'substantive' legitimate expectation (ie the expectation of a substantive benefit or advantage).[183] This broader approach is followed in German law and in European Union (EU) law.[184]

[178] The claimants had argued that the Czech Republic's measures under review were not 'reasonable' in the pursuit of a rational policy 'because the adverse impact on the Claimants' investment did not outweigh the policy's benefits': ibid, para 306. Interestingly, claimants highlighted the various tests under the proportionality principle (in particular, rationality and proportionality balancing) as follows (ibid, para 312): 'proportionality is required not only between the policy objectives and the measures, but also between the benefits to the host State and the impact on investors'.

[179] ibid, para 445. As the actual numbers relating to the drop in profits are redacted, one can only assume that such reduction was not, in the view of the tribunal, 'disproportionate'.

[180] Aniruddha Rajput and Sarthak Malhotra, 'Legitimate Expectations in Investment Arbitration: A Comparative Perspective' in Mahendra Pal Singh and Niraj Kumar (eds) *The Indian Yearbook of Comparative Law 2018* (Springer 2019) ch 13.

[181] Woolf et al, *Judicial Review* (n 6) 699–702; Chintan Chandrachud, 'The (Fictitious) Doctrine of Substantive Legitimate Expectations in India' in Matthew Groves and Greg Weeks (eds) *Legitimate Expectations in the Common Law World* (Hart 2017) ch 11.

[182] The concept of procedural legitimate expectations includes (a) the expectation that a substantive benefit (enjoyed in the past or promised for the future) will continue until the applicant was otherwise notified and afforded an opportunity to comment; and (b) the expectation (based on an assurance from the public authority) that an opportunity to comment would be given before a benefit is withdrawn. See Woolf et al, *Judicial Review* (n 6) 664 citing *Council of Civil Service Unions v Minister for the Civil Service* [1985] AC 374, at 408–9.

[183] Mark Elliott, 'From Heresy to Orthodoxy: Substantive Legitimate Expectations in the United Kingdom' in Matthew Groves and Greg Weeks (eds) *Legitimate Expectations in the Common Law World* (Hart 2017) ch 10.

[184] Schønberg, *Legitimate Expectations* (n 12); Craig, *EU Administrative Law* (n 12) ch 18.

Notwithstanding the differences and evolving nature of the doctrine of legitimate expectations, one common feature that characterizes such doctrine is the relevance of the public interest in determining whether an allegedly legitimate expectation deserves legal protection.[185] Under EU law, it is undisputed that 'even if the applicant is able to prove a prima facie legitimate expectation, this may be defeated if there is an overriding public interest that trumps the expectation'.[186] In English law, it is equally undisputed that 'once established, determining whether a legitimate expectation can lawfully be frustrated depends on whether, in all the circumstances, the public interest is sufficient to override the interest in keeping the promise'.[187]

However, what is disputed, or at least remains unclear, is the standard by which the courts scrutinize the public authority's decision to disappoint a (prima facie) legitimate (or reasonable) expectation. For example, is it a review based on the more deferential 'rationality' test (in English law, the *Wednesbury* unreasonableness test) or is it a review based on the more intrusive 'proportionality balancing' test?[188] According to commentators, the appropriate standard of review may actually be a flexible one, as what really matter is the appropriate intensity of review.[189] In English law, for example, there appears to be a 'sliding scale of review, more or less intrusive according to the nature and gravity of what is at stake'.[190] As succinctly noted by Vanderman, some of the principles stemming from the English case law with regard to the application of the standard of review to determine whether a legitimate expectation should be protected include the following: (a) the more the challenged decision lies in the macro-political or macro-economic field, the less intrusive the court's supervision will be (and the less likely the applicant's expectations will be protected); (b) the more the promise is 'pressing and focussed', the more likely it will be upheld (ie in practice, the number of beneficiaries of such a promise is likely to be small); (c) the method by which the decision is implemented

[185] In English law, in order to create a legitimate expectation, there must exist a clear and unambiguous promise devoid of relevant qualification, to be determined by a fair reading of the promise as reasonably understood by those to whom it was made. Interestingly, the case law shows that most cases will fall at this hurdle: Yaaser Vanderman, 'Substantive Legitimate Expectations' (2016) 21 Jud Rev 174.

[186] Craig, *EU Administrative Law* (n 12) 584.

[187] Vanderman, 'Substantive Legitimate Expectations' (n 185) 174; See also Elliott, 'From Heresy to Orthodoxy' (n 183).

[188] With regard to English law, see Woolf et al, *Judicial Review* (n 6) 685. With regard to EU law, see Craig, *EU Administrative Law* (n 12) 584–6. According to Schønberg, the test in EU law is one of 'significant imbalance': EU courts will not allow a policy change to frustrate an applicant's legitimate expectation 'if there is a *significant imbalance* between the interests of those affected and the policy consideration in favour of the change': Schønberg, *Legitimate Expectations* (n 12) 150 [italics in the original].

[189] Elliott, 'From Heresy to Orthodoxy' (n 183) 10 ('the difficult question invited by substantive legitimate expectation cases is not the somewhat formalistic one concerning whether a "proportionality" or "balancing" or "reasonableness" test should apply. Rather, the essential question concerns the appropriate intensity of review').

[190] Woolf et al, *Judicial Review* (n 6) 687, citing *R v Secretary of State for Education and Employment ex p Begbie* [2001] 1 WLR 1115, para 78.

(ie whether notice periods or transitional arrangements were put in place to cushion the impact on recipients of the promise) is relevant to the question of proportionality and fairness; (d) the burden of evidencing the countervailing public interest is on the public authority.[191]

The key argument put forward in this section is as follows: while the application of the concept of legitimate expectations in investment treaty arbitration is, to be polite, still very much a work in progress, many investment tribunals have, in line with the key feature of a reasonableness-based standard, at least recognized a role for the host State's right to regulate in the public interest in the application of the doctrine of legitimate expectations as part of FET.

(a) Balancing investors' legitimate expectations and host States' right to regulate: sketching two approaches followed by investment tribunals

In Chapter I, it was argued that, despite a handful of early decisions that appeared to read the FET provision to include an obligation of regulatory stability in the strict sense (whether as a distinct requirement of FET or as stemming from the protection of investors' expectations), a large subsequent arbitral practice has denied such interpretation and instead highlighted the relevance of the host State's right to regulate in the public interest.[192] However, as described in part in Chapter I, the way in which arbitral tribunals have actually integrated, in the context of the FET standard, the host State's right to regulate, on the one hand, and the investors' legitimate expectations, on the other hand, is still very much unclear (or at least inconsistent). Arbitral practice seems to follow two approaches in carrying out such integration.

First, several tribunals seem to integrate the host State's right to regulate in the determination of whether investors' expectations are indeed 'legitimate' and 'reasonable'. For example, the *El Paso v Argentina* tribunal emphasized that not all investor's (subjective) expectations can be considered legitimate and reasonable as 'the notion of "legitimate expectations" is an objective concept, that it is the result of a balancing of interests and rights, and that it varies according to the context'.[193] In that case, the claimant had argued that the respondent's modification of the regulatory framework applicable to its investment had frustrated the claimant's legitimate expectations. However, the *El Paso* tribunal rejected the claimant's argument, as it believed that 'the legitimate expectations of a foreign investor can only be examined by having due regard to the general proposition that the State should not unreasonably modify the legal framework or modify it in contradiction with a specific commitment not to do so'.[194] In other words, in

[191] Vanderman, 'Substantive Legitimate Expectations' (n 185) 174. See also Woolf et al, *Judicial Review* (n 6) 687.

[192] See Chapter I above.

[193] *El Paso v Argentina*, Award, 31 October 2011 (n 95), paras 355–56.

[194] ibid, para 364.

the absence of specific commitments, the expectation that 'reasonable' regulatory changes will not occur (eg to address an intervening crisis) is not a 'legitimate' expectation.[195]

This first approach often leads investment treaty tribunals to affirm that, while an investor cannot have a legitimate expectation that existing rules will not be modified (at least in the absence of a specific commitment), the investor has 'a legitimate expectation that, when modifying the existing regulation based on which the investment was made, the State will not act unreasonably, disproportionately or contrary to the public interest'.[196] It is submitted that this is not the most orthodox way to employ the concept of legitimate expectations. Confronted by such an argument, some tribunals have correctly highlighted the 'circularity' of such reasoning. In finding that some of the expectations articulated by the claimant were not 'legitimate expectations' protected under the FET standard, the tribunal in *Crystallex v Venezuela* explained as follows:

> to state that one has a legitimate expectation under the FET to be treated reasonably or proportionally (as the Claimant does [...]) is tantamount

[195] The *El Paso* tribunal concluded, for example, that 'the legitimate expectations of any investor entering the oil and gas market had to include the real possibility of reasonable changes and amendments in the legal framework, made by the competent authorities within the limits of the powers conferred on them by the law': ibid, para 400.

[196] *Charanne and Construction Investments v Spain*, SCC Case No V/063/2012, Final Award, 21 January 2016, paras 499 and 514. This is not the only way, of course. Some tribunals have concluded that investors do enjoy the 'legitimate expectation' that the host State exercises its right to regulate on the basis of the 'original' legal framework. See eg *Suez Sociedad General de Aguas de Barcelona SA and InterAguas Servicios Integrales del Agua SA v The Argentine Republic*, ICSID Case No ARB/03/17, Decision on Liability, 30 July 2010, paras 237–38:

> There is no question that under the legal framework Argentina had the right to regulate the activities of the Concession concerning a broad range of matters, including the tariff structure, investment standards, and performance. But AASA and the Claimants, as participants in any regulated industry, had the legitimate expectation that the Argentine authorities would exercise that regulatory authority and discretion within the rules of the detailed legal framework that Argentina had established for the Concession. But when faced with the crisis, Argentina refused to do this. It still refused once the crisis had abated. Indeed, it enacted various measures directing the regulatory authorities not to respect important elements of the legal framework. Such actions were outside the scope of its legitimate right to regulate and in effect constituted an abuse of regulatory discretion. For the foregoing reasons, this Tribunal finds that Argentina's persistent and rigid refusal to revise the tariff in accordance with the Concession Contract and the regulatory framework, particularly once the crisis had abated and economic growth returned, violated its commitments under the three BITs to treat the Claimants' investments fairly and equitably.

See Teinver SA, *Transportes de Cercanías SA and Autobuses Urbanos del Sur SA v The Argentine Republic* (*Teinver v Argentina*), ICSID Case No ARB/09/1, Award, 21 July 2017, paras 678–79:

> the Tribunal finds that Claimants have not demonstrated on an objective basis any legitimate expectations in respect of the regulatory regime [...]. This does not, however, exclude the expectation that the conduct of Respondent subsequent to Claimants' investment would be fair and equitable. In this regard, the Tribunal accepts that Claimants could expect that Respondent would comply with its laws and regulations and act transparently, grant due process and refrain from taking arbitrary or discriminatory measures or exercising coercion.

> to saying that one has a legitimate expectation to be treated 'fairly and equitably.'[197]

In other words, one could argue that, notwithstanding any reference to the doctrine of legitimate expectations, a reasonableness review would nonetheless be applicable under the FET standard based on the prohibition of arbitrary, unreasonable or disproportionate conduct.[198]

A second approach, which appears to be more in line with the orthodox understanding of legitimate expectations in domestic law, is the one followed by the tribunal in *Saluka v Czech Republic*. There the tribunal, chaired by the late Sir Arthur Watts, appears to distinguish between a determination of whether a legitimate and reasonable expectation exists, on the one hand, and whether the frustration of such expectation is justified (the latter inquiry akin to, for example, the so-called 'public interest defence' in EU law). This view is based, first of all, on the *Saluka* tribunal's identifying the correct terms of the required balancing exercise as follows:

> the determination of a breach of [the FET provision] requires a weighing of the Claimant's legitimate and reasonable expectations on the one hand and the Respondent's legitimate regulatory interests on the other.[199]

[197] *Crystallex International Corporation v Venezuela*, ICSID Case No ARB(AF)/11/2, Award, 4 April 2016, paras 550–51. See also *MTD Equity Sdn Bhd and MTD Chile SA v Republic of Chile*, ICSID Case No ARB/01/7, Decision on Annulment, 21 March 2007, para 67.

[198] See eg *Charanne v Spain*, Final Award, 21 January 2016 (n 196), paras 512–17 and *El Paso v Argentina*, Award, 31 October 2011 (n 95), paras 371–73. However, as analysed in Chapter I, many other decisions remain ambivalent (even if they often cite in support the *Charanne* and *El Paso* decisions) with regard to whether the tribunal's focus is on the measure's reasonableness or on the measure's modification of the applicable regulatory framework. See recently *Antin Infrastructure Services Luxembourg Sàrl and Antin Energia Termosolar BV v Kingdom of Spain*, ICSID Case No ARB/13/31, Award, 15 June 2018, paras 555–57.

[199] *Saluka v Czech Republic*, Partial Award, 17 March 2006 (n 111) para 306. See also *InterAgua v Argentina*, Decision on Liability, 30 July 2010 (n 196), para 216 ('Thus in interpreting the meaning of "just" or "fair and equitable treatment" to be accorded to investors, the Tribunal must balance the legitimate and reasonable expectations of the Claimants with Argentina's and particularly the Province's right to regulate the provision of a vital public service'); *Perenco Ecuador Ltd v The Republic of Ecuador and Empresa Estatal Petróleos del Ecuador (Petroecuador)*, ICSID Case No ARB/08/6, Decision on Remaining Issues of Jurisdiction and Liability, 12 September 2014, para 560:

> Many cases hold that a central aspect of the analysis of an alleged breach of the fair and equitable treatment standard is the investor's reasonable expectations as to the future treatment of its investment by the host State. [...] The search is for a balanced approach between the investor's reasonable expectations and the exercise of the host State's regulatory and other powers.

For an example of a different kind of balancing see *El Paso v Argentina* (n 95), para 358 ('a balance should be established between the legitimate expectation of the foreign investor to make a fair return on its investment and the right of the host State to regulate its economy in the public interest').

Second, and more fundamentally, in applying the standard, the *Saluka* tribunal clearly distinguishes between (the existence of) legitimate expectations and whether the frustration of such expectations is justified (ie reasonable). The *Saluka* tribunal identifies its two-prong task as follows:

> The Tribunal will assess the legitimacy and reasonableness of these expectations and, if they were legitimate and reasonable, whether they have been frustrated by the Czech Republic without reasonable justification.[200]

It must be admitted that not many investment treaty tribunals appear to have followed the more orthodox approach,[201] and there is, moreover, a lot of uncertainty even with those decisions that appear to have followed such an approach. The uncertainty often lies in the way the tribunal relates the investor's legitimate expectations and the host State's right to adopt reasonable, non-arbitrary, proportionate measures in order to achieve a legitimate policy goal.

For example, the tribunal in *Crystallex v Venezuela* seems at first to distinguish between the investor's FET claim based on 'legitimate expectations' and the investor's FET claim based on 'arbitrariness, lack of transparency and consistency'.[202] However, having concluded that the host State had created at least a legitimate expectation in the investor (that the permit procedure with regard to the exploitation of gold relating to the entire project would go ahead), the *Crystallex* tribunal appears to base its finding that the host State had indeed frustrated such legitimate expectations on the determination that the host State had *unlawfully* (ie arbitrarily) denied the permit.[203] In other words, what the tribunal appears to say is that the host State violated the FET standard because its frustration of the investor's legitimate expectations was not justified (ie as the relevant conduct was arbitrary).[204]

[200] *Saluka v Czech Republic* (n 111) paras 348 and 350.

[201] *CEF Energia BV v Italy*, SCC Arbitration V (2015/158), Award, 16 January 2019, para 236; *Greentech Energy Systems et al v Italy*, SCC Case No. V 2015/095, Final Award, 23 December 2018, para 454; *Ioan Micula, Viorel Micula, S European Food SA, S Starmill SRL and SC Multipack SRL v Romania*, ICSID Case No ARB/05/20, Final Award, 11 December 2013, para 529; *Joseph Charles Lemire v Ukraine*, ICSID Case No ARB/06/18, Decision on Jurisdiction and Liability, 10 January 2010, paras 273, 284–85:

> the object and purpose of the Treaty is not to protect foreign investments per se, but as an aid to the development of the domestic economy. And local development requires that the preferential treatment of foreigners be balanced against the legitimate right of Ukraine to pass legislation and adopt measures for the protection of what as a sovereign it perceives to be its public interest.

See Gebhard Bücheler, *Proportionality in Investor-State Arbitration* (OUP 2015) 200–1.

[202] See *Crystallex v Venezuela*, Award, 4 April 2016 (n 197), paras 546–75 and 576–614, respectively.

[203] ibid, para 575.

[204] An alternative reading may more simply be that the tribunal took a holistic approach of the various strands of the investor's FET claim: ibid, para 545('while resort to the elements of which FET is composed may be a useful tool to assess the facts in concrete cases, including this one, it is the overall evaluation of the state's conduct as "fair and equitable" that is the ultimate object of the Tribunal's examination').

On the other hand, the tribunal in *Micula v Romania* first appears to highlight the orthodox balancing exercise between the protection of the investor's legitimate expectations and the substantively and procedurally lawfulness of the host State's conduct.[205] However, having determined that Romania had violated the claimants' legitimate expectations with respect to the availability of the relevant incentives,[206] the majority of the *Micula* tribunal seems to imply that this is enough to establish a violation of the FET standard, without the need to determine whether Romania had acted reasonably in terminating the incentives regime.[207]

However, notwithstanding the existence of these two formally different approaches with regard to integrating the protection of the host State's right to regulate with the protection of the investor's legitimate expectations, the difference may often disappear in practice. Even under the unorthodox approach, the tribunal's review will often not simply be about the reasonableness or proportionality of the host State's regulatory measure generally, but will specifically focus on the reasonableness of the regulatory *change* implemented by the host State,[208] which may entail many of the same questions that characterize the so-called 'public interest defence' in the orthodox understanding of legitimate expectations (such as, for example, whether the decision frustrating the legitimate expectation had been implemented in ways that mitigate the adverse impact on the recipient of the promise).[209]

[205] *Micula v Romania*, Final Award, 11 December 2013 (n 201), para 529:

> The BIT's protection of the stability of the legal and business environment cannot be interpreted as the equivalent of a stabilization clause. In the Tribunal's view, the correct position is that the state may always change its legislation, being aware and thus taking into consideration that: (i) an investor's legitimate expectations must be protected; (ii) the state's conduct must be substantively proper (e.g., not arbitrary or discriminatory); and (iii) the state's conduct must be procedurally proper (e.g., in compliance with due process and fair administration).

[206] The test applied by the tribunal in order to determine the existence of a 'legitimate expectation' was not disputed between the parties and involved the following three conditions (ibid, para 668): 'the Claimants must establish that (a) Romania made a promise or assurance, (b) the Claimants relied on that promise or assurance as a matter of fact, and (c) such reliance (and expectation) was reasonable'.

[207] ibid, para 726 ('Although the majority of the Tribunal has found a breach of legitimate expectations, in order to provide a complete ruling on Romania's compliance with its obligation to provide fair and equitable treatment, the Tribunal will address the Parties' remaining arguments with respect to this standard'). While the respondent seems to have argued as a defence that it acted reasonably, the tribunal nonetheless states that the 'Respondent has acknowledged that the Tribunal may find a breach of the BIT if it finds that Romania promised that the incentives would remain unchanged for ten years and the Claimants reasonably relied on that expectation': Ibid, para 727.

[208] See eg *Impregilo SpA v The Republic of Argentina*, ICSID Case No ARB/07/17, Award, 21 June 2011, para 291 ('The legitimate expectations of foreign investors cannot be that the State will never modify the legal framework, especially in times of crisis, but certainly investors must be protected from unreasonable modifications of that legal framework').

[209] In *Impregilo*, the tribunal concluded that Argentina had violated the FET standard by failing to restore 'a reasonable equilibrium' between rights and obligations in the concession, which had been negatively affected by the emergency legislation adopted by Argentina to confront the economic crisis: ibid, paras 330–31.

(b) Balancing exercise and standard of review

The analysis now turns to addressing the particular balancing test applied by those investment treaty tribunals adopting the more orthodox approach in order to protect investors' legitimate expectations as part of the FET standard.[210] In other words, and to paraphrase from the relevant question under EU law,[211] what is the standard of review that investment treaty tribunals have applied to determine whether there was an overriding public interest sufficient to defeat an otherwise legitimate expectation?

Some tribunals seem to have adopted a deferential standard of review when balancing the investor's legitimate expectations with the host State's right to regulate. These tribunals appear to focus on whether the host State's conduct under review (that has frustrated the investor's legitimate expectations) was itself 'reasonable'. The *Saluka* tribunal, for example, concluded that the Czech Republic had violated the FET obligation because it had frustrated the investor's reasonable expectation that the host State would provide financial assistance in an even-handed and consistent manner so as to include, rather than exclude, the foreign investor's bank. Crucially, the tribunal found that the respondent had not offered a reasonable justification for the different treatment accorded to the foreign investor's bank.[212]

Other tribunals seem to have adopted a somewhat stricter standard of review by referring to the 'proportionality' of the host State's conduct as a relevant factor in the balancing exercise.[213] For example, the tribunal in *Blusun v Italy* stated that if it becomes necessary to modify lawfully granted subsidies (which, in the absence of a specific commitment, is in principle permitted), 'this should be done in a manner which is not disproportionate to the aim of the legislative amendment, and should

[210] For the kind of review undertaken by those tribunals following the 'unorthodox' approach to legitimate expectation, see eg *Charanne v Spain*, Award, 21 January 2016 (n 198), where the tribunal was confronted with certain regulatory changes introduced by Spain in 2010 in the photovoltaic industry, including (a) the elimination of regulated tariffs from the 28th year; (b) the requirement of additional technical requirements; and (c) limits on the operating hours. Having determined that there was no specific commitment by Spain vis-à-vis the investor with regard to the stability of the applicable legal framework and that the legal order in force at the time of the investment could not in itself generate legitimate expectations, the *Charenne* tribunal accepted that an 'investor has a legitimate expectation that, when modifying the existing regulation based on which the investment was made, the State will not act unreasonably, disproportionately or contrary to the public interest': ibid, para 514. With regard to 'proportionality', the tribunal focuses its review on whether the regulatory changes at issue 'are not capricious or unnecessary and do not amount to suddenly and unpredictably eliminate the essential characteristics of the existing regulatory framework': ibid, para 517. Pointing to the 'limited amendments to the regulatory framework' and the 'economic rationality' of the changes introduced by Spain, the *Charanne* tribunal ultimately found that the investor have not demonstrated that the 2010 norms under review would violate the legitimate expectations under the Energy Charter Treaty by being unreasonable, arbitrary, contrary to public interest or disproportionate, unfair or inconsistent: ibid, paras 534 and 539.

[211] Craig, *EU Administrative Law* (n 12) 584–5.

[212] *Saluka v Czech Republic*, Partial Award, 17 March 2006 (n 111) para 498.

[213] *Lemire v Ukraine*, Decision on Jurisdiction and Liability, 10 January 2010 (n 201), paras 284–85.

have due regard to the reasonable reliance interests of recipients who may have committed substantial resources on the basis of the earlier regime'.[214] However, in finding that the host State's measures under review were not disproportionate, the *Blusun* tribunal appears to have set a high bar for a finding of lack of proportionality. With regard to, for example, one of the measures under review (the *Romani* decree), the tribunal highlighted that there were 'genuine fiscal need' and 'valid rural planning concerns' and that the reduction in incentives, while substantial, was not in itself crippling or disabling, and it was 'proportionately less than the reduction in the cost of photovoltaic technology during 2010'.[215]

The tribunal in *CEF Energia v Italy* appears to have adopted a proportionality balancing test in determining whether a measure (aimed at reducing government incentives in the photovoltaic industry) taken by the host State in contrast with the assurances of stability relied upon by the investor is in breach of the FET provision. The tribunal refers to the relevant test as '"balancing and weighing" the expectations of the Claimant as a foreign investor protected by Article 10(1) ECT, with the right of Respondent as host State to adapt its regulatory framework to changing circumstances'.[216] While a majority of the tribunal emphasized that the host State's measure at issue was not 'unreasonable', it still found a breach of the FET provision, as it did not consider that 'the reasons adduced by the Respondent to justify the cut of the tariff granted for a 20-yaer period to the Claimant's investment [...] can prevail over the legitimate expectations of Claimant'.[217] Interestingly, the majority in *CEF Energia v Italy* emphasized some of the relevant criteria in the exercise of proportionality balancing by noting that 'the greater the level of engagement as between a sovereign and an investor [...] ultimately resulting in legitimate expectations which are clear in both scope and origin, the more rigorous the scrutiny must be of acts which, even if reasonable, cut across those legitimate expectations'.[218]

Some uncertainty with regard to the standard of review may be seen in another recent decision involving Italy's reduction of incentives in the photovoltaic

214 *Blusun SA, Jean-Pierre Lecorcier and Michael Stein v Italian Republic*, ICSID Case No ARB/14/3, Final Award, 27 December 2016, paras 319 and 372.

215 ibid, para 342. See *InterAgua v Argentina*, Decision on Liability (n 196), para 215, where the majority appears to base its finding that Argentina's emergency legislation to address the economic crisis (ie prohibiting any tariff increases) violated the FET standard on the fact that the public authorities could have implemented alternative measures (such as implementing tariff increases while at the same time applying social tariffs or subsidies to the poor), which would have had a lesser impact on the foreign investment. See Henckels, *Proportionality and Deference* (n 14) 105–6, who contrasts the majority's application of a 'necessity' or 'least-restrictive means' test with the dissenting arbitrator's application of a more deferential 'means–ends rationality' test.

216 *CEF Energia v Italia*, Award, 16 January 2019 (n 201), para 237.

217 ibid, para 241.

218 ibid, para 243. The dissenting arbitrator, on the other hand, believed that 'the weighing and balancing exercise between the expectations of Claimant in the stability of the 20-year tariff, on the one hand, and the right of Italy to change it in special circumstances in the public interest [...] should lead to the conclusion that Respondent has not thereby breached Article 10(1) ECT': ibid, para 247.

industry. In *Greentech v Italy*, the investors claimed a breach of the FET standard (in the ECT) principally[219] on the basis of the host State's frustration of the investors' legitimate expectations. These expectations were allegedly based on Italy's explicit promises and implicit assurances that the incentive tariff rates granted to its photovoltaic investment would remain the same for twenty years.[220] The respondent argued instead that the reasonableness and proportionality of the regulatory change (contained in the *Spalma-incentivi* Decree) were a defence to what would have otherwise constituted a violation of legitimate expectations.[221] Specifically, the respondent argued that (a) claimants had profited above that fair remuneration that the system was there to guarantee; (b) the changes were necessary to re-equilibrate the system and equalize it to reduce its excessive social burden; and (c) claimants were only affected to a limited extent.[222]

A majority of the *Greentech* tribunal appears initially to reject the approach being put forward by the respondent that would require the tribunal to balance the investor's legitimate expectation with the host State's right to regulate.[223] In the majority's view, by providing repeated and precise assurances that the tariffs would remain fixed for twenty years, Italy had 'effectively waived its right to reduce the value of the tariffs'.[224] However, the majority goes on and apparently envisages not one but two ways out for respondent (albeit the majority rejects both on the facts of the case). First, while it agreed with the dissenting arbitrator that Italy faced a situation of economic difficulty, the majority set a very high bar for permitting a public interest defence as it concluded that 'none of the circumstances evidenced in the case reach the level of *force majeur*'.[225] Second, the *Greentech* majority still went ahead with a balancing exercise between the host State's right to regulate and the investor's legitimate expectations and, crucially, did so on the basis of a deferential 'rationality' test by focusing on whether there was a 'reasonable and valid justification for the changes'.[226] Nonetheless, the majority of the *Greentech* tribunal

[219] The other two pillars of the claimants' FET claim were the notions of transparency and consistency, first, and good faith, second: *Greentech Energy Systems et al v Italy*, Final Award, 23 December 2018 (n 201), para 405.

[220] ibid, paras 408–15. Furthermore, claimants argued that (ibid, para 416):

> the parties to the ECT accepted limitations on their power to modify legislation governing investments, at least insofar as the legislation generated legitimate expectations of stability by giving explicit assurances of the type described above. Accordingly, […] Italy's clear assurances effectively waived any right to regulate insofar as the subsequent exercise of sovereign prerogative would defeat the expectations that investors had formed based on those assurances.

[221] ibid, paras 425–428.

[222] ibid, para 429.

[223] ibid, para 450 ('While Italy submitted that its "right to regulate" must be balanced against the need to protect investors' legitimate expectations, such arguments appear to miss the point in this context').

[224] ibid.

[225] ibid, para 451.

[226] ibid, para 454.

concluded that the respondent's alleged justifications for the *Spalma-incentive* Decree were unpersuasive,[227] and thus found a violation of the FET standard.

D. Indirect Expropriation and the 'Legitimate' Exercise of Police Powers

In chapter 2, I highlighted the growth of investment treaty decisions that have expressly recognized the relevance of the purpose of a host State measure in order to determine whether that measure constituted an indirect expropriation. According to the so-called 'police powers' doctrine, a host State measure substantially depriving the foreign investor of its investment will not constitute an indirect expropriation if that measure is the result of the legitimate exercise of the host State's right to regulate (or police powers).

The aim of this section is to analyse the ways in which tribunals have assessed the 'legitimacy' of the exercise of regulatory powers. Two arguments are advanced: first, the legitimacy review carried out by tribunals in this context amounts to a review of the reasonableness of the host State's allegedly expropriatory conduct; second, in assessing the existence of an indirect expropriation pursuant to the policy powers doctrine, investment tribunals have principally employed either a (more deferential) means–ends rationality test or a (more intrusive) proportionality balancing test.

1. Several versions of the 'police powers' doctrine

Looking at the many arbitral decisions that have recognized the relevance of the public policy purpose of the allegedly expropriatory measure in order to determine whether that measure amounted to an expropriation, one can easily identify several (slightly) different versions of the so-called 'police powers' doctrine. Three early decisions, often cited in investment arbitral practice, offer good examples. In 2003, the tribunal in *Tecmed v Mexico* affirmed that, in order to establish 'a measure equivalent to an expropriation' it must be first determined whether the claimant 'was radically deprived of the economical use and enjoyment of its investments' and second, whether the host State's actions 'are proportional to the public interest

[227] ibid:

> The primary justification Italy has offered for reducing the tariffs refers to the electricity costs to consumers, including households. However, the decree expressly stated that it was 'intended to reduce electricity rates for customers of medium voltage and low voltage electricity with more than 16.5 kW power available, other than residential customers and public lighting.' Further, Claimants pointed to data showing that electricity costs to consumers have decreased approximately 2–4% as a result of the *Spalma-incentivi* Decree.

presumably protected thereby'.[228] In 2005, the tribunal in *Methanex v USA* stated that 'as a matter of general international law, a non-discriminatory regulation for a public purpose, which is enacted in accordance with due process and, which affects, inter alios, a foreign investor or investment is not deemed expropriatory and compensable unless specific commitments had been given by the regulating government […]'.[229] And in 2006, the tribunal in *Saluka v Czech Republic* excluded host States' duty to pay compensation to the foreign investor 'when, in the normal exercise of their regulatory powers, they adopt in a non-discriminatory manner bona fide regulations that are aimed at the general welfare'.[230]

Based on these statements, scholars have correctly highlighted the different 'structure of inquiry'[231] as well as the different elements of the relevant 'police powers' test, including 'non-discrimination', 'good faith', 'proportionality' and 'specific commitments'.[232]

2. Means–ends rationality (or *bona fide* regulation for a public purpose)

One common approach in determining the existence of an indirect expropriation according to the police powers doctrine is to determine whether the allegedly expropriatory measure is rationally related to a public policy objective. This is a relatively deferential test as it focuses on identifying a minimal connection between the measure under review and its alleged underlying public policy objective.

(a) Host State's measure is a *bona fide* measure

One scenario where this test has found application is in cases when the claimant has alleged that the measure under review had an ulterior (hidden) motive. For example, in *Methanex v USA*, the investor had alleged corruption and protectionist intent behind California's regulation that had banned the sale and use of the gasoline additive, MTBE, on environmental protection (and public health) grounds. Methanex, a leading maker of methanol (which is the key chemical component of

228 *Tecmed v Mexico*, Award, 29 May 2003 (n 82), paras 115 and 122.

229 *Methanex v United States*, Final Award, 3 August 2005, part IV, chapter D, para 7.

230 *Saluka v Czech Republic*, Partial Award, 17 March 2006 (n 111) para 255.

231 Jonathan Bonnitcha, *Substantive Protection under Investment Treaties* (CUP 2014) 243 referring to 'exception structure of inquiry' and 'balancing structure of inquiry'.

232 Prabhash Ranjan, 'Police Powers, Indirect Expropriation in International Investment Law, and Article 31(3)(c) of the VCLT: A Critique of *Philip Morris v Uruguay*' (2019) 9 Asian J Int'l L 98, 112–16. See recently *Marfin Investment Group v The Republic of Cyprus*, ICSID Case No ARB/13/27, Award, 26 July 2018, para 826:

> The Tribunal considers that the economic harm consequent to the non-discriminatory application of generally applicable regulations adopted in order to protect the public welfare do not constitute a compensable taking, provided that the measure was taken in good faith, complied with due process and was proportionate to the aim sought to be achieved.

MTBE), complained that California's ban was the result of a political deal with a rival company that makes ethanol, a substitute for methanol and MTBE as a gasoline additive. Having identified the relevant standard ('a non-discriminatory regulation for a public purpose [...] is not deemed expropriatory'), the *Methanex* tribunal rejected the expropriation claim because the investor had failed to prove that the ban was not a *bona fide* measure. The tribunal stated as follows:

> [...] The terms of Governor Davis's Executive Order and subsequent action by the state of California are inconsistent with Methanex's contention that the California ban was designed to transfer the gasoline oxygenate market to ethanol. [...] the argument for resorting to inference as a way of reaching a conclusion inconsistent with the objective evidence is untenable. The behaviour of the California Government as a whole is inconsistent with Methanex's hypothesis. [...] the Tribunal concludes that the California ban was made for a public purpose, was non-discriminatory and was accomplished with due process. [...] From the standpoint of international law, the California ban was a lawful regulation and not an expropriation.[233]

Similarly, in *Saluka v Czech Republic*, the investor had claimed that the Czech banking regulator's forced administration of its investment, IPB (one of four large banks in the Czech Republic) had not been taken in the public interest since (a) an alternative plan proposed by IPB would have cost far less to Czech taxpayers; and (b) the Czech government's sole purpose for the exercise of its regulatory powers was the transfer of IPB's business to CSOB, one of the other four large banks.[234] Having stated that 'bona fide regulations [...] aimed at the general welfare' do not constitute expropriation for purposes of the investment treaty provision,[235] the *Saluka* tribunal reviewed the totality of the evidence which the regulator had invoked in support of its decision and concluded that the regulator 'was justified, under Czech law, in imposing the forced administration of IPB'.[236]

The *Saluka* tribunal's reasoning shows the rather deferential approach undertaken in reviewing the host State's exercise of regulatory powers, in particular emphasizing the regulator's 'margin of discretion' in the exercise of its responsibility to act and the 'reasonableness' of the regulator's decision-making process.[237]

[233] *Methanex v United States*, Final Award, 3 August 2005, part IV, chapter D (n 229), paras 12–15.
[234] *Saluka v Czech Republic*, Partial Award, 17 March 2006 (n 111) para 249.
[235] ibid, para 255.
[236] ibid, para 271.
[237] ibid, para 272:

> The Czech State, in the person of its banking regulator, the CNB, had the responsibility to take a decision on 16 June 2000. It enjoyed a margin of discretion in the exercise of that responsibility. In reaching its decision, it took into consideration facts which, in the opinion of the Tribunal, it was very reasonable for it to consider. It then applied the pertinent Czech legislation to those facts—again, in a manner that the Tribunal considers reasonable.

The *Saluka* decision highlights, furthermore, that the burden is on the claimant to prove that the allegedly expropriatory measure is an illegitimate exercise of its regulatory power. The *Saluka* tribunal concluded that, in the absence of 'clear and compelling evidence' that the regulator had erred or acted otherwise improperly in reaching its decision, the tribunal 'must [...] accept the justification given by the Czech banking regulator for its decision'.[238]

(b) Host State's measure is a legitimate exercise of its right to sanction violations of domestic law

The rationality test may be said to find application in cases where the respondent has argued that its allegedly expropriatory measure was the legitimate exercise of its sovereign right to sanction violations of the law in its territory. This was the case in *Quirobax v Bolivia*, where the investor claimed both direct and indirect expropriation following the host State's revocation by Presidential decree of several mining concessions held by the investor. The *Quirobax* tribunal asked whether the revocation decree was a legitimate cancellation of the mining concessions in the exercise of Bolivia's sovereign power to sanction violations of Bolivian law and therefore not a compensable (direct and indirect) taking.[239] Having determined that the revocation decree was grounded on (a) a systemic refusal by the investor to provide information to the national tax and customs authorities (thus preventing the audits mandated by law); and (b) discrepancies in the amount of ulexite declared and actually transported in violation of the domestic tax code,[240] the *Quirobax* tribunal then examined whether the investor had indeed committed such violations and rejected the respondent's claim as both claims were 'not supported by the facts'.[241]

(c) Host State's measure is a legitimate exercise of its rights under the investment contract

Similarly, the rationality test may also be said to have been applied by tribunals in several cases where the respondent had argued that its termination of the underlying investment contract (eg a concession) was the legitimate exercise of its rights under the concession contract.[242] This was, for example, the argument put forward by the respondent in *Gold Reserve v Venezuela* to counter the investor's claim that the termination by the host State of its two mining concessions constituted

[238] ibid, para 273. See Jorge Viñuales, 'Sovereignty in Foreign Investment Law' in Zachary Douglas, Joost Pauwelyn and Jorge Viñuales (eds) *The Foundations of International Investment Law* (OUP 2014) 344.

[239] *Quiborax SA, Non Metallic Minerals SA and Allan Fosk Kaplún v Plurinational State of Bolivia*, ICSID Case No ARB/06/2, Award, 16 September 2015, para 201.

[240] ibid, para 209.

[241] ibid, paras 210–11.

[242] It should be emphasized, however, that differently from the cases examined above, this scenario is not normally framed as an application of the 'police powers' doctrine.

(unlawful) expropriation.[243] In particular, and as determined by the tribunal, the reason relied on by the respondent to terminate the investor's concessions was the claimant's failure to commence exploitation in accordance with the provisions of the concessions and the mining law. While acknowledging that a host State's allegation of contractual breach may be a pretext designed to conceal a purely expropriatory nature, the *Gold Reserve* tribunal nonetheless limited its review to whether the reasons cited for the termination of the investor's concessions were 'sufficiently well-founded'.[244] The *Gold Reserve* tribunal concluded that, on balance, the termination of the investor's concessions could not be said to be merely 'pretextual' in light of the nature of the investor's breach. Given the importance of the provision which the investor had not complied with, the *Gold Reserve* tribunal concluded that 'the reasons given by respondent for terminating the concessions were sufficiently well founded that the terminations cannot be considered as a form of expropriation under international law'.[245]

3. Proportionality balancing

A second common approach in determining the existence of an indirect expropriation according to the police powers doctrine is to determine whether the allegedly expropriatory measure is proportional to the public interest being protected by the measure itself. This is a potentially more intrusive test as it involves balancing between the measure's adverse impact on the foreign investment and the measure's beneficial effect on whatever public policy the host State is pursuing.

(a) *Tecmed* and the sensitivity of putting different values on the proportionality scale

As a test to determine the existence of an indirect expropriation, in the context of investment treaty arbitration, proportionality balancing was first, and now famously, employed by the tribunal in *Tecmed v Mexico*.[246] Having concluded that the non-renewal of a hazardous waste facility permit (the Resolution) had a severe effect on the economic value of Tecmed's investment (Cytrar, the locally incorporated company, 99% owned by Tecmed, operating the landfill), the tribunal

[243] *Gold Reserve v Venezuela*, ICSID Case No. ARB(AF)/09/1, Award, 22 September 2014, para 648.

[244] ibid, para 666, citing *Malicorp v Egypt*, ICSID Case No. ARB/08/18, Award, 7 February 2011, para 142.

[245] *Gold Reserve v Venezuela*, Award, 22 September 2014 (n 243), para 667. See *Malicorp v Egypt*, Award, 7 February 2011 (n 244), para 143 ('It follows from the foregoing analysis that, to the Arbitral Tribunal, the reasons on which the Respondent relied in order to bring the Contract to an end appear serious and adequate; the termination, justified in fact and in law, could not be interpreted as an expropriatory measure'). *Tulip Real Estate v Turkey*, Award, 10 March 2014 (n 96), para 417 ('... the evidence offered by the Claimant falls short of establishing a violation of the BIT [Art 5(1) on expropriation], inasmuch as the termination was pursued within the framework of the Contract and in Emlak's perceived commercial best interests').

[246] *Tecmed v Mexico*, Award, 29 May 2003 (n 82).

added that, in order for the host State's conduct to be characterized as expropriation, the tribunal had to consider whether such conduct is 'proportional to the public interest presumably protected thereby'. The *Tecmed* tribunal specified that, in order for the host State's conduct not to be seen as a compensable expropriation, '[t]here must be a reasonable relationship of proportionality between the charge or weight imposed to the foreign investor and the aim sought to be realized by any expropriatory measure'.[247]

Following an extensive (and at times convoluted) examination of the various reasons that lead to the Resolution under review, the *Tecmed* tribunal found that the Resolution failed the proportionality test and thus the tribunal concluded that 'the Resolution and its effects amount to an expropriation in violation of the Treaty and international law'.[248]

Two key findings explain the tribunal's conclusion. First, the violations of the terms of the permit that had been committed by Cytrar were minor in nature ('either remediable or remediated or subject to minor penalties') and, crucially, these infringements never compromised the ecological balance, the protection of the environment or the health of the people.[249] Accordingly, the *Tecmed* tribunal concluded as follows:

> it would be excessively formalistic [...] to understand that the Resolution is proportional to such violations when such infringements do not pose a present or imminent risk to the ecological balance or to people's health, and the Resolution [...] leads to the neutralization of the investment's economic and business value.[250]

The second key finding revolves around the Mexican authorities' need to provide a response to the 'community pressure', principally linked to the location of the landfill (the so-called 'political circumstances'). While these political circumstances were not formally referred to in the Resolution under review, the *Tecmed* tribunal believed that these were indeed the real reasons that prevailed in the decision to deny the renewal of the permit. Accordingly, the tribunal noted that, for purposes of establishing whether Mexico had breached the treaty provision on expropriation, it is necessary 'to evaluate these reasons as a whole to determine whether the Resolution is proportional to the deprivation of rights' sustained by the investor.[251] More specifically, in assessing the proportionality of the host State's action, the *Tecmed* tribunal considered as key whether the community pressure was 'so great

247 ibid, para 122 citing several decisions of the European Court of Human Rights as authority.
248 ibid, para 151.
249 ibid, para 148.
250 ibid, para 149.
251 ibid, para 132.

as to lead to a serious emergency situation, social crisis or public unrest'. The tribunal found that this was not the case as the respondent had not presented any evidence that community opposition to the landfill, however 'intense, aggressive and sustained', was in any way 'massive'.[252]

The *Tecmed* decision clearly underscores the difference between means–ends rationality (is there a reasonable/plausible connection between the measure and its policy objective?) and proportionality balancing (is the measure's adverse impact on the investment out of proportion in light of the measure's policy objective?). And crucially, *Tecmed* shows the potentially more sensitive nature of proportionality balancing, as the tribunal had to weigh the radical deprivation of (the value of) the investment against the Mexican authorities' interest in addressing a relatively small but intense, aggressive and sustained opposition to the landfill. The sensitivity of this assessment is in placing the competing interests on a scale and effectively determining whether one takes precedence over another.

(b) Subsequent arbitral practice and various applications of proportionality balancing

The application of the proportionality test in *Tecmed* has been endorsed subsequently by several other investment treaty tribunals in order to determine whether a host State's measure can amount to indirect expropriation.[253] However, subsequent references to 'proportionality' are often made together with various other requirements. For example, having recognized that 'unreasonable general regulation can amount to indirect expropriation', the *El Paso v Argentina* tribunal defines 'unreasonable' as 'arbitrary, discriminatory, disproportionate or otherwise unfair'.[254]

Similarly, the tribunal in *Philip Morris v Uruguay* summarizes the most commonly mentioned conditions for the legitimate exercise of the State's police powers by combining 'proportionality balancing' with 'means–ends rationality' as

[252] ibid, para 144 (and para 137). The tribunal thus concluded as follows (ibid, para 147):

> The actions undertaken by the authorities to face these socio-political difficulties, where these difficulties do not have serious emergency or public hardship connotations, or wide-ranging and serious consequences, may not be considered from the standpoint of the Agreement or international law to be sufficient justification to deprive the foreign investor of its investment with no compensation, particularly if it has not been proved that Cytrar or Tecmed's behavior has been the determinant of the political pressure or the demonstrations that led to such deprivation, which underlie the Resolution and conclusively conditioned it.

[253] See eg *El Paso v Argentina*, Award, 31 October 2011 (n 95), para 243:

> Another example would be a *disproportionate regulation*, meaning a regulation in which the interference with the private rights of the investors is disproportionate to the public interest. In other words, proportionality has to exist between the public purpose fostered by the regulation and the interference with the investors' property rights, as recognised in *Tecmed*.

See also *LG&E v Argentina*, Decision on Liability, 3 October 2006 (n 156), para 195; *EDF International SA, SAUR International SA and León Participaciones Argentinas SA v Argentine Republic*, ICSID Case No ARB/03/23, Award, 8 October 2009, para 293.

[254] *El Paso v Argentina* (n 95), para 241.

follows: 'the action must be taken *bona fide* for the purpose of protecting the public welfare, must be non-discriminatory and proportionate'.[255] The *Philip Morris* tribunal summarily found that both challenged measures (requiring health warnings to comprise 80% of cigarette packaging and limiting the sale of each brand to one variant) met all these conditions.[256] First, the tribunal applied the means–ends rationality test. Having emphasized that the measures were taken by Uruguay with a view to protect public health in fulfilment of its national and international obligations, the *Philip Morris* tribunal affirmed that both measures had been adopted in good faith, and were not discriminatory, arbitrary or unnecessary. In particular, the tribunal emphasized that the two challenged measures were public health measures which were directed to the reduction of smoking and were capable of contributing to its achievement.[257]

Second, the *Philip Morris* tribunal seems to apply the proportionality test by affirming that both challenged measures 'were proportionate to the objective they meant to achieve, quite apart from their limited adverse impact on [the investor's] business'. In a footnote, the *Philip Morris* tribunal underlines the challenged measures' limited adverse impact by contrasting them with the stricter public health measures at issue in *Methanex* and *Chemtura*.[258]

Another interesting aspect of the *Philip Morris* decision is the link between determining the legitimacy of the host State's exercise of police powers (for the purposes of the expropriation claim) and the tribunal's analysis under the FET standard. The *Philip Morris* tribunal premised its above-mentioned findings by referring to the 'reasons which will be explored in detail in relation to claims under [FET]'.[259] While Philip Morris's FET claim had three prongs (arbitrariness, stability requirement and investor's legitimate expectations), it appears that the *Philip Morris* tribunal's reference is to its arbitrariness analysis, which did include a wide set of principles.[260] In that context, the tribunal emphasized, first of all, that it would review the challenged measures 'taking into account [...] the margin of appreciation enjoyed by national regulatory agencies when dealing with public policy determination'.[261] Furthermore, the *Philip Morris* tribunal focused its analysis on the scientific basis for the two challenged measures and it emphasized the strong

255 *Philip Morris v Uruguay*, Award, 8 July 2016 (n 174), para 305, quoting the *Tecmed* proportionality test in n 404.

256 It should be noted that the *Philip Morris* tribunal's decision on police powers is *obiter dictum* as the tribunal had already found that Uruguay's challenged measures did not have any 'substantial effect' on the claimant's business: ibid, para 287.

257 ibid, para 306. The tribunal also emphasized that the WHO had endorsed the conclusion that both measures were 'potentially effective means to protecting public health': ibid.

258 ibid.

259 ibid.

260 For example, with regard to the SPR measure, the *Philip Morris* tribunal found as follows (ibid, para 410): 'In short, the SPR was a reasonable measure, not an arbitrary, grossly unfair, unjust, discriminatory or a disproportionate measure.'

261 ibid, para 388.

link between Uruguay's challenged measures and the work carried out by the World Health Organization (WHO) in the Framework Convention for Tobacco Control (FCTC).[262] Finally, the tribunal did appear to make an (albeit very brief) assessment about the proportionality of the two measures under review, by concluding that neither was 'a disproportionate measure, in particular given its relatively minor impact on [investor's] business'.[263]

The tribunal in *Deutche Bank v Sri Lanka* also relied heavily on its finding with regard to FET in order to conclude that the actions by the Supreme Court and the Central Bank of Sri Lanka (ordering that no further payment be made under the Hedging Agreement between Deutche Bank and CPC, a host State-owned petroleum company) were not legitimate regulatory actions.[264] Interestingly, while the *Deutche Bank* tribunal had expressly endorsed proportionality balancing as a way to limit host States' discretion to interfere with investments in the exercise of 'legitimate regulatory authority', the tribunal appears instead to focus its analysis on means–ends rationality (as well as certain procedural shortcomings of the host State's actions). The *Deutche Bank* tribunal highlighted in particular the 'excess of powers', 'improper motive' and 'lack of good faith'.[265]

The decision in *PL Holdings v Poland* is a recent further example of a tribunal applying proportionality balancing in order to determine the existence of an (indirect) expropriation. Interestingly, the *PL Holdings* tribunal applied proportionality balancing as part of a broader, structured proportionality analysis involving an assessment of the challenged measures' 'suitability', 'necessity' and 'excessiveness'. The *PL Holdings* tribunal was called upon to determine whether certain measures ordered by KNF, Poland's banking regulator, vis-à-vis FM Bank PBP, the claimant's owned bank, represented an unlawful expropriation of claimant's investment. KNF key measures included the suspension of the claimant's voting rights in FM Bank PBP and ultimately the order to sell its shares in FM Bank PBP. Having determined that the actions taken by KNF represent an expropriation,[266] the tribunal examined whether such actions comply with the principle of proportionality. In that dispute, while the claimant fully conceded a host State's right to regulate (ie adopting measures legitimately needed for safeguard of the public good), the claimant also affirmed that under an international investment treaty, the right to regulate does not entitle States to take measures that are 'disproportionate, arbitrary or discriminatory'.[267] In particular, the claimant noted that an

[262] ibid, paras 396 and 407.

[263] ibid, paras 410 and 420. This is perhaps unsurprising as the tribunal had already concluded that the two measures' adverse impact on the foreign investment was not substantial, at all.

[264] *Deutsche Bank AG v Democratic Socialist Republic of Sri Lanka*, ICSID Case No ARB/09/2, Award, 31 October 2012, para 523.

[265] ibid, paras 522–23.

[266] *PL Holdings Sàrl v Republic of Poland*, SCC Case No V 2014/163, Partial Award, 28 June 2017, para 323.

[267] ibid, para 327: according to the claimant, 'it is for this Tribunal to determine whether the measures in question "were taken in good faith, (ii) were proportionate to the public welfare objective, (iii) were non-discriminatory, and (iv) accorded with basic due process rights"': ibid, quoting the claimant's post-hearing brief.

inquiry of proportionality entails a three-prong inquiry into the 'suitability', 'necessity' and 'proportionality *stricto sensu*' of the measure in question.[268] The *PL Holdings* tribunal accepted the claimant's argument, although it slightly reworded the three-prong test as follows:

> To satisfy the principle, a measure must (a) be one that is suitable by nature for achieving a legitimate public purpose, (b) be necessary for achieving that purpose in that no less burdensome measure would suffice, and (c) not be excessive in that its advantages are outweighed by its disadvantages.[269]

Following an extensive review of the KNF's measures according to the three-prong test, the tribunal concluded that, while the KNF acted in what it considered to be the public good, KNF's measures failed all of the proportionality prongs.[270] In terms of suitability, the tribunal noted that the KNF did not justify its decisions on the basis of the bank's illiquidity or insufficient capitalization, which, according to the tribunal, could have persuasively justified strong action by the regulator for the protection of the banking system (including an order to sell the shares of the bank). Instead, the contemporaneous justifications that had been advanced by KNF concerned changes in the bank's management board and certain irregularities in the management of the bank (including failure to inform the regulator of important personnel changes and certain potential conflicts of interest). However, as rationales for the KNF decisions, the tribunal found these 'unconvincing': the tribunal noted inter alia that (a) the claimant did not fail to keep the regulator informed; (b) the claimant and the bank took promptly all corrective action needed to address the regulator's concerns; and (c) the respondent had failed to demonstrate that the various irregularities threatened the bank's sound and prudent management.[271]

On necessity, the *PL Holdings* tribunal noted that, even if sanctions were warranted based on the irregularities alleged by the KNF, the regulator had at its disposal 'less draconian' means for achieving the legitimate and substantial public interest it considered to be at stake. The *PL Holdings* tribunal found that the respondent had not successfully refuted the various milder remedies and sanctions available that had been 'convincingly' suggested by the claimant.[272] Finally, with

[268] ibid, para 328:

> An inquiry into proportionality in particular entails an inquiry into whether the measure in question: (i) was taken in furtherance of a legitimate and substantial public interest and was a suitable one for serving the legitimate and substantial public interest invoked, (ii) was necessary, in the sense that no less drastic measure would have sufficed, (iii) was disproportionately severe for the Investor, compared to the purposes meant to be achieved (i.e., proportionality *stricto sensu*).

[269] ibid, para 355.
[270] ibid, para 391.
[271] ibid, paras 366–68.
[272] ibid, para 377.

regard to the 'excessiveness' prong,[273] the *PL Holdings* tribunal concluded, based on some of the same findings made under 'suitability' and 'necessity', that the respondent had failed to refute the claimant's contention that the regulator's measures under review were 'excessive'.[274]

(c) Proportionality balancing in the context of the host State's exercise of its rights under the investment contract

Proportionality balancing has also found application in cases where the respondent had argued that its termination of the underlying investment contract was a legitimate exercise of its rights under the contact and thus not an expropriation.[275] In *Vigotop v Hungary*, the investor had claimed that the termination by the host State of a concession contract for the creation of a premier resort consisting of a casino, luxury hotels and various attractions constituted expropriation for purposes of the 1989 Cyprus–Hungary BIT. The tribunal set out a three-stage analysis that appears very similar in substance to the kind of means–ends rationality that was applied in *Gold Reserve* in order to determine whether the termination of a concession contract constituted an expropriation.

According to the *Vigotop* tribunal, the first stage involves determining whether the respondent has a 'hidden political agenda' in terminating the concession contract in order to show that the host State acted in its 'sovereign capacity'. Having concluded that it did, the focus of the *Vigotop* tribunal's analysis moves to whether there are contractual grounds for terminating the contract (this is the second phase). In the *Vigotop* tribunal's view, 'a finding that none of the contractual grounds invoked by the respondent were sufficiently well-founded, while not being dispositive of the expropriation question in itself, could indicate that they were merely a pretext designed to conceal a purely expropriatory measure'.[276] The tribunal found that the fact that claimant had failed to establish it had the legitimate right to possession of, and right to build on, the required land by the date specified in the contract, constituted a contractual ground for terminating the concession contract.[277] In the view of the *Vigotop* tribunal, the third and final stage involves determining whether the respondent exercised its contractual termination right legitimately or whether in the circumstances, it was an abuse intended to avoid the

[273] The *PL Holdings* tribunal identified the issue as follows (ibid, para 384):

> the principle of proportionality requires that a measure taken not be excessive in relation to the purposes meant to be served. There is no question that the measures taken—the forced sale of shares in particular—were exceptionally harsh. The question, in connection with this third prong, is whether the situation facing the KNF was so dire as to justify them.

[274] ibid, para 389. As part of its expropriation analysis, the tribunal also reviewed, and eventually found lacking, the procedural propriety of KNF's conduct: ibid, paras 392–410.

[275] As noted above in section D.2 on means–ends rationality with regard to a similar situation, this scenario is not normally framed as an application of the 'police powers' doctrine.

[276] *Vigotop Limited v Hungary*, ICSID Case No ARB/11/22, Award, 1 October 2014, para 329.

[277] ibid, para 543.

liability to compensate, thus amounting to a 'fictitious' or 'malicious' exercise of its contractual rights.[278] The tribunal concluded that 'on the balance of the evidence', the claimant failed to discharge its burden of proof.

Interestingly, however, the *Vigotop* tribunal continued its analysis and considered the claimant's argument that the termination of the concession was a 'disproportionate response to what were relatively minor purported contractual breaches'.[279] The claimant had relied on the *Occidental v Ecuador II* decision that had found the termination of the investment contract disproportionate (and thus in violation of the FET provision). The tribunal rejected the claimant's proportionality argument, distinguishing in particular the present case with the *Occidental II* dispute:

> Because of the advanced stage of contract performance, the *Occidental* Tribunal was required to determine if the termination was proportional to the breach. By contrast, since contract performance in this case involved only the first, threshold step for performance, which was never consummated, no proportionality analysis can or need be performed.[280]

E. Recent Treaty Practice

When it comes to the key reasonableness-based provisions, a few developments with regard to recent treaty practice are worth emphasizing. While it is true that the non-impairment clause may have been omitted from some recent investment treaties,[281] most of the 'action' has been either with regard to the FET and FPS clauses or with the provision on expropriation.

1. FPS and FET clauses

A survey conducted by UNCTAD on investment treaties concluded between 2011 and 2016 (107) shows that approximately half of them contain a reference to the 'minimum standard of treatment under customary law' in their description of both FET

[278] ibid, para 330.

[279] ibid, para 552.

[280] ibid, para 631.

[281] See eg all investment protection treaties concluded by the EU in the past three years (with Canada, Singapore, Vietnam and Mexico). Interestingly, some of these treaties do seem to expressly merge the coverage of the traditional non-impairment clause in to the fair and equitable treatment obligation. For example, the FET provision in the EU–Singapore Investment Protection Agreement (IPA) specifies that the term 'treatment' in the FET provision should be understood as 'treatment of covered investors which directly or indirectly interferes with the covered investors' operation, management, conduct, maintenance, use, enjoyment and sale or other disposal of their covered investments'. See n 1 in Article 2.4, para 1 of the 2018 EU–Singapore IPA.

and FPS.[282] Such clarification takes inspiration from the interpretative note that the three NAFTA Contracting Parties issued in 2001 to clarify the scope of Article 1105 of NAFTA,[283] and then adopted in both the 2004 United States and Canada model BIT.

One example of such recent formulations is Article 12 of the 2011 Australia–New Zealand Investment Protocol on the Minimum Standard of Treatment states as follows:

> 1. Each Party shall accord to covered investments treatment in accordance with the customary international law minimum standard of treatment, including fair and equitable treatment and full protection and security.
> 2. The obligation in Paragraph 1 to provide:
>   (a) 'fair and equitable treatment' includes the obligation not to deny justice in criminal, civil, or administrative adjudicatory proceedings in accordance with the principle of due process;
>   (b) 'full protection and security' requires each Party to take such measures as may be reasonably necessary to ensure the physical protection and security of the covered investment.
> 3. For greater certainty, the concepts of 'fair and equitable treatment' and 'full protection and security' do not require treatment in addition to or beyond that which is required by the customary international law minimum standard, and do not create additional substantive rights.

First, this elaboration of FPS and FET confirms the reasonableness nature of these two provisions. Paragraph 2(a), for example, appears to focus on the notion of 'procedural reasonableness' by expressly referring to the denial of justice and due process. Similarly, paragraph 2(b) appears to focus on the notion of 'substantive reasonableness' by clarifying that FPS requires States to take measures 'reasonably necessary' to ensure physical protection and security. The phrase 'reasonably necessary' seems to refer to the 'necessity' test and appears to be closer to the stricter approach adopted by investment tribunals with regard to the 'due diligence' standard.[284]

[282] UNCTAD, 'Taking Stock of IIA Reform: IIA Issues Note' (March 2012) 15–19 and UNCTAD *World Investment Report* (United Nations 2017) 121.

[283] NAFTA Free Trade Commission, 'Notes of Interpretation of Certain Chapter 11 Provisions', 31 July 2001, which reads in part:

> Article 1105(1) prescribes the customary international law minimum standard of treatment of aliens as the minimum standard of treatment to be afforded to investments of investors of another Party. The concepts of 'fair and equitable treatment' and 'full protection and security' do not require treatment in addition to or beyond that which is required by the customary international law minimum standard of treatment of aliens. A determination that there has been a breach of another provision of the NAFTA, or of a separate international agreement, does not establish that there has been a breach of Article 1105(1).

[284] Article 9.6 of the 2018 Comprehensive and Progressive Agreement for Trans-Pacific Partnership (CPTPP) takes a slightly different (possibly more deferential) approach with regard to FPS, as it clarifies that FPS requires each contracting party 'to provide the level of police protection required under customary international law'.

Second, with regard to FET, while this language is likely to have the effect of narrowing its overall scope, it does not do much in terms of providing more clarity with regard to the appropriate standard of review. First of all, paragraph 2(a) of Article 12 does not provide an exhaustive list of what 'fair and equitable treatment' includes, thus leaving open the question of the meaning of the FET standard. Second, the link to customary law in both paragraphs 1 and 3 of Article 12 does not provide much in terms of added clarity, as the content of the minimum standard under international customary law remains a relatively controversial question. It may be sufficient, in this regard, to point to two decisions rendered in the context of (the very similar FET provision of) Article 1105 NAFTA: while according to the tribunal in *Glamis v United States* the customary minimum standard requires 'sufficiently egregious and shocking' conduct,[285] the *Merrill & Ring v Canada* tribunal was satisfied with the lower threshold of any act that 'might infringe a sense of fairness, equity and reasonableness'.[286]

One further, more recent, elaboration of the FET is the one found in the 2016 Comprehensive and Economic Trade Agreement (CETA) between the EU and Canada. Article 8.10 provides as follows:

> 1. Each Party shall accord in its territory to covered investments of the other Party and to investors with respect to their covered investments fair and equitable treatment and full protection and security in accordance with paragraphs 2 through 7.
> 2. A Party breaches the obligation of fair and equitable treatment referenced in paragraph 1 if a measure or series of measures constitutes:
>   (a) denial of justice in criminal, civil or administrative proceedings;
>   (b) fundamental breach of due process, including a fundamental breach of transparency, in judicial and administrative proceedings;
>   (c) manifest arbitrariness;
>   (d) targeted discrimination on manifestly wrongful grounds, such as gender, race or religious belief;
>   (e) abusive treatment of investors, such as coercion, duress and harassment; or
>   (f) a breach of any further elements of the fair and equitable treatment obligation adopted by the Parties in accordance with paragraph 3 of this Article.

While there is no express reference to customary law, Article 8.10 of CETA does provide a list of the kinds of conduct that would be in breach of the customary

[285] *Glamis Gold v United States*, Award, 8 June 2009 (n 142), para 616.

[286] *Merrill & Ring v Canada*, Award, 31 March 2010 (n 157), paras 210–13. Interestingly, the *Merrill & Ring* tribunal considered whether Canada's conduct at issue breached the protections provided by Article 1105 NAFTA under two scenarios, depending on the 'low' or 'high' threshold to be applied to establish breach: see ibid, paras 219–46.

minimum standard of treatment.[287] However, unlike the approach in the Australia–New Zealand Protocol, the list provided in Article 8.10 CETA is indeed exhaustive (although it may be modified according to the procedure envisaged in para 3 of Article 8.10).[288]

Furthermore, while the list in paragraph 2 of Article 8.10 CETA does not refer to the frustration of the investor's legitimate expectations as a breach of the FET obligation, paragraph 4 does permit a tribunal, when applying the FET obligation, to 'take into account whether a Party made a specific representation to an investor to induce a covered investment, that created a legitimate expectation, and upon which the investor relied in deciding to make or maintain the covered investment'. This appears to be in line with the way some investment tribunals have understood the customary minimum standard of treatment (particularly as referred to in Article 1105 NAFTA). For example, having identified the conduct that will infringe the minimum standard of treatment, the tribunal in *Waste Management v Mexico* famously stated that '[i]n applying this standard it is relevant that the treatment is in breach of representations made by the host State which were reasonably relied on by the claimant'.[289]

While it can easily be argued that a violation of Article 8.10 CETA cannot simply rely on a finding of frustration of the investor's legitimate expectations,[290] it is very much possible that such a latter finding will still play a relevant role in a determination under Article 8.10 CETA.[291] Crucially, however, these recent treaties leave various questions unanswered such as (a) whether or not an 'overriding public interest' exception is relevant for purposes of protecting investors' legitimate expectations; or (b) how a future tribunal link will link, for example, an allegedly manifestly arbitrary conduct with the frustration of legitimate expectations.

[287] See *Waste Management II*, Award, 30 April 2004 (n 110) para 98:

> the minimum standard of treatment of fair and equitable treatment is infringed by conduct attributable to the State and harmful to the claimant if the conduct is arbitrary, grossly unfair, unjust or idiosyncratic, is discriminatory and exposes the claimant to sectional or racial prejudice, or involves a lack of due process leading to an outcome which offends judicial propriety—as might be the case with a manifest failure of natural justice in judicial proceedings or a complete lack of transparency and candour in an administrative process.

See Newcombe and Paradell, *Standards of Treatment* (n 86) 235–53.

[288] Article 8.10.3 CETA ('The Parties shall regularly, or upon request of a Party, review the content of the obligation to provide fair and equitable treatment. The Committee on Services and Investment, established under Article 26.2.1(b) (Specialised committees), may develop recommendations in this regard and submit them to the CETA Joint Committee for decision').

[289] *Waste Management II*, Award, 30 April 2004 (n 110) para 98.

[290] Interestingly, this has now found express recognition in the 2018 EU–Singapore IPA, Article 2.4 para 3, n 2 ('For greater certainty, the frustration of legitimate expectations as described in this paragraph does not, by itself, amount to a breach of paragraph 2, and such frustration of legitimate expectations must arise out of the same events or circumstances that give rise to the breach of paragraph 2') as well as in the 2018 CPTPP, Article 9.6 para 4 ('For greater certainty, the mere fact that a Party takes or fails to take an action that may be inconsistent with an investor's expectations does not constitute a breach of this Article, even if there is loss or damage to the covered investment as a result').

[291] See *Bilcon of Delaware v Canada*, Award on Jurisdiction and Liability, 17 March 2015 (n 157) and Dissenting Opinion, 10 March 2015 (n 175).

An even narrower approach with regard to FET may be found in the 2016 India's Model BIT, which Article 3, titled 'Standard of Treatment', reads as follows:

> Each Party shall not subject Investments of Investors of the other Party to Measures which constitute:
> (i) Denial of justice under customary international law
> (ii) Un-remedied and egregious violations of due process; or
> (iii) Manifestly abusive treatment involving continuous, unjustified and outrageous coercion or harassment.

First, there is no reference to the very concept of 'fair and equitable treatment'. Second, the exhaustive list of conduct that is prohibited by the Article 3 is even more limited than the one found in the EU–Canada CETA. In particular, there is no reference to 'arbitrary conduct' or to the 'frustration of investor's legitimate expectations'.[292]

2. Expropriation

As noted in chapter 2, starting with the United States and Canada 2004 model BITs, investment treaties have started including a clarification of the concept of (direct and) indirect expropriation. Often contained in a specific annex, such clarifications have embraced a different understanding of indirect expropriation compared to the apparent original focus on the 'effect' of the allegedly expropriatory measure. Rather than focusing exclusively on whether the host State's measure has substantially deprived the investor of (the value of) its investment, a finding of indirect expropriation according to these treaties crucially includes consideration of the soundness and legitimacy of the allegedly expropriatory measure, according to the 'police powers' doctrine.[293] Accordingly, by referring to the public policy objectives of the host State's measure under review as one of the relevant factors of the 'case-by-case fact-based inquiry', recent investment treaties can be said to have adopted a reasonableness-based approach when it comes to the concept of indirect expropriation.

[292] For a historical and critical review of India's investment policy see Prabhash Ranjan, *India and Bilateral Investment Treaties: Refusal, Acceptance, Backlash* (OUP 2019).

[293] Andrew T Guzman and Jan H Dalhuisen, 'Expropriatory and Non-Expropriatory Takings under International Investment Law' (2012) UC Berkeley Public Law Research Paper 5:

> It is our view that a taking that is more than *de minimis* is non-expropriatory if it belongs in either of two categories: (i) takings that promote public welfare (also referred to as 'super' public purpose), a category that includes health, safety, and security; and (ii) takings that are incidental to legitimate, ordinary government action.

For example, paragraph 2 of Annex 8-A on Expropriation of the EU–Canada CETA identifies some of the relevant factors to be taken into consideration in order to determine whether a measure constitutes an indirect expropriation. These include the following:

(a) the economic impact of the measure or series of measures, although the sole fact that a measure or series of measures of a Party has an adverse effect on the economic value of an investment does not establish that an indirect expropriation has occurred;
(b) the duration of the measure or series of measures of a Party;
(c) the extent to which the measure or series of measures interferes with distinct, reasonable investment-backed expectations; and
(d) the character of the measure or series of measures, notably their object, context and intent.

One question that remains open with this type of provision revolves around the very nature (and intensity) of the case-by-case inquiry being put forward in the annex on expropriation. Such language may entail a variety of tests involving different levels of intrusiveness in the regulatory prerogatives of States.[294] At the lower end of the intrusiveness spectrum, the case-by-case approach may simply require the existence of a rational connection between the means used and the governmental objective sought to be achieved (ie the conduct adopted is likely to achieve at least in part the legitimate policy aim). This option does not appear likely as the means–ends rationality test does not focus on the economic impact of the measure, but rather on whether (and possibly, the extent to which) the measure under review contributes to the chosen policy goal.

A second option is to read the case-by-case inquiry as requiring that the conduct chosen by the host State entails the lowest possible burden to achieve the specific policy goal (ie the conduct adopted is the most cost-effective in achieving the legitimate policy aim). A cost-effectiveness test does need to consider both the adverse impact on the investment and the ability of one or more measures to achieve the chosen policy objective.

At the other end of the spectrum, and equally plausible, the case-by-case approach in paragraph 2 of Annex 8-A may entail a proportionality balancing test whereby the tribunal will need to determine whether the measure's negative impact on the protected investment is disproportionate based on an evaluation of the measure's public policy objective. These three distinct tests are neatly captured by the three prongs—'suitability', 'necessity' and 'strict proportionality'—of the

[294] For example, US constitutional jurisprudence on regulatory takings has not simply evolved over the years, but it is marred by uncertainty and vagueness: David Schneiderman *Constitutionalizing Economic Globalization: Investment Rules and Democracy's Promise* (CUP 2008) 48 et seq.

principle of proportionality, which finds its modern origin in German public law and its application in various domestic, regional and international legal systems.[295]

Furthermore, paragraph 2 does not clarify the intensity of the review to be carried out by an investment tribunal. Should the tribunal subject the public policy action at issue to an intense review or should it grant the respondent host State a so-called 'margin of appreciation'? While there may be other elements in the investment chapter that may provide important clues on such a question (eg the express recognition of the contracting parties' right to regulate), the intensity of the review represents another important (and unclear) variable in the determination of what constitutes indirect expropriation.

Further evidence that recent investment treaties have expressly adopted a 'reasonableness-based' approach in defining indirect expropriation may be found in an additional paragraph that is regularly included in the annex on expropriation. For example, paragraph 3 of Annex 8-A of CETA states as follows:

> For greater certainty, except in the rare circumstance when the impact of a measure or series of measures is so severe in light of its purpose that it appears manifestly excessive, non-discriminatory measures of a Party that are designed and applied to protect legitimate public welfare objectives, such as health, safety and the environment, do not constitute indirect expropriations.

This paragraph clearly relies on the concept of the right to regulate in the public interest (or 'police powers'). It introduces a general principle according to which non-discriminatory measures designed and applied to protect legitimate policy objectives do not constitute indirect expropriations except in the rare circumstance when the impact of the measure is so severe in light of its purpose that it appears manifestly excessive.

The most effective interpretation of this paragraph of the Annex is to read it as establishing a presumption in the context of the case-by-case analysis under the second paragraph according to which non-discriminatory measures for a public purpose do not constitute indirect expropriation. It is a rebuttable presumption, as even such measures may constitute indirect expropriation in the exceptional case of a measure that imposes such manifestly excessive burdens compared to the measure's public policy benefits.

However, two issues remain unclear with regard to this paragraph of the CETA Annex on expropriation. First, it is not clear whether the case-by-case analysis described in paragraph 2 would then only be applicable for the purposes of

[295] Among the vast scholarship on the topic, see Schwarze, *European Administrative Law* (n 11); Mads Andenas and Stefan Zleptnig, 'Proportionality: WTO Law in Comparative Perspective' (2007) 42 Tex Int'l L J 371; Aaron Barak, 'Proportionality and Principled Balancing' (2010) 3 Law & Ethics of Human Rights 1. See recently Henckels, *Proportionality and Deference* (n 14); Bücheler, *Proportionality in Investor-State Arbitration* (n 201); Vadi, *Proportionality, Reasonableness and Standards of Review* (n 2).

determining the exceptional case (according to a proportionality balancing test) or more broadly in order to assess whether a measure falls under the general presumption (ie it is a non-discriminatory measure designed and applied to protect a legitimate public policy).

A second related issue regarding the right to regulate clarification in paragraph 3 revolves around the issue of determining when a non-discriminatory measure may be said to be 'designed and applied' to protect a legitimate public policy. What is the applicable test to determine whether a specific host State conduct qualifies for the presumption in paragraph 3? Once again, there exist several options including good faith, means–ends rationality, and even proportionality balancing. First, it may be enough that the measure at issue be a good faith attempt at addressing a legitimate public policy concern. In international investment law, for example, this test is often linked with the prohibition of arbitrariness (at least in customary international law)[296] and with so-called self-judging clauses.[297] Second, the language chosen in paragraph 3 may entail an assessment of whether the measure at issue is reasonably linked with a legitimate public policy aim pursued by the host State. The test of rationality (or reasonableness in the strict sense) focuses on 'a sufficient causal link between the legitimate objective sought and the behaviour that one seeks to establish as reasonable'.[298] Finally, the applicable test to determine whether a specific host State conduct qualifies for the presumption in paragraph 3 of the Annex may involve proportionality balancing. This reading may be supported specifically if one reads the case-by-case analysis described in paragraph 2 of the Annex as involving such balancing. Furthermore, the apparent reference to proportionality balancing as the basis for reversing the right to regulate presumption (albeit a case involving a 'manifestly excessive' lack of balance) may also support the argument pointing to proportionality balancing as constituting the applicable test for the purpose of establishing the applicability of the right to regulate presumption, in the first place.

To conclude, while the aim of both paragraphs 2 and 3 of the annex on expropriation is to introduce a reasonableness-based definition of indirect expropriation, the scope and operation of such a mechanism remain unclear.

Preliminary Conclusions

This chapter's main findings have been the following. First, an examination of the origin of some of the key standards regularly found in modern investment treaties

[296] See Dumberry, 'The Prohibition against Arbitrary Conduct' (n 140) 117.

[297] See Stephan Schill and Robyn Briese, '"If the State Considers": Self-Judging Clauses in International Dispute Settlement' in Armin von Bogdandy and Rudiger Wolfrum (eds) *Max Planck Yearbook of United Nations Law Vol 13* (Brill/Nijhoff 2009) 61–140.

[298] Corten, 'The Notion of "Reasonable"' (n 7) 613, 623.

such as FPS, non-impairment through arbitrary or unjustifiable measures (non-impairment), and FET seems to show that these various treaty standards share the two distinctive features of 'reasonableness-based provisions': (a) a focus on whether or not the host State's conduct affecting the foreign investment is justified by a legitimate public policy; and (b) consideration (and balance) of a variety of factors depending on the circumstances of the specific case.

Second, while investment treaty tribunals have (at least for the most part) applied 'full protection and security', 'non-impairment through arbitrary or unjustifiable measures' and 'fair and equitable treatment' as reasonableness-based provisions, tribunals have markedly differed with regard to the specific reasonableness test that they have employed in order to review the lawfulness of the host State conduct. For example, in assessing whether host States have exercised 'due diligence' under the 'full protection and security' provision, investment tribunals have adopted a reasonableness-based approach by focusing on a variety of factors, including whether the host State's failure to prevent (or remedy) the act of a third party causing physical harm to the investment could be justified. However, while most tribunals seem to have carried out such assessment affording deference to the host State, some tribunals have adopted a more demanding standard of review.

Similarly, investment tribunals appear to have applied the FET provision (as well as the provision prohibiting the impairment of the investment through arbitrary or unjustifiable measures) as reasonableness-based provisions. When focusing on lack of good faith, arbitrariness and frustration of legitimate expectations, most investment tribunals have relied on an assessment taking into consideration the public policy justification of the host State's measure under review. However, the analysis has also shown a level of inconsistency (and sometimes also uncertainty) with regard to the standard of review that investment tribunals apply, particularly in the context of a claim of arbitrary conduct or frustration of the investor's legitimate expectations. For example, while most tribunals have set a high threshold for a finding of arbitrariness, some tribunals (appear to) have given the concept a broader (more intrusive) reach by carrying out a review based on 'means–ends rationality' or even 'proportionality balancing'. Similarly, in applying the concept of legitimate expectations as part of the FET provision, investment tribunals have so far failed to adopt a clear and consistent approach with regard to the balancing exercise between the protection of investors' legitimate expectations and the host State's right to regulate in the public interest.

Third, while a growing number of investment tribunals have interpreted the provision on indirect expropriation as a reasonableness-based provision, tribunals have shown a similar ambivalence in defining the 'legitimacy' of the exercise of the host State's so-called 'police powers'. In assessing the existence of an indirect expropriation pursuant to the police powers doctrine, investment tribunals have principally employed either a (more deferential) means–ends rationality test or a (more intrusive) proportionality balancing test.

Finally, with regard to recent investment treaties, States' focus has been to achieve the right balance between the need to promote and protect foreign investment and the need to safeguard their right to regulate for pursuing public policy interests. This has led States to give preference to reasonableness-based provisions as these provisions recognize the relevance of the host State's right to regulate. However, while many of these recent treaties have shown a more deferential approach vis-à-vis the host State's right to regulate, several issues remain unsettled. In particular, with regard to key investment protection provisions such as FET, FPS and indirect expropriation, recent treaties have often failed to clarify the specific reasonableness test being chosen, thus leaving the choice of the applicable standard of review to the future adjudicator.

Two preliminary reflection are advanced. First, investment tribunals' failure to identify a coherent practice with regard to the kind of reasonableness review stemming out of investment treaties represents one of the reasons for the increase in the number of critical voices of the investment treaty system. While there may be intrinsic reasons for such failure, including the vagueness of the key investment treaty standards (such as FPS, non-impairment and FET) and the decentralized nature of international investment adjudication, the fact remains that host States' public policy measures may be subject to intense proportionality balancing review, where the very policy objective, and in particular the specific level of protection being pursued by the host State, will be subject to scrutiny.[299]

Second, while there have been positive developments in the past decade in terms of investment policy reforms regarding reasonableness-based provisions, there is still work to be done. While policy makers seem to be aware that investment treaty protection should be about ensuring economic growth, environmental protection and social equity, recent treaties have failed to draw clear boundaries with regard to the applicable standards of review. For example, references to the concept of legitimate expectations have not been accompanied by the need to balance the protection of investor's legitimate expectations with the host State's right to regulate in the public interest. Similarly, the more elaborate definition of indirect expropriation may entail quite intrusive forms of proportionality balancing. Furthermore, there needs to be stronger rationalization and coordination of the various reasonableness based provisions, both in existing and future treaties as the extent of the overlap, confusion and inconsistency between the various reasonableness standards analysed in this chapter is a concern.[300]

[299] Interestingly, the Court of Justice of the European Union (CJEU) seems to have recently drawn a line with regard to the kind of review that investment treaties (and thus investment tribunals) are allowed to carry out with regard to host State regulation. In Opinion 1/17, on 30 April 2019, the CJEU appears to have identified a substantive benchmark for the investment chapter of the EU–Canada CETA by affirming that the latter is compatible with EU law because it does not permit CETA tribunals 'to call into question the level of protection of public interest determined by the Union following democratic process' (para 156).

[300] This stronger coordination should also include so-called 'public policy exceptions', which have recently been included in investment treaties and which condition their applicability on the basis of

Of course, legal certainty is a relative concept and it would be illusory to expect absolute clarity in the standards of protection required by international law. However, some of the issues that have often not been settled, even in recent treaties, are issues too central to remain unresolved. In particular, should the host State's right to regulate in the public interest be subject to a test based on good faith, means–ends rationality, or proportionality balancing? If the underlying purpose is (still) to strike the right balance between affording a high level of protection to foreign investment and safeguarding the host State's right to regulate in the public interest, this question must be tackled head-on and clearly resolved by policy-makers.[301]

reasonableness tests. See further Caroline Henckels, 'Should Investment Treaties Contain Public Policy Exceptions?' (2018) 59 Boston College L Rev 2825.

[301] See further Federico Ortino, 'Defining Indirect Expropriation: The Transatlantic Trade and Investment Partnership and the (Elusive) Search for "Greater Certainty"' (2016) Legal Issues Econ Integ 351; Federico Ortino, 'Investment Treaties, Sustainable Development and Reasonableness Review: A Case against Strict Proportionality Balancing' (2017) LJIL 71.

Conclusion

This book attempts to sketch the origin and evolution of the key investment protection provisions (mainly standards) found in modern international investment treaties. It argues that these various provisions (including fair and equitable treatment (FET), full protection and security (FPS), expropriation, non-impairment through arbitrary or unjustifiable measures, umbrella clauses) and much of the related controversy (linked with investment tribunals' interpretation of these provisions) can all be captured through three distinct concepts: legal stability, investment's value and reasonableness. The book thus finds that, from the very beginning, the protection afforded to foreign investments by modern investment treaties has been exceptionally broad, including guarantees vis-à-vis the host State's (a) breach of investment contracts and regulatory change (through umbrella clauses and stabilization clauses); (b) substantial deprivation of the value of the foreign investment (through the expropriation provision) and (c) unreasonable conduct (through FET, FPS and non-impairment).

Furthermore, while a growing number of investment treaty tribunals as well as new investment treaties have started to rein in such broad protections, the book finds that the evolution of key investment treaty provisions has been (and in many ways still is) marred by inconsistency and uncertainty. In particular, some of these key treaty provisions have been interpreted by investment tribunals as incorporating different guarantees: for example, while some tribunals have interpreted the provisions on indirect expropriation as a guarantee vis-à-vis the host State's substantial deprivation of the value of the investment, other tribunals have interpreted them as a guarantee vis-à-vis the host State's unreasonable conduct. Similarly, while some tribunals have interpreted the FET provision as a guarantee of legal stability in the strict sense, other tribunals have interpreted them as a guarantee vis-à-vis host State's unreasonable conduct. Furthermore, while there appears to be a growing preference in arbitral practice (as well as treaty practice) for reasonableness-based guarantees, there is still no clarity with regard to the specific reasonableness test that should be employed in order to review the lawfulness of the host State conduct under an investment treaty. For example, whether for purposes of assessing the existence of an indirect expropriation or for purposes of determining a violation of FET, some investment tribunals have employed a (more deferential) means–ends rationality test, while others have employed a (more intrusive) proportionality balancing test.

The Origin and Evolution of Investment Treaty Standards. Federico Ortino, Oxford University Press (2019). © Federico Ortino.
DOI: 10.1093/oso/9780198842637.001.0005

While the challenges facing the investment treaty system are many and the system's future trajectory remains unclear, the hope is that the present study has contributed to a better, more nuanced, understanding of the current system, at least with regard to its investment protection core. Based on the book's above-mentioned findings, one overall conclusion appears relatively uncontroversial: the current state of the law on investment protection is untenable and thus, for the investment treaty system to have a future, at a minimum, that law needs to improve dramatically both in terms of clarity and in terms of its ability to guarantee the host State's legitimate right to regulate in the public interest.

Select Bibliography

Alexandrov, SA, 'The Evolution of the Full Protection and Security Standard' in Kinnear, M (ed) *Building International Investment Law: The First 50 Years of ICSID* (Kluwer Law International 2015) ch 23

Andenas, M and Zleptnig, S, 'Proportionality: WTO Law in Comparative Perspective' (2007) 42 Tex Int'l L J 371

Antony, J, 'Umbrella Clauses since *SGS v. Pakistan* and *SGS v. Philippines*—A Developing Consensus' (2013) 29 Arb Int'l 607

Asteriti, A, 'Regulatory Expropriation Claims in International Investment Arbitrations: A Bridge Too Far?' in Bjorklund, A (ed) *Yearbook of International Investment Law and Policy* (OUP 2012–13) 462

Barak, A, 'Proportionality and Principled Balancing' (2010) 3 Law & Ethics of Human Rights 1

Bernardini, P, 'The Renegotiation of the Investment Contract' (1998) 13 ICSID Rev/FILJ 411

Bonnitcha, J, *Substantive Protection under Investment Treaties: A Legal and Economic Analysis* (CUP 2014)

Bremer, E, 'Incorporation by Reference in an Open-Government Age' (2013) 36 Harv J L & Pub Poly 131

Brower, CN, 'Current Developments in the Law of Expropriation and Compensation: A Preliminary Survey of Awards of the Iran–United States Claims Tribunal' (1987) 21 Int'l L 639

Bücheler, G, *Proportionality in Investor–State Arbitration* (OUP 2015)

Buffard, I and Zemanek, K, 'The "Object and Purpose" of a Treaty: An Enigma?' (1998) 3 ARIEL 311

Cameron, P, *International Energy Investment Law: The Pursuit of Stability* (OUP 2010)

Campbell, C, 'House of Cards: The Relevance of Legitimate Expectations under Fair and Equitable Treatment Provisions in Investment Treaty Law' (2013) 30 J Int'l Arb 361

Caplan, L and Sharpe, J, 'United States' in Brown, C (ed) *Commentaries on Selected Model Investment Treaties* (OUP 2013) 755

Chandrachud, C, 'The (Fictitious) Doctrine of Substantive Legitimate Expectations in India' in Groves, M and Weeks, G (eds) *Legitimate Expectations in the Common Law World* (Hart 2017) ch 11

Chang, A, 'Demystifying Conceptual Severance: A Comparative Study of the United States, Canada, and the European Court of Human Rights' (2013) 98 Cornell L Rev 965

Cheng, B, *General Principles of Law as Applied by International Courts and Tribunals* (CUP 1953)

Christie, GC, 'What Constitutes a Taking of Property under International Law' (1962) 38 BYIL 307

Cordero Moss, J, 'Full Protection and Security' in Reinisch, A (ed) *Standards of Investment Protection* (OUP 2008) 138

Corten, O, 'The Notion of "Reasonable" in International Law: Legal Discourse, Reason and Contradictions' (1999) 48 ICLQ 613

Cotula, L, 'Regulatory Takings, Stabilization Clauses and Sustainable Development' (2008) OECD Investment Policy Perspectives 69

Cotula, L, 'Pushing the Boundaries vs Striking a Balance: Some Reflections on Stabilization Issues in Light of *Duke Energy International Investments v. Republic of Peru*' (2010) 7(1) TDM

Coulombe, LP, 'Duplicating the Umbrella Clause? Some Thoughts on Contractual Expectations and the Fair and Equitable Treatment Standard' in Laird, I, et al (eds) *Investment Treaty Arbitration and International Law Volume 7* (Juris 2014) 101

Craig, P, *EU Administrative Law* (OUP 2012)

de Brabandere, E, 'Host States' Due Diligence Obligations in International Investment Law' (2015) 42 Syracuse J Int'l L & Com 319

Diehl, A, *The Core Standard of International Investment Protection: Fair and Equitable Treatment* (Kluwer Law International 2012)

Dolzer, R, 'Indirect Expropriation of Alien Property' (1986) 1 ICSID Rev/FILJ 41

Dolzer, R, 'Indirect Expropriation: New Developments?' (2002) 11 NYU Env'l J 64

Dolzer, R, 'Fair and Equitable Treatment: A Key Standard in Investment Treaties' (2005) 39 Int'l L 87

Dolzer, R, 'Fair and Equitable Treatment: Today's Contours' (2013) 12 Santa Clara J Int'l L 7

Dolzer, R and Schreuer, C, *Principles of International Investment Law* (2nd edn, OUP 2012)

Dolzer, R and Stevens, M, *Bilateral Investment Treaties* (ICSID & Kluwer Law International 1995)

Douglas, Z, 'Property, Investment, and the Scope of Investment Protection Obligations' in Douglas, Z, Pauwelyn, Z, and Vinuales, J (eds) *The Foundations of International Investment Law: Bringing Theory into Practice* (OUP 2014) 62

Draguiev, D, 'Bad Faith Conduct of States in Violation of the "Fair and Equitable Treatment" Standard in International Investment Law and Arbitration' (2014) 5 JIDS 273

Dumberry, P, 'The Prohibition against Arbitrary Conduct and the Fair and Equitable Treatment Standard under NAFTA Article 1105' (2014) 15 JWIT 117

Elliott, M, 'From Heresy to Orthodoxy: Substantive Legitimate Expectations in the United Kingdom' in Groves, M and Weeks, G (eds) *Legitimate Expectations in the Common Law World* (Hart 2017) ch 10

Ellis, E, (ed), *The Principle of Proportionality in the Laws of Europe* (OUP 1999)

Emiliou, N, *The Principle of Proportionality in European Law: A Comparative Study* (Kluwer Law International 1996)

Endicott, T, 'Arbitrariness' (2014) XXVII Canadian J L & Jurisprudence 49

Epstein, R, *Takings: Private Property and the Power of Eminent Domain* (Harvard University Press 1985)

Fee, JE, 'Unearthing the Denominator in Regulatory Taking Claims' (1994) 61 University of Chicago L Rev 1535

Foltea, M, *International Organizations in WTO Dispute Settlement: How Much Institutional Sensitivity?* (CUP 2012)

Fontanelli, F, 'Necessity Killed the GATT—Art XX GATT and the Misleading Rhetoric about "Weighing and Balancing"' (2012/13) 5 Eur J Legal Studies 36

Fortier, Y and Drymer, SL, 'Indirect Expropriation in the Law of International Investment: I Know It When I See It, or Caveat Investor' (2004) 19 ICSID Rev 293 (and (2005) 13 Asia Pacific L Rev 79)

Frank, S, 'Stabilisation Clauses and Foreign Direct Investment: Presumptions versus Realities' (2015) 16 JWIT 88

Frid de Vries, R, 'Stability Shaken? Israeli High Court of Justice Strikes Down the Stabilization Clause in the Israeli Government's Gas Plan' (2017) 18 JWIT 332

Gehne, K and Brillo, R, 'Stabilization Clauses in International Investment Law: Beyond Balancing and Fair and Equitable Treatment' (2014) NCCR Trade Working Paper No 2013/46

Giannakopoulos, C, 'The Right to Regulate in International Investment Law and the Law of State Responsibility: A Hohfeldian Approach' in Pazartzis, P and Merkouris, P (eds) *Permutations of Responsibility in International Law* (Brill 2019) 148

Gill, J, Gearing, M and Birt, G, 'Contractual Claims and Bilateral Investment Treaties: A Comparative Review of the *SGS* Cases' (2004) 21 J Int'l Arb 397

Guzman, AT and Dalhuisen, JH, 'Expropriatory and Non-Expropriatory Takings under International Investment Law' (2012) UC Berkeley Public Law Research Paper 5

Harbo, TI, 'Introducing Procedural Proportionality Review in European Law' (2017) 30 LJIL 25

Heiskanen, V, 'Arbitrary and Unreasonable Measures' in Reinisch, A, (ed) *Standards of Investment Protection* (OUP 2008) 104

Henckels, C, *Proportionality and Deference in Investor–State Arbitration: Balancing Investment Protection and Regulatory Autonomy* (CUP 2015)

Henckels, C, 'Should Investment Treaties Contain Public Policy Exceptions?' (2018) 59 Boston College Law Review 2825, Symposium Edition, *Reforming International Investment Law: Opportunities, Challenges, Paradigms.*

Hickman, TR, 'The Reasonableness Principle: Reassessing its Place in the Public Sphere' (2004) 63 CLJ 166

Higgins, R, *The Taking of Property by the State: Recent Developments in International Law,* in Collected Courses of the Hague Academy of International Law (The Hague Academy of International Law 1982)

Hirsch, M, 'Between Fair and Equitable Treatment and Stabilization Clause: Stable Legal Environment and Regulatory Change in International Investment Law' (2011) 12 JWIT 783

Hoffmann, A, 'Indirect Expropriation' in Reinisch, A (ed) *Standards of Investment Protection* (OUP 2008) ch 11

Kläger, R, *Fair and Equitable Treatment' in International Investment Law* (CUP 2011)

Koivurova, T, 'Due Diligence' in Rudiger Wolfrung (ed) *The Max Planck Encyclopedia of Public International Law* (OUP 2010)

Kriebaum, U, 'Partial Expropriation' (2007) 8 JWIT (2007)

Kriebaum, U, 'FET and Expropriation in the (Invisible) EU Model BIT' (2014) 15 JWIT 454

Levinson, RB, 'Time to Bury the Shocks: the Conscience Test' (2010) 13 Chap L Rev 307

Limão, N and Maggi, G, 'Uncertainty and Trade Agreements' (2015) 7 AEJ: Microeconomics 1

López Escarcena, S, *Indirect Expropriation in International Law* (Edward Elgar 2014)

Lowenfeld, A, *International Litigation and the Quest for Reasonableness* (OUP 1996)

Maniruzzaman, AFM, 'National Laws Providing for Stability of International Investment Contracts: A Comparative Perspective' (2007) 8 JWIT 233

Mann, FA, 'British Treaties for the Promotion and Protection of Investments' (1981) 52 BYIL 241

Maynard, S, 'Legitimate Expectations and the Interpretation of the "Legal Stability Obligation"' (2016) 1 EILAR 99

McLachlan, C, Lis Pendens *in International Litigation* in Collected Courses of the Hague Academy of International Law (Hague Academy of International Law 2009)

McLachlan, C, Shore, L and Weiniger, M, *International Investment Arbitration: Substantive Principles* (2nd edn, OUP 2017)

Menaker, A, 'Benefitting from Experience: Developments in the United States' Most Recent Investment Agreements' (2005) 12 UC Davis J Int'l L & Pol'y 121

Metzger, S, 'Multilateral Conventions for the Protection of Private Foreign Investment' (1960) 9 J Pub L 133

Miles, K, *The Origins of International Investment Law: Empire, Environment and the Safeguarding of Capital* (CUP 2013)

Montt, S, *State Liability in Investment Treaty Arbitration: Global Constitutional and Administrative Law in the BIT Generation* (Hart 2009)

Morrone, A, 'Constitutional Adjudication and the Principle of Reasonableness' in Bongiovanni, G, Sartor, G, and Valentini, C (eds) *Reasonableness and the Law* (Springer, 2009) 215

Mostafa, M, 'The Sole Effects Doctrine, Police Powers and Indirect Expropriation under International Law' (2008) 15 Aust J Int'l L 267

Murphy, C, 'Lon Fuller and the Moral Value of the Rule of Law' (2005) 24 L Phil 239

Nadakavukaren Schefer, K, *International Investment Law* (2nd edn, Edward Elgar 2016)

Naniwadekar, MC, 'The Scope and Effect of Umbrella Clauses: The Need for a Theory of Deference?' (2010) 2 Trade, Law and Development 169

Nassar, N, *Sanctity of Contracts Revisited: A Study in the Theory and Practice of Long-Term International Commercial Transactions* (Martinus Nijhoff 1995)

Newcombe, A and Paradell, L, *Law and Practice of Investment Treaties: Standards of Treatment* (Kluwer Law International 2009)

OECD, *Draft Convention on the Protection of Foreign Property and Resolution of the Council of the OECD on the Draft Convention* (OECD 1967)

OECD, *Intergovernmental Agreements Relating to Investment in Developing Countries* (OECD 1984)

Ortino, F, 'Italy' in Brown, C (ed) *Commentaries on Selected Model Investment Treaties* (OUP 2013) 321

Ortino, F, 'Refining the Content and Role of Investment "Rules" and "Standards": A New Approach to International Investment Treaty Making' (2013) 28 ICSID Rev 152

Ortino, F, 'The Investment Treaty System as Judicial Review' (2013) 24 Am Rev Int'l Arb 437

Ortino, F, 'Defining Indirect Expropriation: The Transatlantic Trade and Investment Partnership and the (Elusive) Search for "Greater Certainty"' (2016) 43 Legal Issues of Economic Integration 351

Ortino, F, 'Investment Treaties, Sustainable Development and Reasonableness Review: A Case against Strict Proportionality Balancing' (2017) 30 LJIL 71

Ortino, F, 'The Obligation of Regulatory Stability in the Fair and Equitable Treatment Standard: How Far Have We Come?' (2018) 21 JIEL 845

Paine, J, 'On Investment Law and Questions of Change' (2018) 19 JWIT 173

Paparinskis, M, *The International Minimum Standard and Fair and Equitable Treatment* (OUP 2013)

Paulsson, J and Douglas, Z, 'Indirect Expropriation in Investment Treaty Arbitration' in Horn, N and Kröll, S (eds) *Arbitrating Foreign Investment Disputes: Procedural and Substantive Legal Aspects* (Kluwer Law International 2004) 157

Pereira de Souza Fleury, R, 'Umbrella Clauses: A Trend Towards its Elimination' (2015) 31 Arb Int'l 679

Perez-Aznar, F, 'Investment Protection in Exceptional Situations: Compensation-for-Losses Clauses in IIAs' (2017) 32 ICSID Rev/FILJ 696

Pinchis, M 'The Ancestry of "Equitable Treatment" in Trade: Lessons from the League of Nations during the Inter-War Period' (2014) 15 JWIT 13

Pinchis, M, 'Fair and Equitable Treatment in International Trade and Investment Law: 1918–1956' (Phd dissertation, King's College London 2017)

Ponce, JE and Cevallos, R, 'Good Faith in Investment Arbitration' (2016) 13 TDM 5

Potestà, M, 'Legitimate Expectations in Investment Treaty Law: Understanding the Roots and the Limits of a Controversial Concept' (2013) 28 ICSID Rev/FILJ 88

Poulsen, L, *Bounded Rationality and Economic Diplomacy: The Politics of Investment Treaties in Developing Countries* (CUP 2015)

Rajput, A and Malhotra, S, 'Legitimate Expectations in Investment Arbitration: A Comparative Perspective' in Pal Singh, M and Kumar, N (eds) *The Indian Yearbook of Comparative Law 2018* (Springer 2019) ch 13

Ranjan, P, *India and Bilateral Investment Treaties: Refusal, Acceptance, Backlash* (OUP 2019)

Ranjan, P, 'Police Powers, Indirect Expropriation in International Investment Law, and Article 31(3)(c) of the VCLT: A Critique of *Philip Morris v. Uruguay*' (2019) 9 Asian J Int'l L 98

Regan, D, 'The Meaning of "Necessary" in GATT Article XX and GATS Article XIV: The Myth of Cost–Benefit Balancing' (2007) 6 World Trade Rev 347

Reinisch, A, 'Expropriation' in Muchlinski, P, Ortino, F, and Schreuer, C (eds) *The Oxford Handbook on International Investment Law* (OUP 2008) 410

Reinisch, A, 'The Future Shape of EU Investment Agreements' (2013) 28 ICSID Rev/FILJ 179

Reisman, M and Digon, R, 'Eclipse of Expropriation' in Rovine, AW (ed) *Contemporary Issues in International Arbitration and Mediation—The Fordham Papers 2008* (Martinus Nijhoff 2009) 27

Roberts, A, 'Clash of Paradigms: Actors and Analogies Shaping the Investment Treaty System' (2013) 107 AJIL 45

Sabanogullari, L, *General Exception Clauses in International Investment Law: The Recalibration of Investment Agreements via WTO Flexibilities* (Nomos Verlag 2018)

Sacerdoti, G, 'Bilateral Treaties and Multilateral Instruments on Investment Protection' (1997) 269 Recueil des Cours, Tome 269

Salacuse, JW, *The Three Laws of International Investment: National, Contractual, and International Frameworks for Foreign Capital* (OUP 2013)

Sattorova, M, *The Impact of Investment Treaty Law on Host States: Enabling Good Governance?* (Hart 2018)

Sauvant, K and Ortino, F, *Improving the International Investment Law and Policy Regime: Options for the Future* (Ministry for Foreign Affairs of Finland 2013)

Schill, S, 'Deference in Investment Treaty Arbitration: Reconceptualizing the Standard of Review through Comparative Public Law' (2012) 3 JIDS 577

Schill, S, 'Enabling Private Ordering—Function, Scope and Effect of Umbrella Clauses in International Investment Treaties' (2009) 18 Mich J Int'l L 1

Schill, S, *The Multilateralization of International Investment Law* (CUP 2009)

Schill, S (ed), *International Investment Law and Comparative Public Law* (OUP 2010)

Schill, S and Briese, R, '"If the State Considers": Self-Judging Clauses in International Dispute Settlement' in von Bogdandy, A and Wolfrum, R (eds) *Max Planck Yearbook of United Nations Law Vol 13* (Brill/Nijhoff 2009) 61

Schneiderman, D, *Constitutionalizing Economic Globalization: Investment Rules and Democracy's Promise* (CUP 2008)

Schønberg, S, *Legitimate Expectations in Administrative Law* (OUP 2000)

Schreuer, C, 'Travelling the BIT Route: Of Waiting Periods, Umbrella Clauses and Forks in the Road' (2004) 5 JWIT 231

Schreuer, C, 'Protection against Arbitrary or Discriminatory Measures' in Rogers, CA and Alford, RP (eds) *The Future of Investment Arbitration* (OUP 2009) 188

Schreuer, C, 'Full Protection and Security' (2010) 1 JIDS 353

Schwarze, J, *European Administrative Law* (revised 1st edn, Sweet & Maxwell 2006)

Schwarzenberger, G, 'The Abs-Shawcross Draft Convention on Investment Abroad: A Critical Commentary' (1960) 9 J Pub L 147

Shemberg, A, 'Stabilization Clauses and Human Rights' (2009) International Finance Corporation Annual Report

Sinclair, A, 'The Origin of the Umbrella Clause in the International Law of Investment Protection' (2004) 20 Arb Int'l 411

Sornarajah, M, *The International Law on Foreign Investment* (3rd edn, CUP 2010)

Sourgens, FG, 'Reason and Reasonableness: The Necessary Diversity of the Common law' (2014) 67 Maine L Rev 73

Sprankling, JG, *The International Law of Property* (OUP 2014)

Stone, J, 'Arbitrariness, the Fair and Equitable Treatment Standard, and the International Law of Investment' (2012) 25 LJIL 77

Stone Sweet, A and Mathews, J, 'Proportionality Balancing and Global Constitutionalism' (2008) 47 Colum J Transnat'l L 73

Sullivan, C, 'Treaty of Friendship, Commerce and Navigation: Standard Draft' (Unpublished: United States Department of State 1971)

Trachtman, J, 'Trade and ... Problems, Cost–Benefit Analysis and Subsidiarity' (1998) 9 EJIL 32

Tudor, I, *The Fair and Equitable Treatment Standard in the International Law of Foreign Investment* (OUP 2008)

UNCTAD, *Bilateral Investment Treaties in the Mid-1990s* (United Nations 1998)

UNCTAD, *Fair and Equitable Treatment* (United Nations 1999)

UNCTAD, *Taking of Property* (United Nations 2000)

UNCTAD, *Scope and Definition: A Sequel* (United Nations 2010)

UNCTAD, *Scope and Definition* (United Nations 2011)

UNCTAD, *2012 World Investment Report: Towards a New Generation of Investment Policies* (United Nations 2012)

UNCTAD, *Fair and Equitable Treatment: UNCTAD Series on Issues in International Investment Agreements II* (United Nations, 2012)

UNCTAD, 'Taking Stock of IIA Reform' Issues Note (March 2016)

UNCTAD, *World Investment Report* (United Nations 2017)

UNCTC, *Bilateral Investment Treaties* (Graham & Trotman in cooperation with the United Nations 1988)

Vadi, V, *Proportionality, Reasonableness and Standards of Review in International Investment Law and Arbitration* (Edward Elgar 2018)

van der Walt, AJ, *Constitutional Property Clauses: A Comparative Analysis* (Kluwer Law International 1999).

Van Harten, G, *Investment Treaty Arbitration and Public Law* (OUP 2007)

Vanderman, Y, 'Substantive Legitimate Expectations' (2016) 21 Jud Rev 174

Vandevelde, KJ, *Bilateral Investment Treaties: History, Policy, and Interpretation* (OUP 2010)

Vandevelde, KJ, *The First Bilateral Investment Treaties: US Postwar Friendship, Commerce, and Navigation Treaties* (OUP 2017)

Vidigal, G and Stevens, B, 'Brazil's New Model of Dispute Settlement for Investment: Return to the Past or Alternative for the Future?' (2018) 19 JWIT 475

Viñuales, J, 'Sovereignty in Foreign Investment Law' in Douglas, Z, Pauwelyn, J, and Vinuales, J (eds) *The Foundations of International Investment Law* (OUP 2014) 344

Voirin, P and Goubeaux, G, *Doit Civil—Tome 1* (LGDJ 2013)

Voon, T, '*Philip Morris v. Uruguay*: Implications for Public Health' (2017) 18 JWIT 320

Wälde, T, 'The "Umbrella Clause" in Investment Arbitration: A Comment on Original Intentions and Recent Cases' (2005) 6 JWIT 183

Wälde, T and N'Di, G, 'Stabilising International Investment Commitments' (1996) 31 Tex Int'l L J 215

Waldron, J, 'The Rule of Law and the Importance of Procedure' (2011) 50 Nomos 3

Weiler, T, *The Interpretation of International Investment Law: Equality, Discrimination and Minimum Standards of Treatment in Historical Context* (Martinus Nijhoff 2013)

Woolf, H, Jowell, J, and Le Sueur, A, *De Smith's Judicial Review* (7th edn, Sweet & Maxwell 2016)

Wouters, J and Duquet, S, 'The Principle of Reasonableness in Global Administrative Law' (2013) Jean Monnet Working Paper 12/13

Yannaca-Small, K, 'Interpretation of the Umbrella Clause in Investment Agreements' (2006) OECD Working Papers on International Investment

Zachary, D, 'Nothing if not Critical for Investment Treaty Arbitration: *Occidental, Eureko* and *Methanex*' (2006) 22 Arb Int'l 27

Index